Motherhood and Creativity in Contemporary Self-Life Writing

This book aims to study the representation of motherhood in self-life writing by English-speaking authors. It highlights the particular issues women writers are faced with when they try to combine their vocation as artists with their duties towards their children. For those women who claim their right to be both mothers and writers, several cultural myths need to be taken down, chief among which are the representations that we have of what being an artist should be like, as well as the role a mother should have towards her children. This book looks at self-life writing by women from English-speaking countries to reveal the common themes and tropes which recur in texts written on the subject of motherhood, by looking at them from both a literary and a cultural perspective. It also aims to demonstrate that a new generation of women writers is taking up the subject and forging a new literary tradition.

Alice Braun is a senior lecturer at the Université de Paris Nanterre in France. She has been researching self-life writing by women and is the author of several articles on Janet Frame, Rachel Cusk, Sylvia Plath, and Doris Lessing. Lately, she has been working on the representation of motherhood in literary texts, and particularly childbirth.

Routledge Research in Women's Literature

Becoming Wollstonecraft
The Interconnection of Her Life and Works
Brenda Ayres

Conflict and Colonialism in 21st Century Romantic Historical Fiction
Repairing the Past, Repurposing History
Edited by Hsu-Ming Teo and Paloma Fresno-Calleja

Motherhood and Creativity in Contemporary Self-Life Writing
Writers and Mothers
Alice Braun

For more information about this series, please visit: www.routledge.com/Routledge-Research-in-Womens-Literature/book-series/RRWL

Motherhood and Creativity in Contemporary Self-Life Writing
Writers and Mothers

Alice Braun

NEW YORK AND LONDON

First published 2025
by Routledge
605 Third Avenue, New York, NY 10158

and by Routledge
4 Park Square, Milton Park, Abingdon, Oxon, OX14 4RN

Routledge is an imprint of the Taylor & Francis Group, an informa business

© 2025 Alice Braun

The right of Alice Braun to be identified as author of this work has been asserted in accordance with sections 77 and 78 of the Copyright, Designs and Patents Act 1988.

All rights reserved. No part of this book may be reprinted or reproduced or utilised in any form or by any electronic, mechanical, or other means, now known or hereafter invented, including photocopying and recording, or in any information storage or retrieval system, without permission in writing from the publishers.

Trademark notice: Product or corporate names may be trademarks or registered trademarks, and are used only for identification and explanation without intent to infringe.

Library of Congress Cataloging-in-Publication Data
Names: Braun, Alice, 1980– author.
Title: Motherhood and creativity in contemporary self-life writing : writers and mothers / Alice Braun.
Description: New York, NY : Routledge, 2025. |
Series: Routledge research in women's literature |
Includes bibliographical references and index.
Identifiers: LCCN 2024016972 (print) | LCCN 2024016973 (ebook) |
ISBN 9781032609829 (hardback) | ISBN 9781032609836 (paperback) |
ISBN 9781003461388 (ebook)
Subjects: LCSH: Women authors–Biography–History and criticism. |
Mothers–Biography–History and criticism. |
Autobiography–Women authors. |
Literature, Modern–History and criticism. |
Motherhood in literature. | Motherhood. |
LCGFT: Literary criticism.
Classification: LCC PN471 .B73 2025 (print) |
LCC PN471 (ebook) | DDC 920.72091752–dc23/eng/20240525
LC record available at https://lccn.loc.gov/2024016972
LC ebook record available at https://lccn.loc.gov/2024016973

ISBN: 978-1-032-60982-9 (hbk)
ISBN: 978-1-032-60983-6 (pbk)
ISBN: 978-1-003-46138-8 (ebk)

DOI: 10.4324/9781003461388

Typeset in Sabon
by Newgen Publishing UK

To Paul, Sarah, and Tim BP

Contents

Acknowledgements	*viii*
Introduction: A soundproof room of one's own	1
1 The impossible subject	11
2 To have and have not	52
3 On pregnancy and childbirth	85
4 Mother writing	117
5 Bad mothers	150
Conclusion: Throwing the baby out with the bathwater	173
Index	*177*

Acknowledgements

This book is the result of a decade of academic work and has become a reality, thanks to the support of my colleagues at the Université Paris Nanterre, who have welcomed me as a member for 20 years now and who have granted me the time to focus on my research, which was necessary for me to bring this work to completion. I am also grateful to my research affiliation group, the Centre de Recherches en Études Anglophones (CREA), for allowing me to pursue my line of work and providing support and advice. I am forever indebted to Cornelius Crowley for his careful proofreading and for all his insightful suggestions all along the process of thinking through and carrying out this project. In spite of his immense knowledge, he refuses to be an intellectual model or an authority, so I will say that he very much acted as a midwife by guiding me through the symbolic pregnancy and delivery of this book, accompanying me throughout and encouraging me to trust my instincts. I would also like to thank Brigitte Marrec, who took the time to read my work and cheer me on, as well as Charlotte Gould, who provided essential advice and encouragement.

I also want to express gratitude to my friend and colleague Fabienne Moine, whose rigorous approach to academic work has been a model for me, one which I hope one day to be able to emulate. I am also indebted to Claire Bazin, who directed my PhD and who believed in my capacity to become an academic. My thoughts also go to some of the professors whom I have admired as a student and who have urged me on André Topia, Marc Porée, and Carle Bonafous-Murat. I am also lucky to be part of a nurturing community of researchers whose conversation and friendship have been essential, from both an intellectual and a human perspective along the years: Claire Hélie, Élise Brault-Dreux, Julie Loison-Charles, Nicolas Boileau, Laurence Dubois, Corey Scott, and many others. Special thanks go to Charlotte Danino, who invited me to work with her on her "Birthing Stories" venture and who trusted me enough to let me work on the "childbirth in literature" project, which has provided invaluable input for this book.

I also want to thank my colleagues in the Human Science Department at the Université Paris Nanterre, where I have been a teacher for 15 years. Working on a daily basis with specialists in management, economics, sociology, and history has broadened my view on literature and has shaped my approach to academic work. This book would simply not have been the same had it not been for the precious conversations I have had along the years with my colleagues Fabrice Bondoux, Fabrice Tricou, Laure Machu, Lionel Rischmann, Xavier Vigna, Franck Collard, and many others.

I am lucky enough to consider as my friends two amazing authors, whose work and wise words on the subject of motherhood and literature have immensely inspired me in the course of researching this book: thank you Liz Berry and Rachel Bower for being beautiful poets and human beings and for gifting us mothers with your exquisite verse.

Because I value community so much, I am very grateful to the women and mothers who have surrounded me with their friendship over the years, Candice, who has always been and will forever be there, Julie and Sabahe, my fellow "bad mums", and Marianne who on that fateful day found the right words and guided me with infinite gentleness through the first difficult moments of being a mother. You convinced me of the necessity to stick together as mothers and to keep the flow of conversation going: you are an inspiration for this book.

I also want to thank my family and of course my mother Gabriela, whose influence pervades this book, my father, and my brother, the Burton-Page family, with a special thought for Florence, the best gynaecologist and obstetrician in France, who knows and understands women better than any doctor I have ever met.

My never-ending love goes to my husband Tim, who believes in me even more than I do, and to Paul and Sarah: this book is nothing compared to what you have taught me. I could have said that it would have been written more quickly if it had not been for you, but the truth is, this book would not even exist without you.

Introduction
A soundproof room of one's own

In 1929, Virginia Woolf published a foundational text in what we now call "women's studies", *A Room of One's Own* ([1929] 2004). She was trying to establish the reasons why, at the time when she was penning her essay, there was still so little writing by women. What was novel in her approach was that she did not try to find explanations for this fact in the essence of women's identity but rather in their material conditions. For Woolf, we had been under the spell of an illusion, forged under the Romantic period, which held that the artistic vocation descended on the writer regardless of his class, or his gender, when in fact, creativity was always dependent on one's being given the right conditions in which to write:

> It may seem a brutal thing to say, and it is a sad thing to say: but, as a matter of hard fact, the theory that poetical genius bloweth where it listeth, and equally in poor and rich, holds little truth.
> (Woolf [1929] 2004, 160)

If women are to start writing on an equal footing with men, they need what men have been enjoying for centuries: a good education, sufficient money to support their literary careers, and a dedicated space to which they can retreat, away from the necessities of domesticity, epitomised by the family sitting-room where authors like Jane Austen or Emily Brontë had been writing their masterpieces. That special room became the symbol of the autonomy of women writers, the promise that they could gain access to the same literary opportunities as their male counterparts.

Yet what exactly is this room supposed to be like? Is it an office? Or a bedroom? In the preface to her translation of Woolf's essay, French author Marie Darrieussecq explains why she decided to break with the tradition of translating Woolf's "room" by the French equivalent *"chambre"*, which in fact means "bedroom". Instead, she explains, Woolf's room should be translated by the French *"lieu"*, which is closer to the English "place"

(Woolf 2015, 2). The semantics matter here: why do we assume that a woman writer should be relegated to her bedroom? The bedroom is the place where we sleep and love, where mothers breastfeed their children, it is the locus of domesticity and intimacy. For Darrieussecq, talking about the necessity for female authors to have their own space is a truly groundbreaking proposition, as it meant that women could claim to exist outside of the relationships with their families, as individuals in their own right.

For Woolf, women have historically been unable to write because they did not have access to that specific place, but we tend to forget that she also believed this room needed to be "quiet", even "sound-proof" (Woolf [1929] 2004, 113). A generation later, US poet Sylvia Plath was one of those authors who had taken heed of Virginia Woolf's ideas, and who believed in the possibility for women to cultivate their poetic vision, yet she quickly stumbled on a major hurdle: even in that special room, the author can still hear the sound made by her small children in the next room. Even if she has put them to bed, on her own, because she is now a single mother, in the hope that she may get some work done eventually, they still wake up, cry for her to come take care of them, and vie for her attention. In the poem "Ariel", written in 1962, only a few months before Plath would take her own life, the poetic persona pictures herself galloping on a horse named after the Shakespearean epitome of creativity, flying away from material contingencies to reach pure spirituality. Yet in order to do that, she finds that she must let "the child's cry melt into the wall" (Plath 1981, 239). This wall is the wall of the bedroom where Plath would retreat to write her poems at night. For Plath's biographer Heather Clark, Ariel reads as one of the major poems about the difficulties of reconciling motherhood and creativity (Clark 2020, 795): in order to pursue her vision, the poet needs to ignore her children's cries in the other room. This is something that Virginia Woolf had probably not thought about when she wrote *A Room of One's Own*: the (bed)room is never entirely soundproof, in other words, no woman writer can truly shut herself from her family duties, especially if she is a mother as well as a writer.

In this book, I want to show that motherhood is the last frontier of female writing. Since Virginia Woolf wrote her essay, part of her wishes for the future of female literary creation has actually been achieved: a century later, there is now a solid tradition of women writing in all the available genres: novelists, playwrights, poets, essayists, and academics. Women write fiction, and they also increasingly write of their own experiences as authors. Yet for all the writing we now have by women writers, little writing has been produced, at least until recently, on the topic of mothering in fiction and in self-life writing by women – and by men. I say "little" with regard to how common the experience is among women. There are mothers in literature, as we will see, but they do not often get to speak in their own voices (see Podnieks and O'Reilly 2010; Podnieks 2020). There may be several explanations for this fact, some more material, and some more cultural. One is that writers who are also mothers to young children simply do not have the time to write about their own experiences. As the children grow older, amnesia sets in, and they end up moving on to other topics (see Marni Jackson's preface in Cowan, Lam, and Stonehouse 2008). Another is that only a few books on the topic of motherhood actually get published because of a suspicion among the publishing world that such works are too "niche" and would not find their readership. Maybe some authors hold back from actually writing about their own experience of motherhood because they worry their books would not be published or read or else that they would be accused of neglecting their children as Rachel Cusk would find out (2008).

Yet the reality is that things are now changing at last. In the last 20 years, there has been a vast increase in the number of works of fiction and self-life writing on the subject of motherhood, to the point that it has garnered the attention of the mainstream media, as evidenced by articles such as "Why all the books about Motherhood?" by Lauren Elkin (2018), "In a Raft of New Books, Motherhood from (Almost Every Angle)" by Parul Seghal (2018) or "Millennials Are Exploring Motherhood – in a New Generation of Books" by Rhiannon Lucy Cosslett (2020). It seems that since the beginning of the 21st century, motherhood is coming out of the bedroom where it had been confined for too long and into the spotlight: for some critics, there has particularly been a "boom" in motherhood memoirs given the sheer volume of titles that have been published in recent years (Hewett 2020). The memoir has indeed become very popular of late (Rak 2004), and I would argue that, as a genre, it fits the subject of motherhood very well: unlike the autobiography which is supposed to cover its author's entire lifespan, the memoir allows to dwell on a particular aspect of one's life, particularly moments of crisis. There had been motherhood memoirs written in the second half of the century, with the examples of Adrienne Rich's *Of Woman Born: Motherhood as Experience and Institution* ([1976] 1995), as well as Jane Lazarre's *The Mother Knot* ([1976] 1997), but these had been subsumed under the category of feminist writing. I would say one of the books which had a major impact on writing about motherhood was Rachel Cusk's *A Life's Work: On Becoming a Mother* (2001). In the field of maternal studies, Cusk's memoir on the disillusions of a writer who becomes a mother has had a fundamental impact on how we think about motherhood in literature, on a par with Adrienne Rich's book. I certainly have clear memories of reading it one summer of 2015, the clueless and somewhat desperate mother of a one-year-old, and realising that she was laying out in great detail and with typically Cuskian wit, every single thought and emotion that had gone through my mind since the time my son had been born. I had already been working on self-life writing by women for some years: I decided there and then that I would now focus my work on the representation of motherhood.

As I started looking for works written in the first person by authors who had become mothers, I came across a whole variety of genres: there have been memoirs, of course, as well as autobiographies, autobiographical novels, and essays, works that pertain to the new genre of autotheory. I also found a great number of poems written on the topic, in anthologies, as well as individual collections. Yet as I started collecting names and titles, I realised that many of the authors who were writing about their experience of motherhood belonged to very homogeneous social categories: they were for the most part middle-class, heterosexual, white women and Western-born, or Western-educated. In the corpus I have been working on, most of the authors are women who write in English: most of them were born in an English-speaking country, whether it is the UK, the US, Canada, or Ireland. I have also chosen to include a couple of writers who write in a foreign language because their work is so relevant to the subject, in particular French author Marie Darrieussecq and Turkish author Elif Shafak. I would like to be able to say that this corpus is comprehensive and encompasses most of the writing that has been done on the subject of motherhood in the first person, but I have unfortunately left out a number of authors, whose work I was not able to get to in time, and also because my choice of authors has largely been based on personal preferences. The fact that most of the works I came across were written from very similar sociocultural points of view is testimony to the fact that the voices of minorities are still underrepresented, not only in writing about motherhood but also in the publishing world in general. Yet the texts which were written by women belonging to different categories (I'm thinking here of Maggie Nelson, or Alice Walker) definitely provided challenges to some of my main contentions and opened up new avenues of reflection, which prevented my arguments from becoming too predictable.

While the following analyses look at some of the issues which recur in self-life writing by women on the topic of motherhood, the main problem I have tried to study is that of combining a career as a writer and a role as a mother. Like Woolf, I take a very material look at what being a writer entails: how do women writers manage to nurture their creativity at a time in their lives when they are so busy taking care of their children? What amount of time do they have at their disposal, where and when do they write, and can they count on the support of the other parent, do they have enough money to hire a babysitter, or leave their children in day care? Nevertheless, this book should not be read as an advice book in any way, as I have no guidance to offer to anyone. Neither do the authors whose book I will be studying: with a few exceptions, most of them feel like they are scrambling, muddling through, failing at being a good mother or a good writer. Yet I do hope that the study of texts by these women will give the readers a sense that they are not alone in finding it extremely difficult to nurture their creativity while being a mother, and that the companionship with other women who have written about their difficulties will bring some sense of relief and inspiration. One thing which I have found rather striking, as I scan the corpus I have put together to write this book, is the need to form a community of experience. Another common fact is that the female authors who write about their experience of being a mother often refer to other authors who have been through the same conundrums. For this reason, it is impossible to work on their literary production on a solely aesthetic basis, as if the facts of their lives did not matter to their writing. Today's mother writers often turn to their literary foremothers and, for this reason, Virginia Woolf, Sylvia Plath, Doris Lessing, and Rachel Cusk will be familiar figures who will guide us along the way. To quote once again from Woolf in *A Room of One's Own*: "For we think back through our mothers if we are women. It is useless to go to the great men writers for help, however much one may go to them for pleasure" (Woolf [1929] 2004, 88).

In fact, Woolf's "great men writers" will be present in this study alongside their female counterparts. As I contend throughout this book, in Western culture, being a mother is completely at odds with the representation we have of what being an artist is like. Mothers are portrayed as nurturing, domestic, and conservative: they feed and love, but they also teach rules and prepare their children for their membership in the adult world. Artists, on the other hand, are transgressive, they live by rules they have themselves created, or so they believe, they are disaffiliated and self-contained. Even if the figure of the female artist has been allowed to emerge in the 20th century, she has evolved under rules which had been created by men. As Rachel Cusk wonders, "Can a Woman Who Is an Artist Ever Just Be an Artist?" (2019). Another recurring character in this book is the Romantic artist: a Promethean figure, he is the master of his own creation and therefore needs answer to no one (see Spira 2020). Unlike the artists who came before him, he does not depend on a patron or on a creative collective (see Wolff [1981] 1993). His latest avatar is the "art monster" (Dederer 2023), the artist who dedicates his life to his writing, while relying on others to carry out the domestic tasks of daily life, or on the contrary, who chooses to eschew moral norms and engages in a systematic "deregulation of all the senses", like Rimbaud. I agree this figure is a bit of a caricature, but it gathers together all the cultural traits we associate with the Western artist and in particular the writer. The women writers who have tried to follow in his footsteps while also being mothers have had to pay a heavy price, in their private lives and in the eyes of society, who have often cast far harsher judgements on them than on their male counterparts.

More generally, I feel that these texts cannot be considered as if they had been written in a vacuum. As Doireann Ní Ghriofa explains in her own memoir of motherhood and literary obsession (2020), she writes while folding laundry, cleaning the house, and generally taking care of her children. In this instance, and in the case of many of the texts I will be studying, context matters. Like Jane Austen and Emily Brontë, Doireann Ní Ghriofa creates in the middle of her house, with her children around her. There is not enough space in her house for her to have a soundproof room of her own, with a desk and a typewriter, or a computer. Mostly, she tells us, she writes on her phone, in her car, or in the bathroom. Writing by mothers in many cases completely redefines the way we imagine what a writer is, what she does, and how she does it.

Chapter overview

In Chapter 1, entitled "The Impossible Subject", I try to inscribe the question of the conflict between creativity and motherhood within the context of "maternal studies", a field of research which has emerged in the last few decades, alongside the boom of motherhood memoirs. I try to trace the evolution of the cultural discourse around motherhood by deconstructing the concept as it appeared in the wake of the Industrial Revolution in the West, and by looking at how it has been dealt with by the different "waves" of the feminist movement. If motherhood is the last frontier of female writing, I argue that it is also the "impossible subject" of feminism, to quote from Patrice DiQuinzio's work on the subject (2013). Indeed, I try to show how motherhood has always been a stumbling block for feminist critics inasmuch as it was often perceived as a hindrance to the liberation of women from patriarchy. Even if Adrienne Rich's work and her essential distinction between motherhood as experience and institution has laid out the foundations for a new, and more nuanced, vision of motherhood in our culture, there are still debates around the possibility for women to achieve a balance between their desire for self-fulfilment and their duties to their children, with an emphasis on the question of work. I try to show that guilt is one of the main affects which recur in the evocation of motherhood in cultural criticism and in self-life writing on the subject. I also contend that mothers are the impossible subject by showing that the way we have constructed the presumed subjectivity of motherhood is at odds with our definition of the individual in the liberal era: unlike non-mothers, their self is constructed as relational and incomplete. I then try to demonstrate that the role of maternal texts is precisely to open the possibility for a maternal subjectivity to emerge through writing and particularly self-life writing.

Chapter 2, which is entitled "To Have and Have Not", looks at the specific case of women writers who hesitate on whether they should become mothers or not. I interrogate some of the cultural assumptions which underpin their inner debates, and I dwell more specifically on the question of "matrophobia", which is the hatred, personal and/or cultural, aimed at one's mother, or the figure of the mother, in keeping with some of the debates among feminists themselves. I am particularly interested in demonstrating that the women who hesitate on whether they should have children or not are under the influence of our common representations of what an artist *should* be, which is at odds with our representations of what being a mother entails. What I have found interesting in the study of some texts by women who write about their hesitation is that they all try to inscribe themselves in an alternative female literary tradition, and they turn to their "literary foremothers" for advice. I dwell on two texts by Canadian writer Sheila Heti and Turkish writer Elif Shafak, who both portray their doubts and hesitations, in order to highlight the common tropes in their texts. In particular, both authors represent their conundrum as a confrontation with conflicting interior voices which they project outside of them via different literary devices. Both writers also engage in a dialogue with their mothers, real and symbolic, in order to make their decisions.

"On Pregnancy and Childbirth" is the third chapter of this study. It looks once again at the question of maternal subjectivity, this time in the context of pregnancy and childbirth. I try to take a historical view of the way the medical discourse of obstetrics has taken over both experiences, with both positive and negative results. On the one hand, childbirth in particular has both become much safer and less painful than it used to be, but the reverse side of the coin is that women have increasingly felt deprived of the very language that would enable them to express their experiences. I first look at the question of pregnancy, and how it is experienced by female authors as mostly an encounter with ideological presumptions of what an expectant mother should do. I then move on to the issue of childbirth to show that its representation has evolved in parallel with the way pregnant and birthing women have been considered by the medical institution. The first major evolution, I argue, was for them to manage to be represented at all in literary texts, when up until the 20th century, childbirth in particular, would be elided in literary representation, or recounted from the point of view of a male observer. As women increasingly took control of their own narratives, they started inscribing childbirth as an event within their writing. As I have found, it would take some time before women felt they could write about this event in the first person. In this respect, there are many instances in which female authors represent the event as if it was happening outside of them, which reveals both the ambivalent attitudes of newly liberated women towards an event which they still considered as incompatible with their autonomy, as well as the enduring control which the medical discourse still held over childbirth.

In Chapter 4, which is entitled "Mother Writing", I ask the question of whether there is such a thing as a distinct maternal form of writing. I look first at the disorienting effect new motherhood can have on women who were writers before they had children, and I go on to wonder if the conditions in which they are now required to write as mothers – characterised essentially by interruption – have a concrete impact on the way they write. I find that motherhood is best conceived of as a type of work, which takes place in a specific sociocultural context, rather than an identity. This distinction is essential if we are to understand whether there is anything distinctive in texts written by mothers. It does not imply that there is anything essential in their roles as mothers, but rather with the conditions in which they write, and the material as well as social hurdles they have to overcome. I then take a look at the genre of the motherhood memoir to highlight some of its recurring themes and tropes, showing that one of their stated aims is also to create a community of textual traces to share with other mothers, and possibly non-mothers alike.

Chapter 5 is devoted to the figure of the "Bad Mother" and tries to delineate its contours. In our culture, a mother is considered "bad" if she is selfish, or she fails in any way to place her children's welfare before her own, which creates a conundrum for mothers who are also writers, and who want to continue dedicating themselves to their vocations as artists. I compare the figure of the Bad Mother with that of the "Art Monster", a term coined by Jenny Offill (2014), which has been taken up by several cultural critics, particularly to interrogate the different standards to which we hold male and female artists. I look at the legacy left by such major artistic figures as Joan Didion, Sylvia Plath, and Doris Lessing, who have all been accused of having neglected their children, an accusation which is rarely levelled at male artists. I am also interested in the way other writers have been shamed publicly, not for having actually been found lacking as to their parental duties but for having dared to present motherhood in a less-than-positive light in their writing. I then borrow from recent psychoanalytic work on mothering the concept of "maternal ambivalence" as it is developed in particular by Rozsika Parker ([1995] 2005) to show that it provides the most apt entry point for a depiction of the conflicted feelings we often find portrayed in first-person narratives of motherhood.

Because the scope of this study necessarily extends beyond the texts themselves to the material conditions as well as the cultural context in which they were written, I had to use other tools than just those of literary criticism and aesthetics: I tried to diversify my approaches in order to account for the full range of questions raised by the issues of creativity combined with motherhood. I therefore used insights drawn from women's studies, philosophy, sociology, anthropology, psychoanalysis, and history, depending on the aspect of the question I was looking at. Issues relating to the specific subjectivity of mothers, for example, call for the use of philosophy and psychoanalysis, while the chapter dedicated to pregnancy and childbirth required a historical overview of the evolution of obstetrics. This diversity of approaches seems to me essential to account for the complexity of the issues women writers are faced with.

On a final note, I would add that this book was almost ten years in the making, which is the time it took for my children to grow from babies into children, with their own personalities, starting to demand some form of autonomy. Like many mother writers before me, it seemed at first impossible to get any form of writing done while they were in my life, claiming my time and attention, and I gradually got the sense that the time when they needed my full presence would eventually come to pass, probably more quickly than I thought. I have written this book wracked with the same sense of guilt felt by many of the mother writers whose texts I have studied, especially on the days when I could have kept them at home rather than work on my project. I hope that the readers, whether they are mothers or non-mothers, will find some comfort in reading about the delights and the travails of motherhood when one is also an artist. I hope I will be able to prove that motherhood and creativity may not be antagonistic endeavours and that there is enough room in most women's lives for both.

Works cited

Clark, Heather L. 2020. *Red Comet: The Short Life and Blazing Art of Sylvia Plath*. New York: Alfred A. Knopf.
Cosslett, Rhiannon Lucy. 2020. 'Millennials Are Exploring Motherhood – in a New Generation of Books'. *The Guardian*, 16 August 2020, sec. Opinion. www.theguardian.com/commentisfree/2020/aug/16/millennial-women-motherhood-books-novels-women-birth
Cowan, Shannon, Fiona Tinwei Lam, and Cathy Stonehouse. 2008. *Double Lives: Writing and Motherhood*. Montreal: McGill-Queen's University Press.
Cusk, Rachel. 2001. *A Life's Work: On Becoming a Mother*. New York: Picador.
———. 2008. 'I Was Only Being Honest'. *The Guardian*, 21 March 2008, sec. Books. www.theguardian.com/books/2008/mar/21/biography.women
———. 2019. 'Can a Woman Who Is an Artist Ever Just Be an Artist?' *The New York Times*, 7 November 2019, sec. Magazine. www.nytimes.com/2019/11/07/magazine/women-art-celia-paul-cecily-brown.html
Dederer, Claire. 2023. *Monsters: A Fan's Dilemma*. New York: Alfred A. Knopf.
DiQuinzio, Patrice. 2013. *The Impossibility of Motherhood: Feminism, Individualism and the Problem of Mothering*. London: Routledge.

Elkin, Lauren. 2018. 'Why All the Books about Motherhood?' *The Paris Review*, 17 July 2018. www.theparisreview.org/blog/2018/07/17/why-all-the-books-about-motherhood/

Hewett, Heather. 2020. 'Motherhood Memoirs'. In *The Routledge Companion to Motherhood*, edited by D. Lynn O'Brien Hallstein, Melinda Vandenbeld Giles, and Andrea O'Reilly, 191–201. Abingdon; New York: Routledge.

Lazarre, Jane. (1976) 1997. *The Mother Knot*. Durham, NC: Duke University Press.

Ní Ghriofa, Doireann. 2020. *A Ghost in the Throat*. Dublin: Tramp Press.

Offill, Jenny. 2014. *Dept. of Speculation*. London: Granta.

Parker, Rozsika. (1995) 2005. *Torn in Two: The Experience of Maternal Ambivalence*. London: Virago.

Plath, Sylvia. 1981. *The Collected Poems*. New York: Harper & Row.

Podnieks, Elizabeth. 2020. 'Matrifocal Voices in Literature'. In *The Routledge Companion to Motherhood*, edited by D. Lynn O'Brien Hallstein, Melinda Vandenbeld Giles, and Andrea O'Reilly, 176–90. Routledge Companions. Abingdon; New York: Routledge.

Podnieks, Elizabeth, and Andrea O'Reilly, eds. 2010. *Textual Mothers, Maternal Texts: Motherhood in Contemporary Women's Literatures*. Waterloo: Wilfrid Laurier University Press.

Rak, Julie. 2004. 'Are Memoirs Autobiography? A Consideration of Genre and Public Identity'. *Genre* 37 (3–4): 483–504. https://doi.org/10.1215/00166 928-37-3-4-483

Rich, Adrienne C. (1976) 1995. *Of Woman Born: Motherhood as Experience and Institution*. 2nd ed. Women's Studies. New York: Norton.

Sehgal, Parul. 2018. 'In a Raft of New Books, Motherhood From (Almost) Every Angle'. *The New York Times*, 24 April 2018, sec. Books. www.nytimes.com/2018/04/24/books/review-mothers-jacqueline-rose.html

Spira, Andrew. 2020. *The Invention of the Self: Personal Identity in the Age of Art*. London: Bloomsbury Academic.

Wolff, Janet. (1981) 1993. *The Social Production of Art*. 2nd ed. Communications and Culture. Basingstoke: Macmillan.

Woolf, Virginia. (1929) 2004. *A Room of One's Own*. Great Ideas. Harmondsworth: Penguin.

———. 2015. *Un lieu à soi*. Translated by Marie Darrieussecq. Paris: Denoël.

1 The impossible subject

Introduction

In 2015, Maggie Nelson published a memoir which would completely revolutionise the genre of motherhood memoir. Here was a lesbian woman documenting her journey through IVF, pregnancy, and childbirth, all the while reflecting on the values associated with motherhood in our culture. What was truly revolutionary in this work was not so much Nelson's portrayal of a queer family, as her wish to inscribe her personal testimony within the cultural conversation at large by including critics and theorists in the conversation. Hers was not the first book to analyse the values associated with motherhood in our culture, of course, since Adrienne Rich had already paved the way for such a reflection with her 1976 book *Of Woman Born: Motherhood as Experience and Institution* (Rich [1976] 1995), but Nelson was definitely taking the already existing genre of the motherhood memoir to new territories by pushing motherhood to the forefront of the cultural conversation. As she navigates concepts such as "sodomitical maternity" and examines the work of visual artist A.L. Steiner's "Puppies and Babies", she reflects on the reasons why the more highbrow audiences of cultural production have always turned up their noses on representations of motherhood in art (with the notable example of the Mary and Jesus) and quotes in a parenthesis *The New York Times Book Review*'s cover article on Mother's Day of 2012 which opened on the following lines (Nelson 2015, 88–89):

> No subject offers a greater opportunity for terrible writing than motherhood. [...]
> To be fair, writing about children is tough. You know why. They're not that interesting. What is interesting is that despite the mind-numbing boredom that constitutes 95 percent of child rearing, we continue to have them.
>
> (Newman 2012)

DOI: 10.4324/9781003461388-2

The piece, which was actually a review of Anne Enright's (2012) motherhood memoir, *Making Babies: Stumbling into Motherhood* (Enright 2012), perfectly encapsulates our common perception of motherhood as a subject: it is boring, trivial, better left within the confines of the nursery. With such stringently negative connotations attached to an experience which is however central to the lives of millions of women, how are the female authors who also happen to be mothers expected to include it in their writing? And for those women, like Nelson, and before her Adrienne Rich or Rachel Cusk, who decide to make their experience of motherhood an essential part of their writing and a privileged point of view from which to examine our culture, are there not better things to do than sit down in a room and write when there are children to attend, feed, play with, teach, and love? Even Maggie Nelson, for all the freedom of tone and scope she deploys in her writing, stumbles upon a roadblock: "I cannot hold my baby at the same time as I write" (Nelson 2015, 45).

Motherhood, I want to contend in this chapter, is an impossible subject, "a minefield", in the words of anthropologist Sarah Blaffer Hrdy (Hrdy 1999) and this is largely why women writers are finding it so difficult to reconcile motherhood and creativity: beyond the basic material question of who holds the baby while her mother is writing, which we will get to in time, I would like to draw an overview of the current discourse around motherhood in our culture in order to show that, even when women do find the time and the mental space to write about their experience of being pregnant and interacting with young children, they are faced with such cultural prohibitions that they are often tempted to renounce writing altogether. Some of those prohibitions come from deeply ingrained representations we have of mothers' subjectivity, or rather their lack of; as Susan Rubin Suleiman reminds us, quoting Hélène Deutsch: "Mothers don't write, they are written […] this is the underlying assumption of most psychoanalytic theories about writing and about artistic creation in general" (Suleiman [1979] 2011, 116). Mothers have been the subject of countless pages of writing, fictional and otherwise, but very rarely have they been the authors of their own experience, precisely because they have been constructed as a canvas over which the child can project her emotions: love, resentment, craving, mourning, frustration. Moreover, those writers who are also mothers must contend with social and cultural expectations of what a mother should be, that is a subject entirely devoted to her children, devoid of self and blissfully happy to boot.

Of course, the claim that motherhood is an "impossible subject" is slightly provocative and can seem to be contradicted by facts, given the volume of writing which has been produced on the subject in the last 50 years or so. On top of the boom of motherhood memoirs which has taken place over the last 20 years, there are now a great number of books, ranging from philosophy, sociology, anthropology, literary criticism, and cultural studies which have been published on the subject of motherhood. So why make the claim after all? Because, as I will try to demonstrate, any work that engages with the topic inevitably gets caught in a number of paradoxes and contradictions. Is motherhood compatible with feminism? Should women engage in the workforce and seek self-fulfilment, or would that mean harming her child in any way? Is there a specific maternal voice, or is that to engage in essentialism? All these questions are relevant to my reflection about creativity and motherhood, because for one, the female authors who decide to write about their experience of motherhood are very often aware of the writing that has been done on the subject, and if not, they arrive for the most part to the same conclusions. Looking at the work that has been produced as part of the new field of maternal studies gives us invaluable insight enabling us to understand some of the conundrums female authors find themselves entangled in when they try to reconcile being writers and mothers.

Dealing with guilt: the field of maternal studies

De-naturalising and re-historicising motherhood

The year 1976 was a landmark year for what was to become the field of maternal studies as it was the year when Adrienne Rich published her foundational study *Of Woman Born: Motherhood as Experience and Institution*. In the book, which is part autobiographical essay, part critical study, Rich borrows insights from medical history, anthropology, philosophy, and cultural studies in order to make a major distinction, one which would completely reconfigure our thinking about motherhood in culture. For Rich, women's access to the experience of being a mother is interfered with by the patriarchal institution of motherhood.

> Throughout this book I try to distinguish between two meanings of motherhood, one superimposed on the other: the *potential relationship* of any woman to her powers of reproduction and to children; and the *institution*, which aims at ensuring that that potential – and all women – shall remain under male control.
> (Rich [1976] 1995, 13)

In a 2004 collection of essays celebrating the legacy of Rich's text, scholar Andrea O'Reilly, who can be credited for much of the construction and legitimisation of maternal studies as a field, given the extensive work she has produced on the topic, commented that one of the major contributions made by Rich was to have deconstructed the institution of "motherhood" and paved the way for the introduction of "mothering" as a practice that is "female-defined and centered and potentially empowering to women" (O'Reilly 2004, 2). In all the critical studies that one can encounter as part of an exploration of maternal studies, Rich's text is the one that is the most often cited and has had the most influence. This is not just because it was the first major cultural study of motherhood, the book's breadth of scope, as well as the choice to introduce autobiographical elements, make *Of Woman Born* a text of reference, even 45 years after it was published.

Another of the major contributions made by Rich consisted in "de-naturalising" such notions as "maternal instinct", demonstrating how white, Western, middle-class motherhood was constrained by very precise cultural scripts. Only a few years later, in 1980, Elisabeth Badinter would also publish an influential, albeit controversial, book on the same subject, claiming that mother love was only a recent construction, and one which had been dictated by the socio-economic realities of the late 18th century (Badinter 1980). Although Badinter was strongly criticised at the time, mostly by historians who believed her work had been plagued by anachronisms and historical inaccuracies (Bernos, Fouquet, and Knibiehler 1981), she nevertheless took to task one of the most enduring clichés about motherhood, which was that mothers were "naturally" cut out – one could even say genetically programmed – to take proper care of children. Anthropologist Sarah Blaffer Hrdy, who wrote another major study about motherhood across time and culture, echoes Badinter:

> It is not true that women instinctively love their babies, in the sense that they automatically nurture each baby born. Neither do other mammals – although when they *do* care it is hard to explain their behavior as anything other than instinctive. In other words, there is probably no mammal in which maternal commitment does not emerge piecemeal and chronically sensitive to external cues. Nurturing has to be teased out, reinforced, maintained. Nurturing itself needs to be nurtured.
> (Hrdy 1999, 174)

Even though the concept of maternal instinct has been debunked time and time again, it has not completely disappeared and still informs most of our representations of motherhood. Yet the existence of this cultural script, according to which women are made for motherhood and naturally attuned to the needs of her children, supposes that anyone who departs from that script runs the risk of being considered as abnormal, freakish – a monster. And for those women who fail to confirm to the expectations of motherhood, this creates an enormous amount of guilt. In fact, if motherhood is an institution, guilt is the emotion which guards its doors and polices its inmates. As Rich herself discovers:

Soon I would begin to understand the full weight and burden of maternal guilt, that daily, nightly, hourly, *Am I doing what is right? Am I doing enough? Am I doing too much?* The institution of motherhood finds all mothers more or less guilty of having failed their children; and my mother, in particular, had been expected to help create, according to my father's plan, a perfect daughter.

(Rich [1976] 1995, 223)

All of the works I have come across can eventually be read as studies in guilt: why do women feel guilty? How can they stop feeling guilty? Where does the guilt come from? In many ways, the women who work on motherhood, the majority of whom are mothers themselves, seem to be working through their own guilt. Deconstructing motherhood as a cultural construct is one major step towards achieving that: the perception that most of the qualities women are expected to possess in order to be considered as "good mothers" are actually historically and culturally situated can lift some of the fears of being considered a monster, when, for example, a mother does not feel immediate love for her child or does not wish to renounce finding self-fulfilment outside of the relationship with her child.

A commonplace view regarding the cultural construction of motherhood, as we know it today in the Western English-speaking sphere, is that it appeared in the 19th century. For Ann Dally, "There have always been mothers but motherhood was invented" (Dally 1983, 17), and it was specifically invented in the Victorian era, at a time when the Industrial Revolution was reconfiguring the traditional model of the family. Once again the attempt to situate motherhood in a precise historical context is part of an effort to help women cope with "a crisis in motherhood", which, she claims, makes women responsible for all the ills which befall society, and to deconstruct some of our "illusions" about how mother should behave. In *The Mother/Daughter Plot*, Marianne Hirsch also associates the emergence of a new discourse about motherhood with the birth of industrial capitalism:

As representations of the child's vulnerability and need for nurturing and protection became more prominent, motherhood became an "instinct," a "natural" role and form of human connection, as well as practice. As the private sphere was isolated from the public under industrial capitalism, as women became identified with and enclosed within the private sphere, motherhood elevated middle-class and upper-class women into a position of increased personal status, if decreased social power.

(Hirsch 1989, 14)

This theme of critical writing about motherhood was carefully analysed by Petra Bueskens, who studies how the transition into modernity transformed women's role within the home. As liberalism and capitalism gave men access to new rights as individuals, women, and in most cases, mothers, ended up caught in a bind. If the liberal individual is free to find self-fulfilment outside of the community and outside of the home, what happens to the mothers? They could of course in theory find employment outside of the home, but who would pick up their mothering duties while they were away? For Bueskens, the institution of motherhood was created as the result of a moral panic over the possible dereliction of the family once women were given the chance to leave the home and claim their rights as individuals (Bueskens 2018, 9). This original contradiction, Bueskens argues, is responsible for the "double burden" or "double shift" that has been documented in many studies about domestic and emotional labour in the family. There are of course differences to be noted between social classes, as there has been a substantial participation of working-class women in the workforce in the UK and US between 1850 and 1950. I would add that most of Bueskens's remarks apply to middle- and upper-class women.

The latest tool of oppression: on "intensive mothering"

Many of the recent works of critical theory that have analysed perceptions of motherhood in our culture have focused on the concept of "intensive mothering", a term coined by Sharon Hays in her book *The Cultural Contradictions of Motherhood*. She defines it as "a gendered model that advises mothers to expend a tremendous amount of time, energy and money in raising their children" (Hays 1996, x). A natural by-product of the logic that confined the duties of childcare within the home and under the sole supervision of the mother, in the context of the late 20th century, when women were then expected to work outside of the home on top of taking care of their children, it added further pressure on women to succeed in their parenting as well as in their professional careers. This concept, which was taken up by critics in a slew of recent books, served as the basis for the description of the ideology which Western middle-class mothers must now labour under. As Hays and later Ennis (Ennis 2014) explain, it essentially amounts to making mothers solely responsible for every aspect of their child's development and envisions motherhood as self-sacrificial. As Andrea O'Reilly explains in her introduction to the collection of essays examining the legacy of Adrienne Rich's work:

> The ideology of natural-intensive mothering enacted in the patriarchal institution of motherhood has become the official and only meaning

of motherhood, marginalizing and rendering illegitimate alternative practices of mothering.

(O'Reilly 2004, 7)

Susan Douglas and Meredith Michaels have shown that women's entry into the workforce is not necessarily contradictory with the ideology of intensive mothering: mothers are expected to overperform in the care of their children, just like they would in the workplace. The neoliberal logic of individual competition now also extends to mothers who compare their performance to that of other mothers and engage in an impossible arms race to perfection:

> This book is about the rise in the media of what we are calling the "new momism": the insistence that no woman is truly complete or fulfilled unless she has kids, that women remain the best primary caretakers of children, and that to be a remotely decent mother, a woman has to devote her entire physical, psychological, emotional, and intellectual being, 24/7, to her children. The new momism is a highly romanticized and yet demanding view of motherhood in which the standards of success are impossible to meet.
>
> (Douglas and Michaels 2005, 4)

Judith Warner goes even further and contends that the ideology surrounding motherhood has become so "unmoored from reality" that it has turned into a form of "theology" (Warner 2007, 407). Like Bueskens, Warner also dates the emergence of this new set of prescriptions – call it intensive mothering or "new momism" – which mostly developed in the second half of the 20th century to the late 18th century and the social anxiety caused by the revolution in the structure of the family in Europe. Interestingly enough, O'Reilly suggests that the development of this ideology coincides with the boom of motherhood memoirs:

> I argue that this literary genre was born from a new ideology of motherhood, what Sharon Hays has termed "intensive mothering" and Susan Douglas and Meredith Michaels call the "new momism". More specifically, I contend that, as this new ideology made possible a public voice on motherhood, it simultaneously limited what that voice could say about motherhood.
>
> (Podnieks and O'Reilly 2010, 205)

Writers who are also mothers also suffer under the impossible prescriptions of "motherhood-as-religion", yet it has also given them something to write back at. Writing as a mother also means contending with the discourse which pervades our culture and is responsible for the impossible standards mothers are expected to meet. Turkish writer Elif Shafak, who is the author of *Black Milk: On Motherhood and Writing*, a book which reads like a partly fictional motherhood memoir, sums up the contradiction:

> Today, we do not speak or write much about the face of motherhood that has been left in the shadows. Instead, we thrive on two dominant teachings: the traditional view that says motherhood is our most sacred and significant obligation and we should give up everything else for this duty; and the "modern" women's magazine view that portrays the quintessential "superwoman" who has a career, husband and children and is able to satisfy everyone's needs at home and at work.
> (Shafak 2013, 252–53)

For Susan Maushart, the pressure put on mothers to achieve perfection has created among them a "conspiracy of silence" and has encouraged them to don "the mask of motherhood"; she claims that mothers have created a sort of *faux self* in order to eschew self-blame and guilt:

> The mask of motherhood is what mutes our rage into murmurs and softens our sorrow into resignation. The mask of motherhood is the semblance of serenity and control that enables women's work to pass unnoticed in the larger drama of human life.
> (Maushart 2007, 463)

For Elizabeth Podnieks, writing about motherhood *as* a mother implies a removal of that particular mask in order to reach the truth of the experience of motherhood and tell it in an authentic way (Podnieks 2020, 177).

The web of contradictions: mothers who work

The contradiction at the heart of the ideology of intensive mothering is that mothers are expected to give themselves entirely to the care of their children, but when it comes to joining the ranks of the workforce, the proverbial jury is still out. Thus, the most guilt-inducing question of all remains the following: should a mother find paid employment outside of the home? Should she even be allowed to thrive outside of the family? Does that mean abandoning her children and failing them as a result? The question of mothers seeking paid employment and work in general is of particular relevance for women writers who are also mothers. Also, theirs is an atypical type of work, and it is one which requires very strict conditions for it to be able to happen. This question is at the heart of Rachel Cusk's memoir, entitled *A Life's Work: On Becoming a Mother*. In the introduction, the narrator explains that becoming a mother blew up her illusions about gender equality:

> This experience forcefully revealed to me something to which I had never given much thought: the fact that after a child is born the lives of its mother and father diverge, so that where before they were living in a state of some equality, now they exist in a sort of feudal relation to each other. A day spent at home caring for a child could not be more different from a day spent working in an office. Whatever their relative merits, they are days spent on opposite sides of the world. From that irreconcilable beginning, it seemed to me that some kind of slide into deeper patriarchy was inevitable: that the Father's Day would gradually gather to it the armour of the outside world, of money and authority and importance, while the mother's remit would extend to cover the entire domestic sphere.
> (Cusk 2001, 11)

For Bueskens, the "sequestration" in the home imposed by modern motherhood has created the irreconcilable rift between the private space and the public space where most civil and economic activity takes place. In the case of the narrator in Cusk's memoir, the conundrum is made even more complicated by the fact that a writer's work does not necessarily require removing oneself to a distinct place and is often performed from the home. While she was under the illusion that she would be able to carry on working from home with her child in the next room, she realises with dismay that the home has become a domestic space, which means that she will not be able to get any work done anymore. Or does it? At the end of the memoir, the narrator concludes that mothering her children is "the hardest work I have ever done" before she confesses – with some portion of guilt – that she may not have done a perfect job of it.

For Ruth Quiney, much of the sense of shock and horror experienced by the narrator in Cusk's memoir comes from the perceived contradiction between her new role as a mother and the self she had previously constructed as independent and productive:

> However, the suffering and crises of subjective identification to which the writing bears witness paradoxically confirm the continuing inscription of the mother as epitome of private, sacrificial femininity, oppositional to the cleanly bounded, productive post-Enlightenment subject.
> (Quiney 2007, 21)

According to the narrator in Cusk's memoir: "Looking after children is a low-status occupation. It is isolating, frequently boring, relentlessly

20 *The impossible subject*

demanding and exhausting. It erodes your self-esteem and your membership of the adult world" (Cusk 2001, 13). For contemporary women, and in particular female authors who have managed to make writing a career, becoming a mother is felt like a breach of the feminist contract which would allow them to find self-actualisation in their work. Locked up in the home with her baby, she is no longer a productive member of society. In the introduction, the narrator explains that eventually she was able to reclaim her career as a writer by "demolish[ing] traditional family culture altogether":

> My partner left his job and we moved out of London. People began to inquire about him as if he were ill, or dead. What's he going to *do*? they would ask me avidly, and then, getting no answer, him. Look after the children while Rachel writes her book about looking after the children, was his reply. Nobody else seemed to find this particularly funny.
>
> (Cusk 2001, 13)

Although Cusk's following books, in particular her next memoir *Aftermath* (Cusk 2012), tell us that this family arrangement did not particularly work out because the couple eventually separated, we realise that for a mother to also be a writer necessitates some form of deconstruction of typical family structures. Yet the reason why I felt it was important to dwell on the case of Cusk's memoir is that it addresses the question of work, which is at the centre of many of the critical studies on motherhood.

For Sharon Hays, mothers are torn between two very contradictory ideologies, one that would demand they devote the same energy to their work lives as to their family lives. Women, she contends, are left to choose between two mutually exclusive models: "the warm, nurturing mothers on the one side and cold, competitive career women on the other" (Hays 1996, 16). If they choose to stay at home and devote themselves to their children, they are perceived as unproductive, as well as stifling; yet if they choose to work outside of the home, they are suspected of neglecting their children. Shari Thurer hints at the same contradiction mothers are still labouring under: sending children to day care is akin to abandonment, while keeping them at home means isolating them. Our culture, she notes, is particularly cruel to mothers who choose to have a career but looks down upon stay-at-home mums.

> The public does not warm to mothers who are otherwise engaged, especially when they don't have to be. We grudgingly accept it when a woman "has" to work, meaning that her family's survival depends

on her income. It is when a woman chooses to pursue a career that a shadow is cast over her motherliness.

(Thurer 1995, xviii)

Faced with this barrage of cultural prescriptions (from the media, TV, and film representations, and from advice books), mothers end up facing guilt at every corner they take. Women writers who are also mothers fall prey to very much the same guilt-inducing contradictory logic, as they intend to engage in an activity which does not even have the excuse of being productive, but may seem to outsiders, like the friends of Cusk's narrator, as pure self-indulgence. Anthropologist Sarah Blaffer Hrdy tries to take a longer view on the issue; like Hirsch and Bueskens, she sees a coincidence between the debates around the possibility for mothers to work and the emergence of the discourse over a possible maternal instinct, around the time of the Industrial Revolution. In her introduction to *Mother Nature*, she confesses to having felt torn between the duties of childcare and her desire to get back to her academic work. She claims that observations of other cultures as well as other species, primates especially, show us that there is no such thing as a homogeneous class of mothers, but rather a series of individuals who make decisions based on the resources available to them.

> Female primates have always been dual-career mothers, forced to compromise between maternal and infant needs. It is precisely for this reason that primate mothers including human foragers, have always shared care of offspring with others – *when it was feasible*. Acknowledging infant needs does not necessarily enslave mothers.
>
> (Hrdy 1999, 494)

In this assessment Hrdy is particularly conscious of the long shadow cast by the proponents of "attachment theory", such as Winnicott and Bowlby over the issue. In the chapter of her book entitled "Of Human Bondage", she looks at the feminist critical takes on the way mothers have been bullied into compliance by a number of paradoxical injunctions which induce tremendous guilt and self-doubt. She looks at books such as Diane Eyer's *Motherguilt* (Eyer 1996), which takes to task John Bowlby's theories about bonding and holds them responsible for the shame being heaped on mothers who decide to have a career while mothering their infants. Bowlby, in short, developed a set of ideas which held that small babies needed to form a deep and exclusive bond with their mothers which, in order for them to thrive, had to last well into their first months and years. This theory, dubbed "bonding theory" or attachment theory, became extremely popular in the 1960s and 1970s and quickly coalesced into a movement of its own, generating a new set of recommendations for mothers to best achieve this crucial step in their relationship with their babies: mothers were encouraged to hold their babies close lest they cause them some irremediable hurt. The backlash quickly followed, as documented by Hrdy (Hrdy 1999, 488), who nevertheless tries to situate the debate in its context: at the height of the second wave of feminism, mothers did not want to be reminded that their duties as mothers could mean foregoing some of their individual freedom:

> By endowing human infants with a long mother-centered primate heritage, by envisioning infants with special needs and mothers as creatures especially designed to satisfy them, and by situating an infant's sense of security and self in the availability of this specially equipped mother, evolutionists like Bowlby and Trivers appeared to be imposing on women painful choices no man need ever make: her aspirations versus her infant's well-being; vocation *or* reproduction.
>
> (Hrdy 1999, 490)

Hrdy goes on to show that Bowlby's theories "poured a particular type of acid on mothers' fresh, open wounds": if women had been liberated by feminism, how could they bear being re-enslaved by their children? Hrdy is quick to show that a lot of the backlash against these theories was part of a knee-jerk reaction against observations which had, at the time, been mistaken for prescriptions as to what the healthy development of a child should be. Even if Bowlby personally took a dim view of those mothers who decided to go on working after they had children, his work actually did not exclude the possibility that children could form a special bond with another trusted adult. In other words, for Hrdy, it did not exclude the possibility of confiding the care of children to an "allomother", a father, grandparent, or day-care worker. For Hrdy, such arrangements are more often the norm than the exception in primates and in non-Western cultures: over time, women have rarely been expected to take care of their children alone, but the recent evolution of the family structure has placed mothers in sole charge of the care of her children and locked her in the privacy of her home. Recognising the infant's primary needs at birth does not necessarily entail the mother's sacrifice of her self-actualisation, but the intensely negative reactions around Bowlby's theories hint at the remanence of a series of unresolved issues around motherhood, especially in its relationship with mainstream feminism.

Motherhood as the "unfinished work of feminism"

In her article "The meaning of Motherhood in Black Culture and Black Mother-Daughter Relationships", Patricia Hill Collins argues that debating whether mothers should be allowed to work outside of the home is a luxury that Black women in the US have historically not been able to afford. For Black women to choose to take on full-time parenting meant being branded as "welfare queens" and facing the accusation of living off social benefits. Childcare, she explains, has traditionally been a shared responsibility and mothers have always expected help from a network of "allomothers".

> On the one hand, African-American women have long integrated their activities as economic providers into their mothering relationships. In contrast to the cult of true womanhood where work is defined as being in opposition to and incompatible with motherhood, work for Black women has been an important and valued dimension of Afrocentric definition of Black motherhood. On the other hand, African-American women's experiences as mothers under oppression were such that the type and purpose of work Black women were forced to do greatly impacted on the type of mothering relationships blood mothers and othermothers had with Black children.
> (Collins 1987, 5)

By identifying "the cult of true womanhood" (which is another name for the ideology of intensive mothering as articulated by Hays *et alii*) as an essentially white construct, Collins points at contradictions within feminism, specifically second-wave feminism, which place Black women in an impossible position. Indeed, at the time when she was writing, motherhood had become a hot topic in feminist theory insofar as two seemingly irreconcilable positions had emerged in the debate. She identifies two poles: the traditionalists, who see motherhood as consubstantial with a woman's identity, and those feminists who want to dismantle motherhood as a patriarchal institution and tool of oppression. For Collins, the terms of this debate do not apply to Black motherhood, as racial oppression had historically deprived Black families from the possibility of forming a nuclear unit. Black mothers, she argues, disproportionately parent alone and need to work in order to support their children. The critic bell hooks does not say otherwise, like Collins, she is very critical of the "romanticization of motherhood by bourgeois white women" (hooks [1984] 2007, 147) as well as the feminist discourse which would see motherhood as a tool of oppression. Historically, she reminds us, Black women have found "work in the context of family as humanizing labor", as opposed to the work they were required to perform outside of the home (hooks [1984] 2007, 145).

For Bueskens, the unresolved questions about the possibility for women to work and accomplish themselves outside of the family make motherhood "the central unfinished business of feminism" (Bueskens 2018, 3). In a 2018 *Guardian* article, journalist Amy Westervelt observed that while motherhood was having "its moment in books, TV and even women's magazines", the questions it raises for feminists remain open and do not even seem close to have found a resolution (Westervelt 2018). Back in 1992, Ann Snitow had tried to draw an overview of US feminism's relationship with motherhood and had identified two main positions: "pronatalism" on the one hand and "the criticism of pronatalism": she believes there ensued a vicious fight between those feminists who have claimed motherhood as a fundamental aspect of their identities as women and those who have purported to deconstruct motherhood as a tool of patriarchal oppression, a fight which has resulted in all-round defensiveness. She blames first-wave feminist texts such as Simone de Beauvoir's *The Second Sex* (Beauvoir [1949] 2012), Betty Friedan's *The Feminine Mystique* (Friedan [1963] 2010), or Shulamith Firestone's later text *The Dialectic of Sex* (Firestone 1971) for having set the original tone of defiance, even distaste, among feminists with regard to motherhood. For de Beauvoir, Friedan, and Firestone, who all wrote before abortion and contraception were made widely available to women and enshrined as rights in most Western countries, the possibility of having children kept women away from achieving full independence and equality with men.

Snitow identifies a second period, starting in the mid-1970s, and including Adrienne Rich's work, in which "feminism tried to take on the issue of motherhood seriously, to criticize the institution, explore the actual experience, theorize the social and psychological implications" (Snitow 1992, 34). But it was not until 1979 that the discussion shifted from motherhood as institution to the family as practice: "in this period, feminists speak of 'different voices' and 'single mothers by choice'; the feminist hope of breaking the iron bond between mother and child seems gone, except in rhetorical flourishes, perhaps gone for good in this wave" (Snitow 1992, 34). With the advent of broad societal changes, the discussion shifted from the opportunity of being a mother or not as part of the feminist struggle to the best way of navigating women's widespread participation to the workforce and the possibility to access reliable childcare. In fact, what Snitow reveals is the existence of yet another dividing line between women, this time not over the best way to take care of children, but over whether it is possible to be a mother and a feminist.

The question of childcare is of particular relevance to this debate, as I believe it may hold the key to at least a part of the motherhood conundrum. The year 1976 was not only the year when Adrienne Rich's *Of Woman Born* was published, it also saw the publication of US writer Jane Lazarre's *The Mother Knot*, which is the first book to have been branded with the label of "motherhood memoir". The very title of the book hints at the web of contradictions which at the time still characterised the experience of being a mother in Western societies for those women who tried to be mothers and writers. In the book, the narrator details the emotional turmoil she goes through as she tries to juggle all her different roles while feeling overwhelmed with guilt and a sense of alienation from herself. Around the last part of the memoir, she realises that the resolution of her conundrum hinges upon the possibility of joining a communal day-care centre:

> Was it possible, I asked myself, that the simple fact of a good day-care center, a place where Benjamin loved to go every day and which, therefore, freed me from the guilt of leaving him, was the essence of the liberation which I had mistakenly sought in the unraveling of all of my spiritual and emotional tangles?
> (Lazarre [1976] 1997, 128)

The arrangement allows the narrator to enjoy a few hours every day to get on with her duties as a freelance academic while joining a community of mothers who are going through the same difficulties as she is. Yet at the time when she made the decision to leave her child at the child-care facility in her neighbourhood, she could not help but sense a silent judgemental gaze on the part of those "mothers on the bench", the "perfect" mothers who seem to have mastered the art of intensive mothering. Could she be hurting her child by leaving him in the hands of another woman than her? Or are children just as well taken care of by a network of concerned "othermothers"? For bell hooks, accepting the idea that responsibility for childcare should be shared and not simply the duty of individual women would be a true revolution in parenting (hooks [1984] 2007). Sarah Blaffer Hrdy believes we should be careful here: while human infants need their mothers as well as allomothers in order to thrive, the difficulty is still to be able to enlist women willing to perform those ungrateful duties – "throwing money" at the idea of day care is not going to be sufficient, and the reality is that it's often very difficult to find those women in sufficient numbers (Hrdy 1999, 504).

Nevertheless, although the narrator in Lazarre's memoir cannot help but feel judged by the perfect, self-sacrificing mothers, she refuses to engage in the infamous "mommy wars" and forces herself to look at those women as sitting on the same side of the fence as she is: overwhelmed and tired, they are probably dogged by the same sense of guilt and inadequacy as she is:

> If only those expert mothers might give to many children, more than just their own. Instead, they have been robbed of self-respect by a society which idolizes and damns them, and most recently, by the women's

movement too. I vacillated continually between hating them for their cowardice and loving them for their endurance.

(Lazarre [1976] 1997, 132)

The narrator, a self-professed feminist, sees that in condemning those women she would be engaging in the very type of mother-blaming she has been trying to avoid in her own practice of motherhood. How then, to reconcile feminism and motherhood? And is a woman a feminist in spite of, or thanks to, her experience of motherhood? For Marianne Hirsch, the only way to achieve that reconciliation is to realise that, even if not all women are mothers, they were all someone's daughter. In *The Mother/Daughter Plot: Narrative, Psychoanalysis, Feminism*, Hirsch shows that in cultural representation in general, and in literature in particular, the mother–daughter bond which was at the heart of many fictional representations of women's lives in the 19th and early 20th centuries was increasingly replaced by the bond of sisterhood:

> In the 1970s, the prototypical feminist voice was, to a large degree, the voice of the daughter attempting to separate from an overly connected or rejecting mother, in order to bond with her sisters in a relationship of mutual nurturance and support among equals.
>
> (Hirsch 1989, 164)

Breaking with the figure of the mother was at the time a way for women to break the bonds that attached them to their mothers in order to find the freedom to self-actualise. Yet for Adrienne Rich, the only way to climb out of the spiral of guilt and resentment which separates women from each other, and to truly understand ourselves, is to understand our own mothers (Rich [1976] 1995, 225). Daughters, Rich claims, have been separated from their mothers by the patriarchy and have been taught to despise them as obstacles to their self-actualisation, and no amount of sisterhood can repair the loss of that original bond.

To illustrate her point, Rich takes the example of Doris Lessing's autobiographical novel *A Proper Marriage* (Lessing 1954), in which the heroine Martha Quest, on discovering that she is pregnant, decides that she will be a wholly different mother than her own mother ever was. Martha's mother was a creature of patriarchy, while Martha considers herself as a free spirit. Borrowing from Lynn Sukenick's analysis of the novel (Sukenick 1973), Rich uses the term "matrophobia" to identify that particular form of fear mixed with hatred which many empowered women feel they must harbour towards their mothers, whom they judge as insufficiently liberated:

> Matrophobia can be seen as a womanly splitting of the self, in the desire to become purged once and for all of our mothers' bondage, to become

individuated and free. The mother stands for the victim in ourselves, the unfree woman, the martyr. Our personalities seem dangerously to blur and overlap with our mothers'; and in a desperate attempt to know where mother ends and daughter begins, we perform radical surgery.
(Rich [1976] 1995, 236)

For Lynn O'Brien Hallstein, the discord among feminists over the issue of motherhood can be attributed to the sentiment identified by Rich in Lessing's work and in fact in many other authors; yet to her this "killing of the mother" is not liberating at all. She calls for a radical "purging" of the matrophobia she claims "permeates" the discourse over motherhood and its relationship with feminism. She is specifically conscious of the fact that matrophobia is at the origin of many divisions and misunderstandings within the feminist movement and discourages "feminist scholars from understanding fully the contemporary relationship between feminism and maternity" (Hallstein 2010, 2).

The other pitfall which needs to be navigated in the relationship between feminism and motherhood is that of essentialism. As Patrice DiQuinzio has demonstrated in a 1993 article, the problem of analysing the specific forms of oppression related to motherhood from the point of view of the mother is that it grounds the experience in a biological reality. At a time when contraception and abortion had loosened the ties between femininity and fertility, at least in most Western societies, the possibility of motherhood increasingly appeared as a choice rather than a destiny. For DiQuinzio, claims about a universal female experience grounded in motherhood run the risk of essentialising female gender identity and making it contingent on women's exclusive capacity of bearing children alone (DiQuinzio 2013, 11).

This is the fine line treaded by Sara Ruddick for example. For Ruddick, viewing motherhood as only a form of oppression is in itself exploitative and does not allow feminists to articulate a coherent image of what it is that mothers do (Ruddick 1980, 344). Although she is wary of essentialism and does not wish to see motherhood as consubstantial with womanhood, she does argue that there is such a thing as maternal thinking which is characterised by the specific type of attention the mother will bestow on her child. Maternal thinking, in her view, is not a biological, but rather a social, construct, and it functions as an alternative to other forms of more dominant thinking practices, be they scientific or religious. If women struggle to develop that specific form of relationship to the child, and by extension to the world, it is because of the inauthenticity brought about by patriarchal oppression – which can be complicated by class- and race-based forms of oppression.

For DiQuinzio, the only way to avoid the trap of essentialism is to make sure to situate the experience of motherhood as a set of practices which are contingent on the mother's class, race, or sexual orientation. Patricia Hill Collins's piece on Black motherhood is a good reminder that any universalist take on motherhood runs the risk of ignoring the realities of some subsets of women whose experiences are not represented in culture-specific analyses of motherhood, which are often grounded in the lived experiences of white, middle-class mothers. Typically, the debate over whether mothers should be allowed to work does not concern Black mothers, who have often been relegated to the working class. Nancy Gerber in particular shows that even in the context of mothers' access to the status of professional writers on the part of mothers, the question of class is crucial, and not necessarily taken in consideration in feminist reflections on the compatibility between motherhood and creativity (Gerber 2003).

In a 2003 book entitled *The Impossibility of Motherhood*, Patrice DiQuinzio makes further attempts at pinning down what it is that makes motherhood such a difficult subject to broach in feminist discourse. For her the difficulty hinges upon "the relationship of feminism and individualism", more specifically:

> Feminism has to rely on individualism in order to articulate its claims that women are equal human subjects of social and political agency and entitlement. But, I argue, feminism has found it impossible to theorize mothering adequately in terms of an individualist theory of subjectivity.
> (DiQuinzio 2013, xii)

In other words, in liberalism, the promises of feminist liberation have been predicated on women's access to the same individual rights as men (see Bueskens 2018). Yet it is undeniable that women's individuality is complicated by the experience of motherhood: when she becomes a mother, a woman cannot remain as free of her movements as she used to be, something that men do not experience, or at least not with the same intensity.

For DiQuinzio, the figure of the individual which has come to be the central paradigm of human existence within society was created "in terms consistent with traditional Western conceptions of masculinity" (DiQuinzio 2013, xii–xiii). Jennifer Sinclair explains that motherhood is scripted in our culture as the antithesis of the "modern": while the male version of modernity is constructed on the model of the arrow shooting into the future, mothers' labour is cyclical, conservative, mired in everyday banalities (Sinclair 2005, 87). Although women have historically been able to access, via feminist struggles, a comparable level of individual freedom, motherhood often comes in the way of their full liberation from such recurrent, cyclical demands in everyday time. Wrestling their way out of that dilemma implies for feminist analysts of motherhood, to consider the female identity as "different" from that of men and to claim that difference as the basis on which to claim equal rights with men, which thus creates another dilemma. Yet she argues it implies that feminist theory "must accept the inevitability of the dilemma of difference and its resulting paradoxes in theorizing mothering, and thus must embrace, or at least reconcile itself to, what I call a 'paradoxical politics of motherhood'" (DiQuinzio 2013, xvi).

As the narrator in Cusk's *A Life's Work* notes in the introduction to the memoir, the experience of motherhood is, at least for contemporary women, one of the major encounters with gender inequality. The question of women's access to work is therefore central here: now that women are today relatively free to engage in a career of their own in Western societies, the arrival of children in their lives will unquestionably complicate their engagement in the workforce. In the case of women who have chosen to become writers or even artists, they must comply with the requirements of intensive mothering and shift all their creative energy from their work to the care of their children, lest they face the judgement of society as a whole. Even if they decide to parent in their own terms, they must contend with the material difficulties of raising a small child: the shortage of sleep, constant interruptions, and a gnawing sense of guilt. While one of the obvious solutions would be to solicit more help from the mothers' partners, who are often male, the reality of a child's early life often makes delegating the care of an infant to her father a complicated affair, if the mother is breastfeeding her child for example. This is why I believe that looking at the major rifts within feminist theory around the issue of motherhood is entirely relevant to my reflection on motherhood and creativity. As we look further into specific testimonies around motherhood by female authors, we will see that those debates are replicated within women's individual experiences of motherhood: they often – though not always – labour under the same contradictions and struggle to articulate their work, and their identity as artists, with their duties as mothers.

Mothers as impossible subjects

For Alison Stone, the issues raised by motherhood go far beyond the mere question of work and autonomy, extending to the possibility for mothers to be subjects of their own experience. Once the woman writer who is also a mother has asserted her right to being, or to remaining, an author, is she free to write about her experience? The question is not therefore just whether she can write while being a mother, but if she can express herself *as* a mother. In our culture, that is far from obvious. Looking at Cusk's *A Life's Work*, Stone analyses the despair felt by women such as the narrator at seeing their lives being thrown into disarray once they become mothers: "Having formerly been seen as agents of their own lives and treated by others as centers of agency, suddenly they find themselves perceived as largely subservient to the child(ren) for whom they care" (Stone 2013, 2). Turning from sociocultural to psychoanalytic analyses of motherhood in culture, we find that we in fact end up at what is very much the same point. When they become mothers, women realise that they cannot have equal access to the individual rights guaranteed by liberalism because of their co-dependent relationship with their children.

From a psychoanalytic point of view, the formation of the self and the access to the Symbolic are predicated upon a radical break with the mother's body – and if she is a body only, she is not allowed a voice of her own. Mothers, from a broad psychoanalytic perspective, are "selfless", that is, they must forego their own desires and sacrifice them to the well-being of their children; but more deeply than that, they are denied a self of their own: they must forever remain on the side of the inchoate, the unformed, the pre-Symbolic. From that point of view therefore, a mother cannot be a writer, she is the launching pad for the individuation of her children, which means that she must renounce being individuated herself. For Susan Rubin Suleiman, this view is nothing but a sophisticated way of justifying the moral imperative for mothers to dedicate themselves solely to their children, which precludes any form of creativity outside of their mothering duties: "It took psychoanalysis to transform moral obligations into a psychological 'law,' equating the creative impulse with the procreative one and decreeing that she who has a child feels no need to write books" (Suleiman [1979] 2011, 118–19).

For Alison Stone it is essential to analyse why motherhood has been constructed as the antithesis of selfhood, if we are to understand why it is so difficult for writers to express themselves *as* mothers.

> Apparently, maternity challenges (no doubt to varying degrees for different mothers) one's capacities to speak and make meaning and one's sense of being a single, unified subject. These are felt to be under threat, compromised, or recoverable only with difficulty and at the expense of other, newly acquired dimensions of life as a mother. The abilities that are threatened here may seem disparate, but they are connected by virtue of the modern conception of the subject. The subject is one who actively gives meaning to his or her experience (in speech, writing, or other modes), and who can do so only because at some level he or she identifies as the single agent performing this activity. But in becoming a mother, one ceases to be readily able to identify oneself as a single, unified agent, because one has returned in fantasy to the relational

context of one's early childhood before one achieved subjectivity by breaking from this context.

(Stone 2013, 15)

One source for those reflections on the maternal self can be found in Nancy Chodorow's work. Her book *The Reproduction of Mothering: Psychoanalysis and the Sociology of Gender*, which has remained to this day extremely influential in the field of maternal studies, on a par with Adrienne Rich's *Of Woman Born*, argues that women's sense of self is defined in relationship with the fact that they are mothered by another woman.

From the retention of preoedipal attachments to their mother, growing girls come to define and experience themselves as continuous with others; their experience of self contains more flexible or permeable ego boundaries. Boys come to define themselves as more separate and distinct, with a greater sense of rigid ego boundaries and differentiation. The basic feminine sense of self is connected to the world, the basic masculine sense of self is separate.

(Chodorow 1978, 169)

What Chodorow is trying to say here is that, once again, our definition of selfhood as clearly defined and independent is based in culture, and in history, as we saw earlier, but it is also based on gender differences in the way boys and girls interact with their mothers. By extension this means that if women want to have access to the same type of individuality as men, they must necessarily break with their mothers. It follows logically that in our conception of identity, the maternal is identified with the lack of self: in fact, it is the very antithesis of selfhood.

The French philosophers

The definition of the maternal as the locus of the undefined and the antithesis of selfhood actually originates from the theories of Freud (the oedipal crisis) and Lacan (the entry into the Symbolic). Luce Irigaray, Hélène Cixous, and Julia Kristeva have all built on these premises to articulate their own sense of what the maternal stands for in our culture and have tried to establish motherhood as a specific set of meanings. As Adalgisa Giorgio has shown, all three philosophers start from the same assumption that mothers have been denied the power of saying "I", which has justified their traditional exclusion from our culture (Giorgio 2002, 13). Yet their theories diverge in the way they position themselves with regard to psychoanalysis. For Luce Irigaray, who takes an outsider's stance with regard to Lacan's theories and to Western philosophy in general (see M. B. Walker 2002), the maternal has been unjustly construed as the locus of the amorphous, the undefined, the other to the Platonician ideal order of truth. The fact that the condition for the access to both selfhood and knowledge is the disavowal of the mother is proof of the deep misogynistic currents underlying Western culture (Irigaray 1974, 330). In *Et l'une ne bouge pas sans l'autre* (*The One Doesn't Stir without the Other*), she argues for a recognition of the mother–daughter relationship as an alternative form of access to knowledge (Irigaray 1979, 22). Like Hélène Cixous in *La Jeune née* (*The Newly Born Woman*) (Cixous and Clément 1975) with the concept of *écriture féminine*, Irigaray tries to inscribe specific forms of maternal knowledge and selfhood in our culture by making motherhood a specific vantage point and a specific practice of language.

Julia Kristeva's work on motherhood is often lumped together with Cixous and Irigaray's theories, yet she takes a very different stance, specifically with regard to Lacanian theory. For Kristeva, there is no doubt that the maternal functions as the Other to language and she does not question Lacan's belief that entry into selfhood and language (the Symbolic) is predicated upon a necessary matricidal break with the mother (Kristeva 1999). More specifically, if, as Chodorow also suggests, the mother–child (and even more particularly the mother–daughter) relationship is characterised by undifferentiation, the possibility to access individuation supposes the rejection of the mother and of her body, which must be considered as abject. Unlike Irigaray, Kristeva does not take a hammer to the foundations of psychoanalysis but rather offers a reconsideration of the pre-Symbolic space of the mother–child relationship, which she identifies as the *chora*. For Kristeva, because the relationship between the mother and her child takes place somewhere prior to structured language, it does not imply nothing meaningful is being produced. In her book *La révolution du langage poétique* (*Revolution in Poetic Language*) (Kristeva 1974), she argues that the *chora* can be construed as a site of resistance to symbolic language and claims that avant-garde poetic creation (specifically Surrealism) shatters the codes of meaningful language and operates a return to the pre-verbal, pre-Symbolic *chora*. The maternal, then, is not just a position of submission to patriarchy, its unformed nature poses a threat to the very foundation of the most patriarchal of institution, language.

Of course, the spectre of essentialism is always lurking in the background. As Ewa Ziarek explains, Kristeva's theory of maternal positionality has given rise to a debate among feminist critics. Identifying the maternal with subversion means casting real-life mothers in the role of outsiders, with little possibility to act outside of that script. She wonders: "does [Kristeva's] elaboration of the maternal outside the symbolic order boil down to a crude version of essentialism, if not a mute biologism?" (Ziarek

1992, 92). For Marianne Hirsch, the association between the maternal and the unspeakable does not leave a space for the mother as subject, and even less for the mother as author (Hirsch 1989, 171). Ziarek tries to rescue Kristeva's theory from the accusations of essentialism by demonstrating that the *chora* does not stand completely outside of language and symbolism (since we are able to talk about it and theorise it), and that it can be inscribed within the Symbolic through poetic creation, for instance. Susan Rubin Suleiman also looks at the contradictions within Kristeva's theory of the semiotic: those avant-garde artists who Kristeva claims did take a decisively anti-patriarchal stance in their works by refusing the strictures of symbolic language did so in defiance of the Lacanian Father; but in reality, their relationship with the mother as figure was one of defiance against individual mothers, who were perceived as upholders of traditional values. As she suggests:

> Although surrealism in its heyday (roughly, 1924–1935) was virtually all male, imbued with deeply – even if unconsciously – misogynistic attitudes toward women, the movement eventually became quite open to women artists. This did not, however, change the surrealists' view of the family or of mothers.
> (Suleiman 1994, 274)

In her book, *Cool Men and the Second Sex*, Susan Fraiman makes a very similar point about American counterculture, which, she claims, constructed itself on a celebration of a certain form of independent, wilful masculinity, which supposed a rejection of the maternal coded as conservative, and in other words, "uncool" (Fraiman 2003). To come back to Kristeva, the passage through resistance and avant-garde creation does not rescue motherhood from its association with the unformed and the abject. For Imogen Tyler, Kristeva's association with French feminism is questionable at best, since she plays into the matricidal plot which has been denounced by Irigaray and Cixous.

> Kristeva's theory of abjection is founded on the premise that the maternal *cannot be, cannot speak* and *cannot take up a subject position*, which raises a series of unresolved questions for Anglo-feminist adoption of an abject paradigm to theorize maternal subjectivity.
> (Tyler 2009, 86)

A lot of the misunderstanding about Kristeva's theories comes from a reading of her work as prescriptive, which is an attack often levelled at psychoanalysis in general. But her ideas are in great part informed by her work as a therapist and by an analysis of the words she has heard within

34 *The impossible subject*

her practice (this is mostly true of *Soleil Noir: Dépression et mélancolie*). Similarly, it is tempting for my purpose to want to see motherhood as a subversive position with a privileged access to creativity; yet in her view the maternal can only be construed as a site of resistance if and only if it is mediated by male points of view first. In other words, she describes what it means for men to write as if they were still in a pre-symbolic relationship with their mothers – or as if they were mothers themselves – but she does not look at what it is that mothers would say if they were given the chance to speak. Even when she tries to articulate the specific experience of motherhood in works such as "Stabat Mater" (Kristeva 1983), for example, she envisages the maternal as what stands on the outside – of language, the Symbolic, patriarchy. For Toril Moi, Kristeva's view of femininity in general and of the maternal in particular is not essentialist, yet it locks women in a position of marginality, which, if pushed to the limits of its logic, reinforces traditional patriarchal stereotypes of femininity as the Other to reason and plays into the very hands of what is supposedly being deconstructed (Moi 1993, 166).

Furthermore, although Kristeva was a Marxist, her approach to motherhood is not materialistic enough. If we try to articulate what it means to write *as* a mother, we cannot eschew the question of *how* mothers write. This is in fact a criticism that could be made to all the French feminist critics: for all their talk about the "maternal" as a separate instance and a specific voice, not enough attention is being given to the material conditions in which women can have access to writing. It is definitely not the same thing for an upper-class mother with a live-in nanny to claim her right to be a writer as it would be to a Black working-class mother working two jobs and struggling to find adequate childcare. For Rosalind Jones, this is a criticism that can be levelled at the whole concept of *écriture féminine*, which is that it leaves a lot of women's experiences unaccounted for (Jones 1981).

At this point, it is slightly disheartening to realise that we have not progressed much in our investigation over whether mothers can benefit from the same access to an individual self as men – and I would also add as non-mothers. They seem to be the impossible subject, forever written and fantasised about, projected upon, but always denied a voice of their own. For Michelle Boulous Walker mothers and the maternal body have been identified in the texts of Western philosophy as "the site of a radical silence" (Walker 2002).[1] For Stone, like Chodorow before her, the only way out is to deconstruct the positions of mother and father so as to create a more fluid dynamic between them. For Nancy Chodorow, we can and must dissociate the Lacanian identification of the individual and the Symbolic with the father and of the relational with the mother, and that can only happen if fathers (and life partners in general) shoulder a bigger share of parental duties, which would redress both psychoanalytic and material imbalances. Kelly Oliver suggests that we start placing the maternal body on the side of the "social and lawful" while at the same time reinforcing the association between the paternal function and the embodied and emotional in order to solve the conflicts of motherhood and reinvent the mother–child relationship (Oliver 2000, 2). For Stone, placing the paternal function at the heart of parenting – and not at its outer borders, as a passageway into individual adulthood – is a way to break the hold of essentialising representations of motherhood:

> If we could thus re-imagine the sexes to be continuous in character rather than polar opposites, then this would support a complete sharing of child-caring labor between the sexes, because paternity would no longer signify distance from material and affective life.
> (Stone 2013, 24)

For these authors, that the *tête-à-tête* between mother and child should be broken by the father's active participation in child-rearing means that girls can also project themselves as individuals while at the same time retaining that relational sense of self they obtained from their mothers. And incidentally, it means women have more time to themselves to think and write. It is undeniable that mothers are no longer alone in taking care of their children: they can rely on day-care facilities and more and more, on their partner to fulfil themselves outside of their roles as mothers. Could we say that fathers' involvement in the care of children is one of the factors that has made the boom of mother writing possible?

Mothers as writers

We cannot satisfy ourselves with the diagnosis that mothers are the antithesis of selfhood. If mothers are – literally – selfless, it means they cannot pretend to be speaking in a voice of their own. Nor can we be satisfied with the belief that a woman needs to break with her mother if she is to find her autonomy: that, it has been amply demonstrated, is an illusion to which too many women have fallen prey. Adrienne Rich intuited that reconciling women with their mothers was the remaining work of feminism: "Until a strong line of love, confirmation, and example, stretches from mother to daughter, from woman to woman across the generations, women will still be wandering in the darkness" (Rich [1976] 1995, 246). What this means concretely is that we need to look at mothers as autonomous selves, with their own thoughts and desires, a whole inner room of their own, the door of which their children cannot come knocking to. It is an inner room where she may even end up writing her own story, in her own terms. Clearly, as

Susan Rubin Suleiman has shown, psychoanalysis has been to blame for a lot of our cultural constructions about mothers, by entrenching the idea that they merely exist as backdrops for their children's fantasies (Suleiman [1979] 2011, 116). For Helene Deutsch, Suleiman argues, motherhood functions as an acceptable substitute for the creative drives of women, but it implies that women need to choose between creativity and motherhood, which creates another false dilemma that mothers must overcome if they are to write *as* mothers.

Birthing the self through writing

Yet I think it would be wrong to condemn psychoanalysis as a whole: even if some of the authors who pertain to this critical tradition have tended to frame their observations as laws, it is best considered as a method to analyse human relationships, which allows for evolution and recreation. The work of Jessica Benjamin is testimony to this adaptability: in her work she never takes her forebears' conclusion for granted but is constantly reworking pre-existing theories. In "A Desire of One's Own", she advocates for a redefinition of feminine gender identity that is not just a reaction to men's gender identity (Benjamin 1994). For Shirley Nelson Garner, psychoanalysts must "learn to listen to mothers as well as to children and recollections of childhood. They must consider the limits of psychoanalytic understanding of class and race and reach for a broader perspective" (Garner 1991, 93). Similarly, Suzanne Juhasz, who builds on Benjamin's work, tries to identify a way out of the position of essential marginality to which writers like Irigaray and Kristeva have confined mothers. She reminds us that language acquisition occurs during the pre-oedipal phase, and that mothers teach children how to access the power of language even before the passage into the Symbolic (Juhasz 2003, 397). To that I would also add that by reading stories, or singing songs, mothers have an important role in introducing their children to the imaginary and to aesthetic pleasure, which is not only the domain of the father. In fact, Juhasz argues that the possibility for women to write *as* mothers can facilitate the emergence of a maternal self: "writing from a maternal perspective can construct maternal subjectivity in a linguistic form" (Juhasz 2003, 395).

Mothers are not doomed to wander in selfless limbo and remain silent objects for their children's fantasies. The number of motherhood memoirs that have been published recently attests to the vitality of the maternal voice, even if it means contending with the contradictions of motherhood. The former taboo on the possibility for women to also be writers was for a time transferred onto mothers. While it was one thing for women to take up the pen, there was an unspoken expectation that those women would have to remain childless and that a choice would have to be made between their vocations as artists and as mothers (Suleiman [1979] 2011, 119). Now that second taboo is slowly being lifted: women do not put an end to their writing careers as soon as they become mothers – and if they do, that is often attributable to their material conditions and a lack of proper support. As we will see in the following chapters of this book, that does not mean they do not have to grapple with guilt and ambivalence, but at least we can say that in spite of all, they are writing while being mothers, and some are even writing *as* mothers. I would argue in this last part that writing is what has allowed the maternal self to emerge and assert itself. Specifically, self-life writing (whether it be in the form of memoirs or autobiographies) has allowed mothers to write in their own terms of their feelings, desires, and contradictions.

In their book *Narrating Mothers: Theorizing Maternal Subjectivities*, Brenda Daly and Maureen Reddy advocate for a redefinition of subjectivity that would allow the possibility for mothers to speak in their own voice, but also to escape the false dilemma of creation vs. procreation (Daly and Reddy 1991). Like Juhasz, they believe it is essential that we distinguish between a consciousness perceived to be "relational or intersubjective" and the pre-Symbolic. In other words, we need to finally do away with the notion that, because women and mothers' ego boundaries are constructed as more fluid, they are fated to never have access to full selfhood and to a voice of their own. Emily Jeremiah goes even further by suggesting that the possibility for women to write *as* mothers has a profound effect on our conception of selfhood and should be explored for precisely this reason:

> I will argue not only that mothers can and should write literature, but that mothering and literary production – both profoundly relational practices – can be linked and deployed as challenges to traditional western ideals of rationality and individuality, in subversive and ethically compelling ways.
>
> (Jeremiah 2002, 7)

More specifically, she suggests that the association of literary production and mothering can bring about a reconsideration of traditional representations of masculine selfhood associated with autonomy and authority. While she does acknowledge that one of the main reasons why mothers have been absent from the literary field for so long are essentially financial and practical, she identifies the cultural representations which surround motherhood as being responsible for the negation of their voices. She takes a historical view of the gradual introduction of a form of "maternal aesthetic", which did suppose at one point a form of "strategic essentialism", the main goal of which was to extract the maternal from its marginal position. But in order to overcome the hurdles of both marginalisation and essentialism, she tries to articulate a maternal literary practice which could destabilise the main tenets of Western liberal individualism by placing relationality and dialogue at its centre.

> Aesthetic practice, then, involves relationality, constituting participation in a particular culture. If texts are understood as citational responses to other texts [...], then traditional liberal humanist ideas of authorial autonomy and authority are discredited, and the way is clear for an understanding of the writing subject as engaged in a relationship with other writers and with readers.
>
> (Jeremiah 2002, 12)

The novel Jeremiah takes as an example to prove her point is Sarah Moss's *Night Waking* (Moss 2011). What is truly innovative indeed in this novel is that the plot revolves around the main character's struggle with caring for her two children on a remote island while trying to write a piece of academic work. The constant interruptions, the lack of sleep, and mental space are all dramatised as hurdles she needs to overcome in order to accomplish her work and reach self-fulfilment. While the production of novels like Moss's is essential to placing mothering front and centre and making it worthy of literary representation, I nevertheless think that self-life writing is the genre in which maternal selfhood can fully express itself.

Writing in the first person

Self-life writing is an invaluable resource to help us understand the cultural factors that influence how we think of ourselves as individuals. It is no wonder, then, that Nancy Chodorow's theories have had such a tremendous influence on studies about autobiographical writing by women. By identifying specificities in the formation of self in women, she placed mothers, specifically the relationship one entertains with one's mother, at the centre of the reflections about how autobiographical subjects construct their trajectories to selfhood. Susan Stanford Friedman remarks: "Chodorow's theory of differential gender identity highlights the unconscious equation of masculine selfhood with human selfhood in the concept of isolate identity proposed by writers like Gusdorf and Olney" (Friedman 1998, 77). Once again, autobiographical studies, especially when they take a wider historical perspective, help us to realise that how we define selfhood is very much culturally defined and has evolved through history. Studying autobiographical texts by women allows us to see that they do not construct themselves as individuals in the same way as men. In autobiographical accounts by men, ego formation is predicated upon rupture with one's mother and one's milieu and upon the establishment of strong boundaries that separate the self from others. The affirmation of the ego promised by Western liberalism and its attending matricidal impulse is the script that shapes much of the narrative of male selfhood, but it falls short of representing the experience of women, who view the break with their mother as a far more complicated and fraught process. Mary G. Mason who has been a pioneer in the research about women's autobiographical selves has compared the autobiographical writings of Augustine and Rousseau, which remain the template for most autobiographical narratives today, with writing by Julian of Norwich or Margery de Kempe and she concludes: "… the self-discovery of female identity seems to acknowledge the real presence and recognition of another consciousness, and the disclosure of female self is linked to the identification of some 'other'" (Mason 1998, 321). The self which is revealed or "disclosed" in autobiographical writing by women is constructed as a relationship, or a dialogue, with someone else, whether it be a higher entity, a husband, a child, but it is rarely constructed as isolated. What space does that leave for mothers as subjects of their own autobiographical writing?

The study of autobiographical selfhood is complicated by the fact that most, although not all, authors of autobiographical writings define themselves as artists and inscribe their ego within that framework. As Laura Marcus has shown, the concept of "genius", as it appeared in the 19th century, is crucial to the definition of autobiographical male selfhood (Marcus 1999, 4). The typical autobiographical account by a male artist will depict his struggle to overcome unwanted group affiliations (to cultural group, class, etc.) in order to establish his own unique voice. Arguably then, women's equivalent accounts will depict a far more arduous process, with ties incompletely severed and a self defined in relation with the others around her. In a recent book detailing the history of the concept of self in European culture, Andrew Spira has demonstrated that the figure of the artist has been the model over which our notions of selfhood have been built since the end of the Middle Ages. The figure of the Romantic artist, freed from his ties with patrons and commissioners, and speaking directly from his privileged vantage point of isolated genius has functioned as a mediator to allow individuals to experience their own sensibility (Spira 2020). If the male artist as isolated genius is the blueprint for our representations of the self (and of the artist), how are mothers supposed to fit in? Their story is the opposite of disaffiliation: on the contrary, they must claim their right to self-expression while nurturing strong bonds with children who are dependent on them. Does that mean that, because of those relationships, they cannot claim to the status of artist? Of course not, but the model of the Romantic genius is one that has informed many female authors' sense of what being an artist should be like, especially in a cultural context which, at least for a long time, did not allow them to identify with a sufficient number of literary models (Gilbert and Gubar [1979] 2000; Showalter 1978; Duplessis 1985). In her autobiography, Janet Frame explains how she constructed her sense of self by disidentifying with her mother and identifying with Romantic artists such as Coleridge and the Brontës, forgetting that it was precisely through her mother that she had been introduced to those writers. Yet, convinced that she would be unable to access the status of artist through the sole quality of her writing, she decided to buy into the cultural script of the "mad genius", convincing herself that she was schizophrenic, and ended up being wrongly institutionalised for ten years (Frame 1990).

While Laura Marcus is convinced that subjectivity and identity must be redefined if we are to better account for women's autobiographical selves, she is also wary of essentialism (Marcus 1999, 220). Identifying the specificities of women's ego formation does not mean that all female artists are destined to experience their subjectivities in the same way. In particular, alternative forms of autobiographical writing, exemplifying a broader definition of "self-life writing", have allowed other forms of subjectivity to express themselves and to break the mould of traditional autobiography, which is very much informed by a hegemonic representation of the self:

> Women's autobiographies may also expose the double-edged nature of the psychic construction of femininity. On the one hand, autobiography is a vehicle for the expression of the female self. On the other hand, if women's autobiographies are read "symptomatically", they can reveal the ways in which, in Simone de Beauvoir's phrase, one "becomes" a woman. The narrative character of autobiography seems to have a particular affinity with the developmental accounts informing psychoanalysis, while the "incompleteness" of the process of feminisation is seen to be mirrored in the fractured structures, or sometimes specific contents, of women's autobiographical writings.
> (Marcus 1999, 221)

The notion of fragmentation and incompleteness is crucial here and applies to narratives by women and women who are mothers alike. A lot of the first-person accounts I will be looking at in this study do not fall under the label of autobiography *per se*, apart maybe from Doris Lessing's three-part autobiography. The bulk of the texts I'm interested belong to the category of self-life writing, with memoirs, autobiographical novels, and poems, autotheoretical narratives, etc. As we will see later in the course of this study, what a lot of the texts written by mothers do have in common is that they are written in a far more fragmented form than more traditional autobiographical narratives, which leaves room for interrogation and dialogue, but also does not rely on a stable pre-existing self.

Maternal texts

Is there such a thing as a "maternal text"? Now that mothers have broken out of from the margins and have entered centre stage, do they have something specific to say? What revelations do they have to make? In their book *Textual Mothers/Maternal Texts: Motherhood in Contemporary Women's Literatures*, Andrea O'Reilly and Elizabeth Podnieks argue for a recognition of "matrifocal texts", that is writing with a resolutely "mother-centric" point of view. Building on Marianne Hirsch's work on the "mother/daughter plot", they offer to look at texts by women which do not adopt a traditional "daughter-centric" perspective but rather explore the specific subjectivity of the mother writer (Podnieks and O'Reilly 2010, 2). This shift also supposes adopting a method for "matrifocal readings" that do not stop at the daughter's account of the relationship with her mother but try to recover the mother's experience, much like Adrienne Rich encouraged feminists to reconcile with their mothers in order to overcome their own matrophobia. They also encourage us to take into consideration the intersection between race and motherhood and point to the fact that first-person narratives by Black women do not feature the dramatic break with the mother figure that is so often found in self-life writing by white women. Similarly, as Shirley Nelson Garner suggests, the relationships with their children depicted by Black women writers such as Maya Angelou, for instance, are very different from the accounts one would expect from maternal texts by white, middle-class authors (Garner 1991, 87). In her 1972 essay "In Search of Our Mothers' Gardens", Alice Walker revisits Virginia Woolf's *A Room of One's Own* to show that in order for Black women to stake their claims as artists, they must see themselves first and foremost as heirs to a matrilineal tradition (A. Walker [1972] 1994).

What does it mean to write a matrifocal text, or to read a text from a matrifocal lens? For Elizabeth Podnieks, what matrifocal texts do is to liberate motherhood from the cultural inscriptions which had silenced it for so long. It participates in Susan Maushart's aim of "unmasking motherhood", that is to reveal the complexity of motherhood, buried under layer upon layer of injunctions to maternal bliss, selflessness, and the mimetic rivalry in the pursuit of intensive mothering.

This "unmasking" implicates mothers as "bad" not only for *what* they write but also for the *act* of writing itself. By speaking up, women repudiate proscribed patriarchal imperatives for submissive feminine behavior; their "unfeminine" articulations about the way things really are for mothers have produced narratives that are bold, irreverent, and authentic.

(Podnieks 2020, 177)

Mothers who write are, from that point of view, necessarily "bad" mothers, not because they are possibly neglecting their children, but because they are breaking a taboo, which is that motherhood is a time of silent bliss, and that the mother–child relationship is perfectly self-sufficient. This is a legend that no one really believes, yet it is constantly peddled by the mainstream media and cultural production (see Bassin, Honey, and Kaplan 1994). If we look at the production of maternal texts which have emerged over the last 20 years or so, they mostly seem to gravitate around one particular form, that is the motherhood memoir. As Fahlgren and Williams show, texts like Rachel Cusk or Sheila Heti's motherhood memoirs allow their authors to "rewrite cultural scripts about motherhood" (Fahlgren and Williams 2023, 138).

Motherhood memoirs

Although in this study, I will not only be looking at texts which belong to the genre of the memoir, I felt it was interesting to document the emergence of that particular form of self-life writing as testimony to the growing interest for first-person accounts of motherhood. Why do mothers, when they write in the first person, choose the memoir? I would suggest that it has something to do with the association of the memoir with a minor form of autobiographical writing. Compared with the broad scope of the autobiography, which aims at encompassing the subject's whole lifetime up to the point of writing, the memoir has more modest ambitions and only seeks to represent one aspect of the autobiographical subject's lived experience (see Rak 2004), which is in keeping with the way women writers tend to construct their subjectivity. For Alison Hewett, the first texts that could be said to fall under the umbrella of motherhood memoirs are Adrienne Rich's *Of Woman Born* and Jane Lazarre's *The Mother Knot*, both published in 1976. But the motherhood memoir as a genre really took off in the 1980s and 1990s (Hewett 2020).

Indeed, following into the footsteps of Jane Lazarre, more and more women started writing about their experience of motherhood in the first person: Louise Erdrich with *The Blue Jay's Dance* (1995), Anne Roiphe with *Fruitful: A Real Mother in the Modern World* (1996), Rachel Cusk with *A Life's Work: On Becoming a Mother* (2001), Andrea Buchanan with *Mother Shock: Tales from the First Year and Beyond – Loving Every (Other) Minute of It* (2003), Anne Enright with *Making Babies: Stumbling into Motherhood* (2012), Marie Darrieussecq with *Le Bébé* (2002), Elif Shafak with *Black Milk: On Motherhood and Writing* (2013), Jenny Offill with *Dept. of Speculation* (2014), Maggie Nelson with *The Argonauts* (2015), Rivka Galchen with *Little Labours* (2016), Chitra Ramaswamy with *Expecting: The Inner Life of Pregnancy* (2016), Lara Feigel with *Free Woman: Life, Liberation and Doris Lessing* (2018), and Doireann Ní Ghriofa with *A Ghost in the Throat* (2020). This is by no means an exhaustive list of all the motherhood memoirs which have been published in the last two or three decades, but they form a good a basis on which to start an exploration of the field. To that list of titles, I would also add a growing number of poetry collections which take the experience of motherhood as their main subject, and which also provide insights into how women experience motherhood in a genre which, since Plath and Sexton, has evolved to make more way to women's real-life stories: Kate Clanchy's *Newborn* (2005), Liz Berry's *The Republic of Motherhood* (2018), and Rachel Bower's *Moon Milk* (2018).

What all these memoirs have in common is that they purport to make visible what had been kept silent for so long: the ambivalent feelings of a mother welcoming children in her life and her struggles at maintaining some sort of autonomous self in the midst of those tumultuous first years with a small child. As Jane Lazarre explains in the preface to *The Mother Knot*:

> As long as we have children and raise them – both badly and well, as we must – the story of the mother in her own voice will have to be told and retold. We will have to break the silence and break it again as we try to become real for our children and, at the same time, come more fully to understand our society and ourselves.
>
> (Lazarre [1976] 1997, xvi)

Admittedly, the aim of writing about motherhood in the first person is to force a reckoning upon society as a whole, not just to change the way we view mothers, but also, and this is true of Jane Lazarre's memoir, to push a political agenda, advocating among other things for affordable, abundant childcare, and for a wider array of options for young mothers, who are often forced into the false dilemma of choosing between being a stay-at-home mum or a full-time professional. Giving visibility to the travails of mothers can hopefully raise awareness of their specific needs.

The other aim of motherhood memoirs, Hewett suggests, is to create a community of experience women can identify with. In her piece entitled

"You are Not Alone: The Personal, the Political, and the 'New' Mommy Lit", she argues that the appeal of this new literature, which she identifies as a sub-genre of so-called Chick Lit, is to break the silence around the reality of motherhood, or to borrow once again from Susan Maushart's terminology, to rip away the mask of motherhood. The point is to send out a message to those distraught new mothers that "they are not alone", that their sense of confusion and bewilderment is shared by many other women out there. And that is also why the boom of the motherhood memoir coincided with the emergence of the Internet as a space for shared testimony: as more and more stories started circulating via personal blogs and online literary magazines, a momentum gathered around the possibility for mothers to speak their truth (Hewett 2005, 134).

Ivana Brown has also attempted to identify a series of common themes which are broached in motherhood memoirs. She specifically mentions how most authors depict a sense of being unprepared for the challenges of motherhood, as well as an emphasis on the gendered nature of mothering (something that was felt acutely by the narrator in Rachel Cusk's *A Life's Work* for instance). She wonders if, in some respect, the realisation of gender differences brought upon by the experience of motherhood does not contribute in some ways to entrenching gender stereotypes and reinforcing the link between femaleness and parenting. Andrea O'Reilly goes even further by suggesting that even as maternal texts claim to rip away the "mask of motherhood", they often unintendedly replace it with another one:

> In particular, I will argue that as this discourse makes a critique of patriarchal motherhood possible, it simultaneously censors what can be said in that critique. More specifically I argue that this discourse ultimately reinscribes, or more accurately naturalizes and normalizes, the very patriarchal conditions of motherhood that feminists, including the motherhood memoir writers themselves, seek to dismantle.
> (O'Reilly 2010, 205)

For O'Reilly, motherhood memoirs do not sufficiently engage in a critique of the discourse around intensive mothering or new momism and sometimes even buy into their clichés. If the very fact of writing about motherhood in a cultural context which has so often been hostile to its representations is in itself a revolutionary act, the content of the narratives which belong to the genre does not take on the discourses around motherhood at the root, she contends. It is not enough, in other words, to simply acknowledge that mothering is a deeply gendered activity and that it reinforces gender inequalities, or that mothers' contribution to society is not fairly recognised. Similarly, by portraying their struggle with guilt and inadequacy, mother writers, albeit unconsciously, participate in circulating the same ideology they are labouring under, without questioning it with sufficient vigour. I would argue that more recent works, for instance Maggie Nelson's *The Argonauts*, have attempted just that, in questioning for example our expectations of what a mother should be and in introducing the possibility for a radical approach to motherhood. The same could be said of Sheila Heti's memoir *Motherhood* (2018) in which she comes to grips with the injunction to motherhood and finally decides to opt out. But in general, should we expect mother writers to break their cultural shackles and claim a radical idiosyncratic approach to mothering? In most of the narratives I will be looking at, the mothers who are also writers are still struggling to make their voices heard and are still too busy charting a path for themselves among all the different cultural injunctions for them to take such a revolutionary approach. Yet I believe that as the genre of the motherhood memoir comes into its own and gains cultural momentum, we will start to see more radical takes on what it means to be a mother today.

Conclusion

The first chapter in Anne Enright's collection of autobiographical essays is titled "Apologies All Round". As she embarks on reflections about her own experience of motherhood, she feels the need to extend apologies to all her readers for having dared to broach a subject that is generally taboo:

> Speech is a selfish act, and mothers should probably remain silent. When one of these essays, about pregnancy, appeared in the *Guardian* magazine there was a ferocious response on the letters page. Who does she think she is? and Why should we be obliged to read about her insides? and Shouldn't she be writing about the sorrow of miscarriage instead?
>
> So I'd like to say sorry to everyone in advance. Sorry. Sorry. Sorry. Sorry.
>
> I'd like to apologise to all those people who find the whole idea of talking about things as opposed to just getting on with them mildly indecent, or provoking – I do know what they mean.
>
> (Enright 2012, 1–2)

In this humorous attempt at *captatio benevolentiae*, we find encompassed all the traditional misgivings which surround writing about motherhood: should mothers be allowed to write? Is motherhood an acceptable subject for literature, or is it personal? A similar apologetic tone can be found in the introduction to Rachel Cusk's memoir *A Life's Work*; like Enright, Cusk was subjected to a barrage of outraged reviews and letters to the editor after her book was published and reviewed in publications like *The Guardian*. Cusk is nevertheless under no illusion that her book will be read beyond the community of literary-oriented mothers: motherhood, she believes, is of absolutely no interest to those who have not experienced it:

> I make this explanation with the gloomy suspicion that a book about motherhood is of no real interest to anyone except other mothers; and even then only mothers who, like me, find the experience so momentous that reading about it has a strangely narcotic effect. I say "other mothers" and "only mothers" as if in apology: the experience of motherhood loses nearly everything in its translation to the outside world. In motherhood a woman exchanges her public significance for a range of private meanings, and like sounds outside a certain range they can be very difficult for other people to identify.
>
> (Cusk 2001, 9)

Now that the taboo around the possibility for mothers to speak, in their own voice, about their experience of motherhood, has been lifted, there remains another hurdle. Who will read the motherhood memoirs, apart from the mothers? Who wants to read about life on the other side of the great parenting divide? The boom of the motherhood memoir has been amply documented at this point, but there has been no real study of who really reads those books. Is there a readership among men? Do childless/childfree women read them as well? Do they find them distasteful or inspiring? That to me is another question that remains unanswered. If motherhood is not such an impossible subject after all, it is still weighed down by its association with the domestic, the emotional – the uncool.

I felt that this introductory overview of the issues surrounding motherhood and the specific issue of the motherhood memoir in our culture was necessary to establish before I move on to close readings of first-person accounts by writers who are also mothers and vice versa. A lot of the debates I have been introducing, concerning the contradictions of mothering in 20th- and 21st-century Western culture, intensive mothering, matrophobia, the possibility for mothers to have a self of their own apart from the relationship with their children, the myth of the artist as isolated genius, the taboo on self-expression by mothers, will be useful in the course of my analysis of self-life writing (in prose and in verse) by mothers. Once these notions have been posited, it is now time to look at what individual writers have to say about what it means for them to become a mother.

Note

1 If one excepts the Greek tragic heroine Medea as a companion figure to the pure maternal being of the Virgin Mary.

Works cited

Badinter, Élisabeth. 1980. *L'amour en plus: histoire de l'amour maternel, XVIIe-XXe siècle*. Paris: Flammarion.
Bassin, Donna, Margaret Honey, and Meryle Mahrer Kaplan, eds. 1994. *Representations of Motherhood*. New Haven, CT; London: Yale University Press.
Benjamin, Jessica. 1994. 'A Desire of One's Own'. In *Feminist Studies/Critical Studies*, edited by Teresa de Lauretis, 78–101. Language, Discourse, Society. Houndmills: Macmillan Press.
Bernos, Marcel, Catherine Fouquet, and Yvonne Knibiehler. 1981. 'Elisabeth Badinter, L'Amour En plus. Histoire de l'amour Maternal, XVIIe-XIXe Siècles (Compte-Rendu)'. *Revue d'Histoire Moderne & Contemporaine* 28 (1): 207–9.
Berry, Liz. 2018. *The Republic of Motherhood*. London: Chatto & Windus.
Bower, Rachel. 2018. *Moon Milk*. Scarborough: Valley Press.
Buchanan, Andrea. 2003. *Mother Shock: Tales from the First Year and Beyond--Loving Every (Other) Minute of It*. New York: Seal Press.
Bueskens, Petra. 2018. *Modern Motherhood and Women's Dual Identities: Rewriting the Sexual Contract*. Abingdon; New York: Routledge.
Chodorow, Nancy J. 1978. *The Reproduction of Mothering: Psychoanalysis and the Sociology of Gender*. Oakland, CA: University of California Press.
Cixous, Hélène, and Catherine Clément. 1975. *La Jeune née*. Paris: Union générale d'éditions.
Clanchy, Kate. 2005. *Newborn*. London: Picador.
Collins, Patricia Hill. 1987. 'The Meaning of Motherhood in Black Culture and Black Mother-Daughter Relationships'. *Sage* 4 (2): 3–10.
Cusk, Rachel. 2001. *A Life's Work: On Becoming a Mother*. New York: Picador.
———. 2012. *Aftermath*. London: Faber and Faber.
Dally, Ann. 1983. *Inventing Motherhood: The Consequences of an Ideal*. New York: Schocken.
Daly, Brenda O., and Maureen T. Reddy, eds. 1991. *Narrating Mothers: Theorizing Maternal Subjectivities*. Knoxville, TN: University of Tennessee Press.
Darrieussecq, Marie. 2002. *Le Bébé*. Paris: P.O.L.
de Beauvoir, Simone. (1949) 2012. *Le deuxième sexe I: Les faits et les mythes*. Paris: Gallimard.
DiQuinzio, Patrice. 2013. *The Impossibility of Motherhood: Feminism, Individualism and the Problem of Mothering*. London: Routledge.
Douglas, Susan Jeanne, and Meredith W. Michaels. 2005. *The Mommy Myth: The Idealization of Motherhood and How It Has Undermined All Women*. New York; London; Toronto: Free Press.
Duplessis, Blau Rachel. 1985. *Writing beyond the Ending: Narrative Strategies of Twentieth Century Women Writers*. Bloomington, IN: Indiana University Press.
Ennis, Linda Rose. 2014. *Intensive Mothering: The Cultural Contradictions of Modern Motherhood*. Bradford: Demeter Press.
Enright, Anne. 2012. *Making Babies: Stumbling into Motherhood*. New York: W. W. Norton & Company.
Erdrich, Louise. 1995. *The Blue Jay's Dance: A Birth Year*. New York: HarperCollins.

Eyer, Diane E. 1996. *Motherguilt: How Our Culture Blames Mothers for What's Wrong with Society*. New York: New York Times Books/Random House.
Fahlgren, Margaretha, and Anna Williams. 2023. 'Contested Motherhood in Autobiographical Writing: Rachel Cusk and Sheila Heti'. In *Narratives of Motherhood and Mothering in Fiction and Life Writing*, edited by Helena Wahlström Henriksson, Anna Williams, and Margaretha Fahlgren, 135–51. Palgrave Macmillan Studies in Family and Intimate Life. Cham: Springer International Publishing. https://doi.org/10.1007/978-3-031-17211-3
Feigel, Lara. 2018. *Free Woman: Life, Liberation and Doris Lessing*. London: Bloomsbury Publishing.
Firestone, Shulamith. 1971. *The Dialectic of Sex: The Case for Feminist Revolution*. London: Jonathan Cape Ltd.
Fraiman, Susan. 2003. *Cool Men and the Second Sex*. Gender and Culture. New York: Columbia University Press.
Frame, Janet. 1990. *The Complete Autobiography*. London: The Women's Press.
Friedan, Betty. (1963) 2010. *The Feminine Mystique*. New York: W. W. Norton & Company.
Friedman, Susan Stanford. 1998. 'Women's Autobiographical Selves: Theory and Practice'. In *Women, Autobiography, Theory: A Reader*, edited by Sidonie Smith and Julia Watson, 72–82. Madison, WI: University of Wisconsin Press.
Galchen, Rivka. 2016. *Little Labours*. London: Fourth Estate.
Garner, Shirley Nelson. 1991. 'Constructing the Mother: Contemporary Psychoanalytic Theorists and Women Autobiographers'. In *Narrating Mothers: Theorizing Maternal Subjectivities*, edited by Brenda O. Daly and Maureen T. Reddy, 76–94. Knoxville, TN: University of Tennessee Press.
Gerber, Nancy. 2003. *Portrait of the Mother-Artist: Class and Creativity in Contemporary American Fiction*. Lanham, MD: Lexington books.
Gilbert, Sandra M., and Susan Gubar. (1979) 2000. *The Madwoman in the Attic: The Woman Writer and the Nineteenth-Century Literary Imagination*. 2nd ed. New Haven, CT: Yale University Press.
Giorgio, Adalgisa, ed. 2002. *Writing Mothers and Daughters: Renegotiating the Mother in Western European Narratives by Women*. New York: Berghahn Books.
Hallstein, D. Lynn O'Brien. 2010. *White Feminists and Contemporary Maternity: Purging Matrophobia*. New York: Palgrave Macmillan.
Hays, Sharon. 1996. *The Cultural Contradictions of Mothering*. New Haven, CT; London: Yale University Press.
Heti, Sheila. 2018. *Motherhood*. London: Vintage.
Hewett, Heather. 2005. 'You Are Not Alone: The Personal, the Political, and the "New" Mommy Lit'. In *Chick Lit: The New Woman's Fiction*, edited by Suzanne Ferriss and Mallory Young, 119–40. New York: Routledge. https://doi.org/10.4324/9780203036211
———. 2020. 'Motherhood Memoirs'. In *The Routledge Companion to Motherhood*, edited by D. Lynn O'Brien Hallstein, Melinda Vandenbeld Giles, and Andrea O'Reilly, 191–201. Abingdon; New York: Routledge.
Hirsch, Marianne. 1989. *The Mother/Daughter Plot: Narrative, Psychoanalysis, Feminism*. Bloomington, IN: Indiana University Press.

hooks, bell. (1984) 2007. 'Revolutionary Parenting'. In *Maternal Theory Essential Readings*, edited by Andrea O'Reilly, 145–56. Bradford: Demeter Press.
Hrdy, Sarah Blaffer. 1999. *Mother Nature: Natural Selection and the Female of the Species*. London: Chatto & Windus.
Irigaray, Luce. 1974. *Speculum de l'autre Femme*. Paris: Éditions de Minuit.
———. 1979. *Et l'une Ne Bouge Pas sans l'autre*. Paris: Minuit.
Jeremiah, Emily. 2002. 'Troublesome Practices: Mothering, Literature and Ethics'. *Journal of the Motherhood Initiative for Research and Community Involvement* 4 (2): 7–16.
Jones, Ann Rosalind. 1981. 'Writing the Body: Toward an Understanding of "L'Ecriture Feminine"'. *Feminist Studies* 7 (2): 247–63. https://doi.org/10.2307/3177523
Juhasz, Suzanne. 2003. 'Mother-Writing and the Narrative of Maternal Subjectivity'. *Studies in Gender and Sexuality* 4 (4): 395–425. https://doi.org/10.1080/15240650409349236
Kristeva, Julia. 1974. *La révolution du langage poétique: l'avant-garde à la fin du XIXe siècle, Lautréamont et Mallarmé*. Paris: Éditions du Seuil.
———. 1983. 'Stabat Mater'. In *Histoires d'amour*, 225–47. Paris: Denoël.
———. 1999. *Soleil noir: dépression et mélancolie*. Paris: Gallimard.
Lazarre, Jane. (1976) 1997. *The Mother Knot*. Durham, NC: Duke University Press.
Lessing, Doris. 1954. *A Proper Marriage*. New ed. Children of Violence, Doris Lessing; Book 2. London: Flamingo.
Marcus, Laura. 1999. *Auto/Biographical Discourses: Criticism, Theory, Practice*. Manchester: Manchester University Press.
Mason, Mary G. 1998. 'The Other Voices: Autobiographies of Women Writers'. In *Women, Autobiography, Theory: A Reader*, edited by Sidonie Smith and Julia Watson, 321–24. Madison, WI: University of Wisconsin Press.
Maushart, Susan. 2007. 'Faking Motherhood: The Mask Revealed'. In *Maternal Theory Essential Readings*, edited by Andrea O'Reilly, 460–81. Bradford, Ontario: Demeter Press.
Moi, Toril. 1993. *Sexual/Textual Politics: Feminist Literary Theory (New Accents)*. London; New York: Routledge.
Moss, Sarah. 2011. *Night Waking*. London: Granta Books.
Nelson, Maggie. 2015. *The Argonauts*. London: Melville House UK.
Newman, Judith. 2012. '"Making Babies," by Anne Enright'. *The New York Times*, 11 May 2012, sec. Sunday Book Review. www.nytimes.com/2012/05/13/books/review/making-babies-by-anne-enright.html
Ní Ghriofa, Doireann. 2020. *A Ghost in the Throat*. Dublin: Tramp Press.
Offill, Jenny. 2014. *Dept. of Speculation*. London: Granta.
Oliver, Kelly. 2000. 'Conflicted Love'. *Hypatia* 15 (3): 1–18. https://doi.org/10.1111/j.1527-2001.2000.tb00328.x
O'Reilly, Andrea, ed. 2004. *From Motherhood to Mothering: The Legacy of Adrienne Rich's 'Of Woman Born'*. Albany, NY: State university of New York press.
———. 2010. 'The Motherhood Memoir and the "New Momism": Biting the Hand That Feeds You'. In *Textual Mothers/Maternal Texts: Motherhood in*

Contemporary Women's Literatures, edited by Elizabeth Podnieks and Andrea O'Reilly, 203–13. Waterloo: Wilfrid Laurier University Press.

Podnieks, Elizabeth. 2020. 'Matrifocal Voices in Literature'. In *The Routledge Companion to Motherhood*, edited by D. Lynn O'Brien Hallstein, Melinda Vandenbeld Giles, and Andrea O'Reilly, 176–90. Routledge Companions. Abingdon; New York: Routledge.

Podnieks, Elizabeth, and Andrea O'Reilly, eds. 2010. *Textual Mothers/Maternal Texts: Motherhood in Contemporary Women's Literatures*. Waterloo: Wilfrid Laurier University Press.

Quiney, Ruth. 2007. 'Confessions of the New Capitalist Mother: Twenty-First-Century Writing on Motherhood as Trauma1'. *Women: A Cultural Review* 18 (1): 19–40. https://doi.org/10.1080/09574040701276704

Rak, Julie. 2004. 'Are Memoirs Autobiography? A Consideration of Genre and Public Identity'. *Genre* 37 (3–4): 483–504. https://doi.org/10.1215/00166928-37-3-4-483

Ramaswamy, Chitra. 2016. *Expecting: The Inner Life of Pregnancy*. Glasgow: Saraband.

Rich, Adrienne C. (1976) 1995. *Of Woman Born: Motherhood as Experience and Institution*. 2nd ed. Women's Studies. New York: Norton.

Roiphe, Anne Richardson. 1996. *Fruitful: A Real Mother in the Modern World*. Boston, MA: Houghton Mifflin.

Ruddick, Sara. 1980. 'Maternal Thinking'. *Feminist Studies* 6 (2): 342–67. https://doi.org/10.2307/3177749

Shafak, Elif. 2013. *Black Milk: On Motherhood and Writing*. Translated by Hande Zapsu. London: Penguin.

Showalter, Elaine. 1978. *A Literature of Their Own: From Charlotte Brontë to Doris Lessing*. London: Virago Press.

Sinclair, Jennifer. 2005. 'Motherhood and the Temporal Logic of the Modern'. *Arena Journal* 24: 83–98.

Snitow, Ann. 1992. 'Feminism and Motherhood: An American Reading'. *Feminist Review* 40 (1): 32–51. https://doi.org/10.1057/fr.1992.4

Spira, Andrew. 2020. *The Invention of the Self: Personal Identity in the Age of Art*. London: Bloomsbury Academic.

Stone, Alison. 2013. *Feminism, Psychoanalysis, and Maternal Subjectivity*. London: Routledge. https://doi.org/10.4324/9780203182932

Sukenick, Lynn. 1973. 'Feeling and Reason in Doris Lessing's Fiction'. *Contemporary Literature* 14 (4): 515–35. https://doi.org/10.2307/1207470

Suleiman, Susan Rubin. (1979) 2011. 'Writing and Motherhood. The Mother Tongue'. In *Mother Reader: Essential Literature on Motherhood*, edited by Moyra Davey, 113–38. New York City: Seven Stories Press.

———. 1994. 'Playing and Motherhood or, How to Get the Most from the Avant-Garde'. In *Representations of Motherhood*, edited by Donna Bassin, Margaret Honey, and Meryle Mahrer Kaplan, 272–82. New Haven, CT: Yale University Press.

Thurer, Sherry. 1995. *The Myths of Motherhood: How Culture Reinvents the Good Mother*. New York: Penguin Books.

Tyler, Imogen. 2009. 'Against Abjection'. *Feminist Theory* 10 (1): 77–98. https://doi.org/10.1177/1464700108100393
Walker, Alice. (1972) 1994. 'In Search of Our Mothers' Gardens'. In *Within the Circle: An Anthology of African American Literary Criticism from the Harlem Renaissance to the Present*, edited by Angelyn Mitchell, 401–9. Durham, NC: Duke University Press.
Walker, Michelle Boulous. 2002. *Philosophy and the Maternal Body: Reading Silence*. 1er édition. Routledge.
Warner, Judith. 2007. 'The Motherhood Religion'. In *Maternal Theory Essential Readings*, edited by Andrea O'Reilly, 705–725. Bradford: Demeter Press.
Westervelt, Amy. 2018. 'Is Motherhood the Unfinished Work of Feminism? | Amy Westervelt'. *The Guardian*, 26 May 2018, sec. Opinion. www.theguardian.com/commentisfree/2018/may/26/is-motherhood-the-unfinished-work-of-feminism
Ziarek, Ewa. 1992. 'At the Limits of Discourse: Heterogeneity, Alterity, and the Maternal Body in Kristeva's Thought'. *Hypatia* 7 (2): 91–108. https://doi.org/10.1111/j.1527-2001.1992.tb00887.x

2 To have and have not

Introduction

In 2013, a strange debate took hold of the literary world: in an article published in *The Atlantic*, Lauren Sandler made the case that, in order for a writer to be truly successful, she must limit herself to having one child only. She took several examples out of literary history to illustrate her point: Susan Sontag, Joan Didion, Mary McCarthy, Elizabeth Hardwick, Margaret Atwood, and Ellen Willis only had one child and went on to become the major authors that we know today (Sandler 2013). Having one child only, she concluded, was "The secret to being both a successful writer and a mother" that women supposedly had been trying to discover for decades. Sandler would later expand this idea into a book entitled *One and Only: The Freedom of Having an Only Child, and the Joy of Being One* (Sandler 2014). However, the backlash to the original article was quick to follow, and the comment section on *The Atlantic*'s webpage became a battleground of conflicting opinions, with contributions from such high-profile authors such as Zadie Smith, who replied "the idea that motherhood is inherently somehow a threat to creativity is just absurd" (Flood 2013) and quoted a list of female authors who actually had had more than just one child. She added by way of a conclusion that the real threat "to all women's freedom is the issue of time, which is the same problem whether you are a writer, factory worker or nurse" (Flood 2013). Arguing over the right number of children a female author should have amounts to a false debate, Smith argues, because it shifts the focus away from the real issues faced by writers who are also mothers, that is the fact that the majority of childcare duties still come down to them, even in societies which are supposed to have achieved gender equality. If those women's partners consented to equal contribution to the care of children and if affordable and reliable childcare options were made available to mothers, the number of children would not even be a question.

DOI: 10.4324/9781003461388-3

For Sandler, having more than one child is what takes mothers from the elevated realm of motherhood to the more mundane world of "momishness", the first an experience with the fullness of life, and the second the acquisition of a slightly shameful quality. Rebecca Mead, who took up the issue for *The New Yorker*, sees the article by Sandler as the opening of yet another front in the ongoing "Mommy wars":

> But whether intentionally or not, Sandler's essay is a contribution to the all-too-familiar promotion of divisiveness among women. There is already enough easily fomented and self-righteous side-taking between women who opt for motherhood versus those who do not; between stay-at-home versus work-for pay moms. Now we have new grounds for division: my family structure is more freeing than your family structure.
> (Mead 2013)

Like Smith, Mead concludes that the key to a writer's productivity is not "the head count of her children but the sum of her free hours" (Mead 2013). I would agree with her that mothers, and writers among them, are already bombarded with enough contradictory injunctions as it is, so remarks like Sandler's only add fuel to an abundant fire of guilt. This particular controversy is a good example of the discourse that runs through the media and culture in general, which would oppose creativity and motherhood. Even now that women are finally claiming their right to have both a family and a career as artists, they are still made to examine their life choices to see if they fit in the current narrative about the "right" way of juggling both. Yet, to do justice to Sandler's piece, she does not completely exclude the possibility that motherhood and creativity could coexist; on the contrary, she concludes motherhood can be a way to "create something that would outlast them, to never turn away from a human experience" (Sandler 2013).

An article published very recently by members of the Orlando Project sheds a rather different light on the matter. The piece, entitled "Women Writers Have Had Plenty of Babies", purports to give us a data-driven perspective on the question of whether female authors had consistently made the choice to forgo children and finds that this view is far from representing the truth: "Given the cultural prominence of this idea that you can't be a mother and a writer, it is surprising to learn that, across history, at least in Woolf's Britain, roughly half of women writers have in fact had children" (Bourrier and Brosz 2022). Looking back to examples of female authors as far as the Medieval period, the authors of the study find that not only did women who were also mothers become authors on a par with non-mothers, but the former ended up writing as many books as the latter. Of course, this is a purely statistical view; one flaw we could point at is that the Orlando project study does not include more qualitative metrics such as the influence those different authors may have had over literary history. If we look at those major 19th-century authors quoted by Woolf in *A Room of One's Own*, such as Jane Austen, The Brontës, or George Eliot, the balance is definitely tilted in favour of childless authors. Yet Bourrier and Brosz's study does put a finger on an uncomfortable reality, which is that we have collectively interiorised the belief that in order to achieve a career as an author, a woman must renounce the possibility of having children.

> If the narrative that women writers can't be mothers is, at best, only half true, why do we continue to give this 100-year-old critical chestnut so much weight? Clichés about both writers and mothers are to blame. Writers are supposed to be independent, working in long stretches of unbroken solitude and living a life of the mind. Mothers, meanwhile, are supposed to epitomize selfless care and interdependence. They are also not generally held to be competent at anything other than caregiving: witness the phrase, "so simple, even my mother could do it," and the well-documented bias against mothers in the workforce.
> (Bourrier and Brosz 2022)

The authors of the study are aware, in fact, that even sheer numbers are not sufficient to convince us that women do not need to choose between being writers and mothers – the belief that the two are incompatible is so entrenched in our culture, that for a woman who is a writer, the question of whether to have children or not is a serious one. And as Bourrier and Brosz suggest, the question is not really to know whether she will have the time and mental space to fulfil both roles – rather it is framed in terms of our cultural expectations of what an author is.

One major element which needs to be factored in the discussion is the fact that motherhood is no longer the biological destiny of women in the West. Indeed, contraception and abortion have completely changed the discourse around motherhood: fertility has become decorrelated with femininity and is now discussed in terms of choice rather than necessity.[1] For female authors, especially in the late 20th century, the possibility of having children is not a calamity to be dreaded or simply avoided through celibacy: it is a life choice, which can be deliberated upon. In her book *The Baby on the Fire Escape: Creativity, Motherhood and the Mind-Baby Problem*, Julie Philips follows the lives of a series of "creative mothers", from Alice Neel to Angela Carter. Some female authors do not wonder whether they should or should not have children and become mothers as they follow what Julie Philips calls "the motherhood plot", while others experience motherhood as an obligation they have to contend with:

One of the stories of this book is about how motherhood went from being an accident and an obligation to being a choice, and how profound that effect has been on women's lives. In reading about women writers' careers it's essential to remember how little choice some of them had.

(Phillips 2022, 25)

Other women may of course decide to opt out altogether. If becoming a mother is a choice for mothers, starting from the 1970s onwards, a space opens up for a discussion over whether it is in fact possible to be a mother and a writer. While for some writers there is no decision to be made, and becoming a mother is simply a life event, others approach the possibility with some measure of dread, wondering whether the arrival of a baby in their lives will simply wreck their literary careers. In this chapter I would like to look at the hesitations some female writers have expressed over the possibility of becoming mothers: my main contention is that when they do explore their doubts, they frame their interrogations as part of a dialogue with their mothers, symbolic and/or real. To quote a famous passage from Virginia Woolf's *A Room of One's Own*: "For we think back through our mothers if we are women" (Woolf [1929] 2004, 88).

As we will see in the course of the demonstration, when female writers dither about the possibility of becoming mothers, they do so primarily as daughters: as they arrive on the threshold of motherhood, the writers I will be looking at turn towards their own mothers for guidance. If her mother is a figure of inspiration, the daughter will follow in her footsteps; if her creativity is perceived to have been squandered by motherhood, she will become a symbol of female oppression, a counter-model whom she must disidentify from. Beyond their own actual mothers, many of those writers also engage in a dialogue with their literary mothers: first with the 19th-century trinity composed by Jane Austen, The Brontës and George Eliot, then moving on to Virginia Woolf, Sylvia Plath, and Doris Lessing, who become tutelary figures, guides through the maze of their own doubts. As they examine the lives of other female authors, hoping to find a model to identify or disidentify with, the female writers whose texts I will be looking at place themselves as heirs to a female literary tradition which, as a result, is allowed to emerge.

Among the questions these writers ask themselves are: can I be a mother and a writer at the same time? Will I lose my creativity? Is being a mother compatible with the idea we have of what being a writer entails? This last question also points at some of the cultural assumptions we make about authorship and what it means to be an artist: only when these preconceptions are deconstructed can we allow for a broader definition of what an artist stands for. On the other hand, one of the recurring questions is whether opting out of motherhood means renouncing a crucial life experience which, in turn, could impair one's writing. The internal wars women wage within themselves and detail in their writing is best described by the figure of the *agon*, a struggle of opposing voices, which are continually wrestling for dominance before the final choice imposes itself on them. I will be looking at two texts, Elif Shafak's *Black Milk: On Motherhood and Writing* (2013) and Sheila Heti's *Motherhood* (2018), in which both authors represent their inner wrestling with the decision whether to become mothers, eventually arriving at diametrically opposed decisions, in order to show that although the two authors reach different points, they do follow a similar path. I also want to show that what emerges through the exploration of their inner doubts is how these authors reveal how female authors have internalised the belief that creativity and motherhood are fundamentally incompatible.

Authorising the mother

Choosing between books and babies

Before we embark on a close reading of these texts, I would like to come back to the controversy set off by Lauren Sandler's article. While it did attract a lot of criticism upon its publication, the point she was making was hardly new and had already been made by Alice Walker, who is even quoted in Sandler's piece. In 1979, Alice Walker wrote an autobiographical essay entitled "One Child of One's Own: A Meaningful Digression within the Works", in which she explores the guilt and self-doubt she experienced as a mother to her daughter and justifies her choice to have had one child and one child only. She specifically recounts a dialogue between herself and a "someone" who was asking her if having children was compatible with writing, to which she replied that it was, admitting to feeling surprised by her answer.

> "Why only one?" this Someone wanted to know. "Because with one you can move," I said. "With more than one you're a sitting duck."
> (Walker [1979] 2011, 140)

She then re-enacts a dialogue she had with her own mother, who encouraged her to have another child with whom her daughter could play, leaving her enough time to go about with her tasks. Seeking to disidentify herself with her mother, and her mother's choices, Walker dismisses the advice, which, although it is usually identified with "Women's Wisdom", she decides to view as an instance of "Women's Folly".

The essay was written in praise of poet and scholar Muriel Rukeyser, whom she essentially thanks for her attempts to inscribe the figure of "The Child" within the main themes of the literary canon, along with "Hunger, Nuclear Reactors, Fascists" (Walker [1979] 2011, 139). It is also a reflection on what it is to speak of one's position as a Black woman and a scholar in a society which does not reckon with the fact of her double oppression as both a woman and a member of the Black community, in fact very much intuiting what Kimberley Crenshaw would ten years later come to define as "intersectionality" (Crenshaw 1989). As it stands, with its mixture of cultural analysis and personal anecdotes delivered in a sometimes playful tone, the essay is reminiscent of Virginia Woolf's *A Room of One's Own* – a text she had already started a conversation with in a 1972 essay, "In Search of our Mother's Gardens" (Walker [1972] 1994). Both of Walker's texts attempt to complement Woolf's points about the specific condition of the female artist, by including the reality of the lives of female slaves and their descendants. In "One Child of One's Own", Walker's reflections on motherhood evolve into an examination of the way she was in fact excluded both by white feminism and Black activism. In the context of this double oppression, she realises that her child is not an impediment to her work, like she initially thought she would be, but rather a companion in her struggle: "We are together, my child and I. Mother and child, yes, but sisters really, against whatever denies us all that we are" (Walker [1979] 2011, 154).

The position taken by Walker in this text with regards to the possibility for a mother to also be a writer is reminiscent of the counterpoint argued by such thinkers as Patricia Hill Collins with regards to discussions of motherhood among white feminists. In the context of a society which denies Black women a voice of their own, having children is almost an act of resistance. She specifically distances herself from feminist debates of the time around motherhood and the possibility to both be a mother and a writer. Walker quotes an essay by Tillie Olsen, "Women Who Are Writers in Our Century: One out of Twelve", in which Olsen makes a list of 20th-century female authors who have remained childless and remarks: "Most never questioned, or at least accepted, this different condition for achievement, not required of men writers" (Olsen 1972, 10). Interestingly, further down in her argument, Olsen makes another list of female authors who have had children but only relegates it to a footnote. Walker had read the essay and comments thus: "I discovered these warnings: 'Most women who wrote in the past were childless'–Tillie Olsen. Childless and *white*, I mentally added" (Walker [1979] 2011, 144). The question asked implicitly by Olsen is to know whether childlessness is an essential condition to become a writer, at least for women, or whether it is a cultural prohibition imposed on female authors. For Walker this cultural prohibition is one that she, as a Black female writer, refuses to be subjected to.

The question was not new, and feminists of the time were coming to the realisation that it had been left out of that foundational text, *A Room of One's Own*, which, for all its attempts to take a materialist look at the condition of female artists, did not really delve into the question of motherhood. As Woolf tries to locate a female literary tradition, she – somewhat naively – wonders what brings its authors together:

> Moreover, I thought, looking at the four famous names, what had George Eliot in common with Emily Brontë? Did not Charlotte Brontë fail entirely to understand Jane Austen? Save for the possible relevant fact that not one of them had a child, four more incongruous characters could not have met together in a room – so much that it is tempting to invent a dialogue between them.
> (Woolf [1929] 2004, 77)

The fact that the authors mentioned by Woolf should all have remained childless is only mentioned in passing and as a potentially incidental common factor between them is striking – possibly a reflection of Virginia Woolf's own complicated relationship with motherhood. Nina Auerbach chooses to read Woolf's text as actually establishing a correlation between the choice Austen and Eliot made to remain childless and their successes as writers (Auerbach 1985). Yet, she argues, the choice made by these authors (even though the terms of that choice were very different in the 19th century) was at the origin of a conflation, in the mind of the reader looking back on their lives, between their childlessness and their literary production:

> The vacuum where the adult female should be, the paradox whereby her existence is defined only in reference to children, explains much of our difficulty not only in creating our own lives, but in assessing the lives of women in the past. This difficulty is compounded when we look at the lives of childless women in the nineteenth century, struggling against universal approval of large families and paeans to the holiness of motherhood.
> (Auerbach 1985, 173)

For Auerbach, those 19th-century authors were bestowed "honorary motherhood" by their writing of books, which, she believes, is at the origin of our confusion between books and children. Rebecca Solnit makes a similar point and looks at the reasons why, in the 21st century, female authors are still being asked for some sort of justification for their choice to remain childless, as if motherhood was the only path available for a woman, this time in the name of an ideology which would view motherhood as the main form of self-fulfilment for women and the guarantee for their happiness (Solnit 2015). The question here is to determine whether they wrote books to make up for their lack of children or if they precisely chose to remain childless to protect their autonomy as writers. For Solnit and Auerbach, such authors as Austen and Eliot made a deliberate decision not to have children in order to give themselves entirely to their literary careers – even if in the case of Virginia Woolf, Solnit acknowledges that the reasons for her childlessness may have been slightly more complicated[2]. Susan Rubin Suleiman laments that feminist theorists such as Auerbach have adopted this either/or attitude to writing mothers. For Suleiman, it is time to listen to what mother writers have to say and to give a closer look to the way they perceive the possibility to reconcile motherhood and creativity (Suleiman [1979] 2011, 121).

The question of whether creativity and parenthood are compatible ventures is only addressed when it comes to female writers: as most of the writers I have just quoted remark, no one really questions if a male writer can continue to write books after he has become a father, usually because it is assumed that someone around him will take care of the children while he is busy writing, that someone usually being his wife and the mother of his children. The idea that women should satisfy themselves with either books or babies, but not both at the same time, was for a long time deeply entrenched in our social and cultural representations of what a woman and an artist should be. While it is fair to say that the condition of women has improved since the 19th century, and that it is no longer unheard of for a woman to want to pursue careers both as a mother and as a writer, I want to show that, on top of the usual material questions around how the mother will organise her time between her writing and the care of her children (a point I will be making in Chapter 4), the hesitation felt by female authors is testimony to the remanence of those old, deep-seated beliefs – mainly that motherhood and creativity are in fact irreconcilable.

The childbirth metaphor and the myth of the self-sufficient artist

Susan Stanford Friedman has explored that particular question in her essay "Creativity and the Childbirth Metaphor: Gender Difference in Literary Discourse", in which she argues that the use of the childbirth metaphor to describe literary production, and the underlying equivalence between books and children, has somewhat paradoxically, participated in entrenching the division between creation and procreation.

> The male comparison of creativity with woman's procreativity equates the two as if both were valued equally, whereas they are not. This

elevation of procreativity seemingly idealizes woman and thereby obscures woman's real lack of authority to create art as well as babies. As an appropriation of women's (pro)creativity, the male metaphor subtly helps to perpetuate the confinement of women to procreation.

(Friedman 1987, 64)

For Susan Stanford Friedman, the equivalence between books and babies is a false one: "Babies are never books" (Friedman 1987, 58). Yet, by appropriating the figure of childbirth and the metaphorical power of procreation, male artists, particularly from the Romantic period, participated in obscuring women's reproductive work by sublimating it and cutting it from the biological reality of pregnancy and childbirth. In other words, if male authors producing novels and poems are comparable to women giving birth to their children, it means that women cannot do both, they must either give birth to children and fade into irrelevance, or give birth to their art, which unlike men, will be the consolation prize for having renounced their natural destiny, namely procreation. Few among us remember the exact number of children Wordsworth or Shelley fathered, yet there is still endless discussion over George Eliot's family life and marital choices. Female writers in the 21st century know that they do not really need to choose between their vocations as mothers and artists, yet they still carry with them the cultural memory of that initial cultural prohibition on trying to juggle with both. In society and in culture more broadly, this memory still manifests itself in the debates over whether women can really "have it all" – that is a family life and a career[3] – that still rage among cultural commentators.

Susan Stanford Friedman locates the emergence of the childbirth metaphor during the Romantic period, which was characterised by an appropriation of qualities usually associated with the feminine, such as intuition and emotion, which, again, were sublimated by their association with male intellectual and cultural production. The Romantic period, as we saw in the previous chapter, was also the time when our contemporary representation of the artist started to take shape (see Spira 2020) as the isolated, self-sufficient individual of genius, his artistic production the unmediated expression of his individual sensitivity. As sociologist Janet Wolff has demonstrated, the Romantic period was also the time when artistic production became untethered from the material conditions which made it possible. As a result of the emergence of capitalism and individual liberalism, creativity became a form of work unlike any other: art was no longer the result of collective production or made possible by the help of patrons and commissioners (Wolff [1981] 1993). The artist became the sole source of his creativity, itself the direct product of his individual thoughts and emotions, as he became increasingly disaffiliated from the traditional, collective forms of artistic production. Our image of the artist today remains largely heir to this original break from the collective and from an identification of art with craftsmanship: we perceive the artist as producing his art "in splendid isolation", which is antithetical with how we represent mothers, whose mode of subjectivity is essentially relational.

To put it bluntly, if one were to portray an artist, few among us would portray him screaming at his children in a supermarket, trying to decide about the family's weekly meal plan. Our representation of the artist has him floating above everyday trivialities, only concerned with his quasi-divine mission. One sentence, which has almost reached the status of aphorism, by British critic Cyril Connolly in his 1948 memoir *Enemies of Promise* perfectly captures our traditional view of the relationship between parenthood and creativity: "there is no more sombre enemy of good art than the pram in the hall" (Connolly [1948] 2008). Connolly's memoir explores the different reasons why he felt unable to fully achieve his artistic vision and the "pram in the hall" was a reference, not just to children per so, but to domesticity in general. For Connolly, a writer's life was incompatible with a sustained interest in everyday matters, and he tried to blame "creeping domesticity, marital obligation, interest-free mortgages, all the urgent summonses of hearth and home" for his own failures as an artist (Taylor 2016). For Claire Dederer, who revisits Connolly's quote in her 2023 autobiographical essay *Monsters: A Fan's Dilemma*:

> The image of the pram in the hall took hold of the popular mind, as a kind of synecdoche for all the troubles that family life can bring an artist. All writers struggle to find our way into that blessed place: a room with a door that locks from the inside, against the family.
> (Dederer 2023)

When male writers decide whether they should have children or not, the debate rarely revolves around whether the arrival of children in their lives will have an impact on their literary vocation. As Nancy Huston has shown in *Professeurs de désespoir*, the decision is often contingent on the writer's belief in humanity and his desire to project himself in the future, especially in the context of what she calls 20th-century nihilism, quoting such writers as Cioran, Beckett, or Bernhardt. The so-called nihilist tradition identified by Huston is heir to 18th- and 19th-century representations of the artist, whose vocation is perceived to be sacrificial and all encompassing. For Huston, many of the "nihilist writers" regarded life as an artist as necessarily a monastic life, radically detached from the everyday and entirely dedicated to the artist's vision. Yet this type of lifestyle implies that someone else will put in the labour necessary to take care of everyday necessities, and that someone, Huston suggests, is often a woman (Huston

2004). She contends that the hatred of domesticity and family life that was so rife in mid-20th-century literature was precisely allowed to flourish because the authors who engaged in it were often detached from their reality. Her point, ironic and playful, is that writers like Beckett, Céline and Cioran were able to wallow in nihilistic despair because they had a devoted wife who saw to it that they never had to worry about such trivialities as cooking meals and cleaning the house, and who agreed to renounce having children so that their artist husbands would not be distracted from their literary endeavours. If they had had to clean up after a child, spend endless boring hours in the park, they would probably not have written the same odes to despair, Huston concludes.

If the "pram in the hall sentiment" is still prevalent in our cultural representations of the artist, how can a mother today, even if she is equipped with the tools to make the choice whether to have a child or not, hope to combine motherhood and a status as artist? For the authors who question the possibility of being both at once, they realise they often need to wrestle with their own internalised representations of what an artist is supposed to be. Can she really espouse the life of isolation and self-sacrifice she believes is required of a writer as well as the life of a mother, whose privacy is constantly encroached upon? Of course, being a mother in the 21st century is not remotely the same as it was in the 1950s, for example. If they choose to become mothers, they can reasonably expect to get help from their partners, and they certainly do not face the same stigma as mother writers did in previous generations. Yet the struggles of many contemporary writers' literary foremothers have left a deep mark on their imagination. As we will see in contemporary texts exploring hesitation over motherhood, Sylvia Plath is often convoked as the first martyr of the cause, her tragic life a cautionary tale to those who would later try to combine one's desire to be a mother and one's literary vocation.

Sylvia Plath and the childbirth metaphor

Sylvia Plath's legacy is one that is difficult to handle. The accepted wisdom in the 1970s was that she had committed suicide as the result of her inability to reconcile motherhood with her career as a poet (Dobbs 1977; Juhasz 1978; Schwartz and Bollas 1976). It is true that up until recently, her tragic death remained the main entry point for most of the critical studies of her literary work (Brain 2001). More recent critical works have tried to engage with her work on the basis of its own merit and to decentre the question of her suicide (Brain 2019), yet even while denying one looking at Plath's work through the sole lens of her death, it still casts a long shadow over any engagement with her oeuvre. In her memoir *Monsters: A Fan's Dilemma*, Claire Dederer looks at the figure of the monstrous artist over the 20th century and summarises the conversation thus:

> Our experience of Plath's biography is essentially involuntary, and yet there's a whole area of Plath scholarship that seems largely to consist of smart people telling other smart people to forget about her suicide, and then the other smart people basically saying, "I tried to forget about it and I can't!"
>
> (Dederer 2023, 217)

However hard we try, we still struggle to forget that Sylvia Plath killed herself when she was 30 years old, leaving behind two small children. What we can do instead is refraining from speculating over the exact reasons why she did it and accept that the factors which drive anyone to such an extreme act of violence against themselves are multifarious and complex. What most critics of her work do agree on is that her relationship to motherhood, as expressed in her poetry and her prose is best described as ambivalent.[4] Sylvia Plath's career began in the 1950s, at a time when the cultural script women were expected to conform to still very much revolved around the idea that motherhood was the major achievement in a woman's life, a fulfilment of her biological destiny. Abortion and contraception were not widely available, and marriage was still the main gateway to social visibility and respectability. According to Susan Van Dyne, Sylvia Plath had very much adhered to these scripts, as her letters and journals can attest (Van Dyne 1993, 129).

From what we can gather from biographical knowledge about her, Sylvia Plath did not feel hesitant about whether she should have children or not. In her journals and in her letters, she expressed an unwavering and enthusiastic commitment to her vocation as a wife and mother; she even went as far as making her career as a poet contingent on her becoming a mother. When her gynaecologist barely hinted at the possibility that she might be experiencing fertility problems, she worried in her journals that her career as a mother and as a poet would come to an end:

> Suddenly everything is ominous, ironic, deadly. If I could not have children – and if I do not ovulate how can I? – how can they make me? – I would be dead. Dead to my woman's body. Intercourse would be dead, a dead-end. My pleasure no pleasure, a mockery. My writing a hollow and failing substitute for real life, real feeling, instead of a pleasant extra, a bonus flowering and fruiting.
>
> (quoted in Davey 2011, 21)

Here was a writer who took the childbirth metaphor at face value: if she could not bring forth babies, it would mean that she could not bring forth poems. Yet it is worth noting that, at this stage, Plath was mostly worried about her fertility and had not experienced the upheaval caused by the arrival of a child in her life.

Conversely, barrenness is a running theme in her poems and alludes both to her fears over the failure of producing a child and producing literature, locking together creativity and fertility. Much has been made of the opening lines of "The Munich Mannequins": "Perfection is terrible, it cannot have children" (Plath 1981, 262–63), but poems such as "Two Sisters of Persephone" or "Barren Woman" elaborate further on the symbolism of fertility/infertility in her poems. The first poem opposes two types of creativity: one that is rich, organic, connected with the earth and nature in general, and one that is dry and cold, purely intellectual. "Barren Woman" explores the fantasy of a completely disembodied poetic imagination, the poem a lonely and silent museum, echoing Baudelaire and Mallarmé's fantasies of the pure imagination. But the poem trails into silence and nothingness as the poet fails to bring forth flesh-and-bone children.

Plath's repeated claims in her journals and letters that she wanted to be "an Earth Mother in the deepest richest sense" (quoted in Davey 2011, 20) could lead us to believe that she felt absolutely no hesitation whatsoever as to her desire to become a mother. Yet Heather Clark's biography tells us that, before she became pregnant, Plath went around asking friends and fellow poets if she could possibly become a mother while thriving as a poet. Ruth Whitman says that she was "terrified it would get in the way of her poetry", and that they spoke of "practically nothing else" when they met. Clark also quotes Adrienne Rich, who was still in the throes of young motherhood, and reportedly told Plath that she could do both, but, she admitted, "it's hellishly difficult" (Clark 2020, 545).

Jeanine Dobbs also notes that Plath's relationship to motherhood and domesticity in general was complex and ambivalent: "Plath's life and her writing are filled with anxiety and despair over her refusal to choose [between family and career] and instead to try to have–what most males consider their birthright–both" (Dobbs 1977, 11). In her private correspondence, Plath wavers between enthusiastic celebration of marriage and motherhood and anxiety at the possibility that having children might clash with her poetic vocation (see Braun 2023). Her poems about motherhood, on the other hand, and especially those she wrote before she actually became a mother, usually resort to very dark and violent imagery, featuring monstrous babies and animal-like mothers, suffocated by the needs of their infants. The poem "Stillborn" is particularly revealing in that respect. Written at a time when Plath was pregnant with her first child, it is built on a running metaphor that equates failed poems with stillborn children:

The poem can be read as an echo to infertility poems such as "Barren Woman" as they equate the failure of the babies with a failure of the imagination, which is not incarnated enough. For Plath in these texts, poems are, literally, babies, but she takes that logic to the bitter end as she uses the childbirth metaphor to express her fears of a monstrous birth (also explored in the poem "Thalidomide"), which as Dobbs contends, reveal the deeper anxiety Plath felt about becoming a mother:

> All in all, these early poems, written around the time of Plath's first pregnancy and personally selected for publication in her first collection, reveal degrees of mental stress over the maternal condition. Motherhood may be something monstrous, as the child may be. Signs attending birth are not propitious.
> (Dobbs 1977, 15)

Even if the tone of her poems changed when she gave birth and became a mother, Plath remained extremely ambivalent about the possibility of being a mother and a poet at the same time and frequently complained about the difficulties of juggling both careers, especially after she became a single mother. For Susan Van Dyne, the *Ariel* poems allowed Plath to interrogate and revise the childbirth metaphor, especially by exploring the different facets of motherhood, and the coexistence of contradictory feelings she felt as a mother to her children: "Motherhood was not a stable, unified or transparent category to Plath; rather, what it might mean had to be refigured repeatedly in the *Ariel* poems" (Van Dyne 1993, 144). In fact, most of the poems in Plath's last collection can be read as illustrations of the tensions of trying to reconcile her two roles as mother and poet. I believe that in the end, Plath outgrew the childbirth metaphor and realised that it failed to account for the complexity of her situation as a mother and a writer in the 1950s and 1960s. In *The Bell Jar*, which Plath wrote after she became a wife and a mother, the main character, Esther Greenwood is far more wary of the trap that domesticity could represent for a clever young woman like herself. In fact, she projects her own fears of being trapped by marriage and motherhood on the two mother figures around her: her own mother, and the mother of her boyfriend, Buddy Willard, who she feels squandered her potential by becoming a housewife:

> This seemed a dreary and wasted life for a girl with fifteen years of straight A's, but I knew that's what marriage was like, because cook and clean and wash was just what Buddy Willard's mother did from

morning till night, and she was the wife of a university professor and had been a private school teacher herself.

(Plath 1963, 65)

The ambivalent vision of motherhood which is displayed in *The Bell Jar* and in fact in many of Plath's poems reveals a woman torn between motherhood as institution and mothering as experience, to borrow from Rich's illuminating dichotomy. As much as she would like to borrow from the experience of motherhood for inspiration – the sense of a deep connection with another human being, the joy of bringing forth another human into the world – Plath kept bumping into the walls of the institution of motherhood, its strict schedules, its ideology, and the obligation to sacrifice one's ambition for the wellbeing of one's children. By aiming her feelings of contempt at the archetype of the proper housewife represented by Mrs. Willard, Esther – and Plath herself – is demonstrating hostility towards the mother figure in general. Not to delve too deeply in the biographical once again, it is fair to say that Plath's relationship with her mother was a fraught and painful one: she felt both suffocated by and dependent upon a mother who had sacrificed her career and her health in order to raise her two children on her own after the death of her husband. This figure of self-sacrifice inspired many ambivalent feelings in her daughter, as attested by her journals and the letters they exchanged. The hostility towards the figure of the mother extended even beyond Plath's own mother, as suggested by Susan Van Dyne:

> Finally, the knot of motherhood and writing was itself ensnarled with the tangle of mother-daughter relations. Plath's wish to be a mother was connected to her desire to be mothered, to be connected to a matrilineal heritage by reproducing her mother's choices. Yet here, too, her desire for approval, connection, and continuity was contested by her dread of disappointing the other mothers, like her teachers, who recommended nunlike devotion to career.
>
> (Van Dyne 1993, 131)

Plath's representation of motherhood, Nephie Christodoulides suggests, is one that is elaborated from a position of daughterhood and one that is often contaminated by the blight of feminist thinking about motherhood, which is matrophobia (Christodoulides 2005). Plath's relationship with motherhood was complex and changed as she became a mother, yet her tragic ending participated in entrenching the belief that a woman could not be a mother and a writer at the same time, lest she was driven to insanity and death, and bestowed a sense of finality to a question which had remained very much unresolved in Plath's lifetime.

Matrophobia

Sylvia Plath's representations of fertility and the possibility of motherhood are best understood in the light of the conflicted relationship she had with her mother, as much biographical material can attest. Plath was torn between a desire to become an "Earth mother" a figure of caring and nurturance and a seemingly unreconcilable desire to remain autonomous and keep in touch with her own imagination. Yet she thought of her own mother as everything she did not want to become. Self-effacing to the point of subservience, Aurelia Plath was the very figure of renouncement and sacrifice she rejected for herself. It could be argued that Sylvia Plath suffered from the lack of positive mother figures (both real and symbolic) around her to latch on to in order to forge her own path as both a mother and a writer. The female artists she took her inspiration from, such as Marianne Moore or Elizabeth Bishop, did not have children and did not directly discuss motherhood in their poetry (see Clark 2020).

Adrienne Rich, who knew Sylvia Plath as a young poet, also perceived Plath's relationship with her mother as highly problematic on a personal level but also as symptomatic of the difficulty faced by many women when they try to assert themselves as individuals in their own right, especially as artists (Rich [1976] 1995, 230). For Rich, the fact that so many women should have to struggle with that conundrum can be described as "matrophobia", that is not the hatred of mothers *per se*, but the fear of becoming one's mother (Rich [1976] 1995, 235). As we saw in the previous chapter, matrophobia as a concept was forged by Lynn Sukenick who believed it pervaded most of Doris Lessing's work, from *A Proper Marriage* to *The Golden Notebook* (Sukenick 1973). Matrophobia, I would like to show here, is a powerful force which has been documented in literature dating back to the 19th century but also gives a key through which to understand some of feminism's unresolved issues. It is particularly relevant to this discussion as it also informs the internal debates of the female authors who try to decide whether they should have children or not. If a woman decides to become a mother, she always runs the risk of becoming "like" her own mother.

Matrophobia within feminism

Jane Flax wrote "The Conflict between Nurturance and Autonomy in Mother-Daughter Relationships and within Feminism" in 1978 around the same time Nancy Chodorow wrote *The Reproduction of Mothering*; in that piece, she tried to shed a psychoanalytic light on the feminist debates of her time. Motherhood, she argues, remains a contentious issue among feminists precisely because female autonomy is perceived to be predicated upon a radical break with one's mother, the consequence of which for many liberated women, the goal of achieving self-fulfilment is antithetical with motherhood in general (Flax 1978, 180). For Flax, this is an example of a false dilemma, as she does not believe that women should have to choose between autonomy and motherhood. However, it still informed feminists' representation of mother figures at the end of the 1970s. Unwittingly, those women play into the script of associating autonomy with masculinity instead of forging a distinctly female form of self-actualisation. The girl's oedipal drama, which implies transferring sexual desire from mother to father, is the foundation of patriarchy, according to Flax, and by adhering to male constructions of success, which suppose foreclosing the mother as symbolic figure, they incompletely liberate themselves from patriarchal structures. Like Marianne Hirsch (Hirsch 1981), Flax believes that the focus on sisterhood as the one and only liberating bond among women, to the detriment of the mother-daughter bond, has entrenched the rejection of the mother as a figure of conservatism and imprisonment.

Lynn O'Brien Hallstein has devoted a whole book to the question of matrophobia within feminism: the very metaphor of the "wave", used to describe the different generations of feminism, thus implying a disidentification with previous ideas and models, is in itself matrophobic as it implies each new generation of feminists needs to "kill" the symbolic feminist mothers, that is the women who came before them (Hallstein 2010). This, she argues, has implications in our perception of the mother as figure, who becomes code for what needs to be overcome and broken with in order to achieve true liberation. She attributes this matrophobic trend in feminist debates to an incomplete reading of Adrienne Rich's *Of Woman Born* and an unnecessary split between motherhood as experience and institution. By overfocusing on motherhood as patriarchal institution, and by constantly representing the experience of mothering through the lens of conflict, we tend to forget the liberating potential of mothering as a potentially feminist practice (see O'Reilly 2004).

Matrophobia, Hallstein claims, is particularly ripe within academia, a fact which is powerfully illustrated by a passage in Maggie Nelson's *The Argonauts*. This memoir, written in 2015 by a lesbian writer married to a transgender man, is considered a landmark in the genre of motherhood memoirs because it tackles the questions usually related to motherhood in a completely novel way. The doubts she experiences about whether she should become a mother have a very different resonance: like most female authors, she wonders if she will be able to remain an artist even if she becomes a mother, but she is also aware that she will have to face far more hurdles than other white, heterosexual writers whose pregnancy will not be interfered with by society's judgment and will not depend as much on the medical institution. Reflecting upon the place of mothers within our culture, and more specifically academic culture, she shares her memory of a panel she attended, celebrating the work of US scholar Jane Gallop. Gallop, who wrote influential work upon psychoanalysis and feminism, appears as a messy, yet likeable figure: she has come to present some of her work-in-progress, which consists mainly of pictures of her family life taken by her husband. The respondent was Rosalind Krauss, a much more self-contained and tidy character, who instead of commending her, proceeded to take down Gallop's work in the cruellest way possible:

> The room thickened with the sound of one keenly intelligent woman taking another down. Dismembering her, really. Krauss excoriated Gallop for taking her own personal situation as subject matter, accused her of having an almost willful blindness to photography's long history.
> (Nelson 2015, 50)

Accusations of "mediocrity, naïveté and soft-mindedness" are heaped by Krauss upon Gallop: for Nelson, there is no doubt that Gallop is being put in the dock for her celebration of motherhood and domesticity, which are considered by Krauss as fundamentally incompatible with any serious academic exploration of art history. Nelson decides to remember this incident as an "object lesson" in how radical feminism can be hostile to mother figures.

> I didn't have a baby then, nor did I have any designs on having one. [...] But I was enough of a feminist to refuse any kneejerk quarantining of the feminine or the maternal from the realm of intellectual profundity. And, as I remember it, Krauss was not simply quarantining; she was shaming. In the face of such shaming, I felt no choice. I stood with Gallop.
> (Nelson 2015, 51–52)

According to Nelson, Krauss treats motherhood as something that has "rotten" her colleague's mind, a disease for which Gallop must be quarantined, lest she contaminate the rest of the audience with her shameful ideas and representations. The violence described by Nelson is inflicted by one woman upon another, and although it may be the result of other forms of rivalry, it exemplifies the tension within academia, and more generally feminists, between mothers and non-mothers. The incident reveals the way motherhood has been portrayed within the feminist movement even to this day as a form of betrayal of feminist principles, with mothers being suspected of being traitors to the cause. It did not discourage Nelson from having children, but this is the kind of conflict that could have a chilling effect for those women who wish to include their maternity within their feminist practice. In fact, the story recounted by Nelson could be analysed through the prism of what Susan Fraiman has described as the hegemony of "coolness" within academia and the arts in general. Rosalind Krauss presents herself as a stylish, authoritative figure, while Gallop displays pictures of herself in which she appears as clumsy and ill-dressed, in other words, she is the "uncool" to Krauss's cool. Susan Fraiman has written about the figure of the "cool" cultural worker, the fashionable film director or star academic: most of them are men and have constructed their persona around a form of typically male individualism whose model is the "teen rebel". For her this is a figure that has constructed itself in frontal opposition with the maternal, coded as uncool.

> The cool subject identifies with an emergent, precarious masculinity produced in large part by youthful rule breaking. Within this stricture of feeling, the feminine is maternalized and hopelessly linked to stasis, tedium, constraint, even domination. Typed as "mothers", women become inextricable from a rigid domesticity that bad boys are pledged to resist and overcome. A defining quality of coolness, then, is that a posture of flamboyant unconventionality coexists with highly conventional views of gender – is, indeed, articulated through them.
> (Fraiman 2003, xii–xiii)

For Fraiman, the posture assumed by proponents of progressive politics starting from the 1960s and 1970s is predicated upon a rejection of the maternal as reactionary. As the Romantic artist of the 19th century was increasingly replaced by the cool avant-garde artist with ties to leftism and even revolutionary ideas, the mother remained a figure of rejection insofar as she would always be too sentimental, too conservative, forever removed from the heroic aesthetic of the individualistic, self-contained artist and/or academic. Similarly, for Jennifer Sinclair, motherhood is represented in our culture as the "anti-modern": the labour of women has been identified with cyclical, or "natural" time (see also Kristeva 1981), their lives following the ebb and flow of their fertility, while men "are associated with linear, progressive time" (Sinclair 2005, 85). Quoting from Henri Lefebvre, Sinclair shows that the domain of the mother is the "quotidian", her realm is the everydayness of running the lives of those people in her care. Her labour as a mother is repetitive, trivial, and is perceived to be dumbly following ancestral codes, while on the other hand, male individuality self-actualises through a projection into the future, a conquest of the unknown.

> A valorization of change, movement and the future render the desire to mother and mothering as, in the sense I have been developing,

anti-modern, since motherhood and mothering imply the (mere) repetition of what women have always done, anchoring them in the same role tradition has assigned to them.

(Sinclair 2005, 87)

In *The Bell Jar*, Esther's boyfriend Buddy tries to talk some sense into her by reminding her of his own mother's wisdom: "What a man is is an arrow into the future and what a woman is is the place the arrow shoots from" (Plath 1963, 67). The fact that Buddy should be repeating his mother's words like a mantra ("until I was tired", Esther comments) is indicative of his own lack of confidence but also demonstrates how some women have internalised their role as keeper of the home to the point of being complicit with an ideology that oppresses them. Esther is not fooled and knows that through Buddy's voice, the real enemy she is being confronted with is the Mother: whether it is her own mother or her boyfriend's, she is the one who is keeping her behind and forbidding her from achieving her own hopes of becoming a writer.

Matrophobia in literature

G.B. Stewart has analysed several autobiographical novels by women and finds that a recurring pattern in those narratives is the way that women writing in the first person feel the need to disidentify with their mothers in order to become their own person and more specifically stake their claims as artists. Using psychoanalysis, and following Chodorow and Kristeva, she enquires into the passage from pre-oedipal fusion to the forever incomplete severance of ties with the mother: in some cases (as we can see in Doris Lessing's autobiographical novels for example), the mother may transmit, or "telegraph" her resentment at her own condition, to her daughter who will interpret it as the imperative to rebel against it, especially if she wants to become an artist.

> The problem of individuation is of the utmost importance for women writing autobiographical novels of the artist as heroine, for they are describing the process of their own or of their heroine's individuation. When one examines these novels as a genre, the relationship of mother and daughter looms in mythic proportions.
>
> (Stewart 1979, 130)

In the autobiographical *Künstlerroman*, the female artist must follow the same script of disaffiliation and affirmation of one's identity as her male counterpart, yet it implies a radical break with her mother who must be repudiated, excised even, from her own self, which is a far more painful process than it would be for male artists. This particular cultural script, which can be found in many novels dating back to the tradition of the 19th-century novel, has been identified and analysed by Marianne Hirsch in *The Mother/Daughter Plot: Narrative, Psychoanalysis, Feminism* (1989). Hirsch is particularly interested in the opposition between creativity and procreativity which can be found as a common pattern in many novels written by women:

> I would argue that in conventional nineteenth-century plots of the European and American tradition the fantasy that controls the female family romance is the desire for the heroine's singularity based on a disidentification from the fate of other women, especially mothers.
> (Hirsch 1989, 11)

Mothers are the primary negative model for women's emancipation, which also means that they are not entitled to a voice of their own, especially in the 19th century, and well into the 20th century. Hirsch also explains:

> Women writers' attempts to imagine lives for their heroines, which will be different from their mothers' make it imperative that mothers be silent or absent in their texts, that they remain in the prehistory of plot, fixed both as objects of desire and as examples not to be emulated.
> (Hirsch 1989, 34)

Like Irigaray, Hirsch believes that the subtext for the rampant matrophobia within literature is actually the matricidal impulse which underpins most of Western culture: the mother must be killed, symbolically or otherwise, in order for the individual to forge her own path, especially if she is to write and be accepted as an author by society. Hirsch does see an evolution between the Victorian and the Modernist plot: in Virginia Woolf's *To the Lighthouse* or in Colette's *Sido*, the figure of the mother is both powerful and creative – yet her creativity is associated with the quotidian and the banal, her work or art is her domesticity and her studio is her home. On top of that, Hirsch notes that those mother portraits are often elegies, a shrine constructed for the regretted mother after her death. Following the usual psychoanalytic script, the mother in those narratives is idealised through her daughter's eyes, but she does not get to express herself in the first person.

In the last part of this chapter, I would like to take a closer look at two autobiographical narratives by women who hesitate as to whether they should have children or not. My point is that, however different these two narratives and their authors may be, they both represent their internal debates around motherhood as a kind of *agon*, a wrestling between different instances of themselves, and with the mother figures who they have looked up to for inspiration.

Agonising over motherhood

Turkish writer Elif Shafak's (2013) *Black Milk: On Writing and Motherhood* and Canadian writer Sheila Heti's (2018) *Motherhood* have very little in common, apart from the fact that they address their authors' struggle with the idea of becoming a mother. Shafak's style is full of wit and humour and the narrative often borrows some of its plot lines from the codes of magical realism, while Heti's memoir follows the meanderings of the narrator's musing about whether she should have children or not and, in many ways, relates more to the genre of autofiction (Shirm 2022). More importantly perhaps, the two memoirs have two very different outcomes: while Shafak eventually becomes a mother, Heti decides, Bartleby-style, that she'd rather not. Yet despite these differences, the two books have many features in common, including the theme of having to wrestle with an uncomfortable decision, the relationship to one's mother, symbolic or otherwise, and the parallel between creativity and procreativity.

Wrestling with a decision

In order to represent their personal dilemmas, both Shafak and Heti resort to narrative devices that allow them to stage their internal debates by exteriorising them into separate instances of themselves. The narrator in *Black Milk* is inhabited by a "mini-harem" of tiny creatures whom she can visit at will but who also regularly appear alongside her in everyday circumstances. Each "thumbelina" or "mini-woman" represents a different facet of herself and is named after the different aspects of her personality: Little Miss Practical, Miss Highbrowed Cynic, Miss Ambitious Chekhovian and Dame Dervish. These four original characters who all vie for the narrator's attention and try to take the upper hand on her life are later joined by Miss Blue Belle Bovary and Mama Rice Pudding as the narrator moves on with her life, gets married and considers children. The narrator stages herself descending into the deepest recesses of herself in order to consult them but whenever she reaches a new stage in her life, they appear outside of her and discuss what they believe the right course of events should be for the narrator, based on their monomaniac personality. When she starts feeling an inkling of a desire to become a mother, as made visible by the narrator's rapprochement with Mama Rice Pudding, some of the other thumbelinas stage a *coup d'état* and enrol the narrator in an academic program that would take her away from Turkey and into a US university where she can work as a full-time intellectual. A running theme through the book is about the different regimes the narrator and her mini-harem experiment with, in order to coexist; after a dictatorship and a queendom, they settle into a democracy which allows each to have her voice heard in the concert within the narrator's mind. As she announces in the introduction to her memoir: "This book is the story of how I faced my inner diversity and then learned to be One" (Shafak 2013, x).

As she reaches the end of her 30s and she realises the window of her fertility is closing, the narrator in Heti's memoir feels cornered into making a decision: should she have children while it is still time when she so obviously does not desire to have any? The paradox here, as explained by Mark Currie, is that the narrator is struggling with a negative decision: she is not deciding to do something, but rather *not* to do something (Currie 2022, 1). Like Shafak's narrator, Heti's feels the need to exteriorise her decision-making and goes in search of some sort of external truth about herself she feels may be out there, ready to be found. Therefore, she resorts to the Chinese divination system called *I Ching* which works through the flipping of coins and tries to extract some sort of guidance from pure contingency, resulting in conversations which give the narrator – and the reader – the illusion of wisdom when they in fact rely on chance only:

> Is art a living thing – while one is making it, that is? As living as anything else we call living?
> *yes*
>
> Is it as living when it is bound in a book or hung on a wall?
> *yes*
>
> Then can a woman who makes books be let off the hook by the universe for not making the living things we call babies?
> *yes*.
>
> (Heti 2018, 24)

The universe, whose absolution she is seeking here, has no more wisdom to impart than the fortune-tellers and card readers she consults in search for answers to her questions. What the narrator does understand, eventually, is that the answer lies not in her future, but in her past. As the narrative progresses, the narrator slips into a crippling depression which she only manages to climb out of when she realises that what she needs is not to have a baby but to repair the relationship with her own mother (Shirm 2022). One of the recurring figures in the memoir is the biblical story of Jacob wrestling with the angel: like Jacob, the narrator is wrestling with a force that is stronger than herself, and yet unknowable, outside of reach, and like Jacob, she comes out of that struggle stronger and armed with more knowledge about herself than she had to begin with. The last page of the narrative consists in just one final sentence, in which she rephrases the original Biblical text: "Then I named this wrestling place

Motherhood, for here is where I saw God face-to-face, and yet my life was spared" (Heti 2018, 284). The book's name, therefore, signals the place where a struggle took place, between the narrator and the forces governing her destiny. The fact that the book should be called *Motherhood* when its outcome is the narrator's decision not to have children is ironic but signals that the decision *not* to have children still implies an engagement with the reality of motherhood. As she herself reflects:

> What is the main activity of a woman's life, if not motherhood? How can I express the absence of this experience, without making central the lack? Can I say what such a life is an experience of *not* in relation to motherhood? Can I say what it *positively* is?
> (Heti 2018, 159–60)

The narrator in Heti's memoir is aware that the question she is asking is a deeply gendered one – many of the questions she asks herself have to do with the fear that she may be missing out on an experience which is central to the lives of so many other women. She is aware that she is engaged in a struggle against her biological urges as well as the cultural scripts which to this day prescribe the necessity for a woman to have children (Fahlgren and Williams 2023, 138): "There is something threatening about a woman who is not occupied with children. There is something at-loose-ends feeling about such a woman. What is she going to do instead? What sort of trouble will she make?" (Heti 2018, 32).

Both Heti and Shafak's narrators question the possibility of becoming mothers not just as women but also as writers. Their main line of questioning has to do with the possibility of combining motherhood and creativity, and both wonder, in slightly different ways: is having a child the same thing as "having" a book?

Books and babies

The question the narrator in Shafak's memoir tries to answer throughout her narrative is whether she will manage to continue leading the life of a writer if she becomes a mother. The qualities required to be a good novelist, she used to believe, are the capacity to abstract oneself from the world, lead a life of the mind and escape into the world of the imagination:

> For weeks, months and sometimes years on end, we retreat into the novels we write; we stay inside that imaginary cocoon surrounded by imaginary characters, writing destinies, thinking we are God. As we develop plots, add sudden twists, create and destroy characters, we can easily end up presuming we are the center of the world. Self-absorption

and an inflated ego are the two most harmful side effects of our profession. That is why we make poor lovers and even poorer wives and husbands. Writers are primarily asocial creatures – though we can easily forget that with a bit of fame and success. The novel is the loneliest form of art, as Walter Benjamin once said.

(Shafak 2013, 4)

Even though she is settled at Mount Holyoke University, where she can devote her life to thinking and writing, the narrator in *Black Milk* remains in touch with the maternal side of herself in the guise of Mama Rice Pudding. The other thumbelinas, wary of her remaining attachment to the idea of having a family, stage another intervention and ask her to commit once and for all to "a life of the brain" which would require her to relinquish any ties with her body. One night under a tree, she is required to take an oath:

> I've traveled wide, I've traveled far, and I've placed writing at the center of my life. At last I've reached a decision between Body and Brain. From now on I want to be only, and only, Brain. No longer will the Body hold sway over me. I have no want for womanhood, housework, wife work, maternal instincts or giving birth. I want to be a writer, and that is all I want to pursue.

(Shafak 2013, 143)

She immediately stops menstruating, as if her brain had truly taken over her body. Down the line she meets the man who would soon become her husband, and she becomes pregnant. As she nears the end of her pregnancy, the narrator wonders if books really are comparable with babies and finds that the metaphor does not pass the test of real life: babies, she notices, require a tremendous amount of care from their parents, while books very early on "stand on their own feet":

> once the books are born, their authors do not really need to keep an eye on them or discuss them; just like books do not need to give interviews, pose for photographers or tour around. It is we writers and poets who crave the recognition and the praise. Otherwise books are in no need of being nursed by their authors.

(Shafak 2013, 203)

The narrator in Heti's memoir also wonders if it is indeed possible to be married and a parent while living an "avant-garde life" (Heti 2018, 34). She documents the many conversations with her partner Miles, who also subscribes to the belief that the life of a writer is incompatible with the life of a parent:

> If you can get that existential satisfaction from parenthood, would you feel as much desire to make art? He said that one can either be a great artist and a mediocre parent, or the reverse, but not great at both, because both art and parenthood take all of one's time and attention.
>
> (Heti 2018, 35)

One of her main preoccupations in the narrative is to justify her choice not to have children in the eyes of society and of her social milieu. She compares herself with her religious cousin, who has had six children, while she has written six books. She wonders: "Maybe there is no great difference between us, just the slightest difference in our faith—in what parts of ourselves we feel called to spread" (Heti 2018, 85). By entertaining this thought, the narrator gives credit to the belief that books are an acceptable substitute for a childless woman and that a female writer needs to make a choice between two separate vocations. Yet as she pushes her reflection further, she also understands that there is a fundamental difference between art and children:

> Art is eternity backwards. Art is written for one's ancestors, even if those ancestors are elected, like our literary mothers and fathers are. We write for them. Children are eternity forwards. My sense of eternity is backwards through time.
>
> (Heti 2018, 120)

Along a similar line, Heti constructs the narrator's progress through her decision-making around the cycles of her fertility as she names the last chapters of the memoir after the different phases of a woman's cycle: PMS, bleeding, follicular, ovulating, etc. She definitely grounds women's subjectivity and capacity at artmaking in a gendered relationship to time, at least in the terms defined by Kristeva (Kristeva 1981) and Sinclair (Sinclair 2005): cyclical, oriented towards conservation and revisitation of the past. In developing that representation of art, Heti makes space for a distinctive artistic practice.

Thinking back through their mothers

Heti's book is not designed to function as a substitute for motherhood – as the narrator acknowledges towards the end: "Maybe that's why I'm writing it–to get myself to the other shore, childless and alone. This book is a prophylactic. This book is a boundary I'm erecting between myself and the reality of a child" (Heti 2018, 193). It is in fact not written from the perspective of a mother but of a daughter. What she finds in the end is that the truth about herself is not lodged into an unknowable future which she tries to have access to but in the past relationship with her mother and her mother's mother. As Gretchen Shirm argues, the whole book also reads as an inquiry into the intergenerational trauma carried from one woman to the next (Shirm 2022): her grandmother, a survivor of the Holocaust who failed to have the professional career she was hoping for, transmitted to her daughter the taste for hard work and intellectual pursuit, which she in turn transmitted to the narrator: "My mother works hard, and I work hard, too. I took the lesson of hard work from her. That is what a mother does: she sits in her room and works hard" (Heti 2018, 40). As she revisits her childhood, the narrator remembers that she was in fact raised by her father and that she often felt actively rejected by her mother. She realises that by not having children she is in fact "honoring her mother" (Heti 2018, 200), fulfilling her mother's failed wish to remain childless and dedicated to her work. When the narrator finishes the book, she sends the manuscript to her mother, who replies with an email thanking her for enshrining the memory of her own mother: "You never knew her, and you are the one who will make her alive forever" (Heti 2018, 283), ending her message with a display of maternal tenderness the narrator had very rarely encountered from her when she was a child. Writing the book in an act of love that flows back from the present back up to the past, a restoration of lives unrecorded, the reparation of a broken bond (Shirm 2022, 316–18).

The narrator in Elif Shafak's memoir also "thinks back through her mothers", to borrow Virginia Woolf's quote from *A Room of One's Own*, but she does not restrict herself to her actual ancestors. Her representation of motherhood, she acknowledges, is split between her mother who, although she was modern and secular, had nevertheless advised her to become "dependent" on someone in order to get by in life (Shafak 2013, 125), and her grandmother, who entertained traditional beliefs. As a woman, she identifies most with her mother, but as an artist, she feels closer to her grandmother (Shafak 2013, 127). Yet the women she turns to the most for advice and guidance are her symbolic, literary mothers: in the course of the narrative, she looks at the lives of many English-speaking, Turkish, and Japanese writers, including, Sylvia Plath, Doris Lessing, Alice Walker, Ursula K. Le Guin, and many more. She goes through the essays and the biographical knowledge she manages to gather about each of them as she goes about foraging for wisdom in her quest towards motherhood. In her *Journal de la création*, which is part pregnancy journal, part literary memoir, Nancy Huston also revisits the lives of several female literary figures as she progresses through the stages in her pregnancy. Like Shafak, she tries to mine their life stories in order to find some form of guidance, not just as a mother, but as a writer who is also a mother (Huston 1990).

The narrator confronts another mother figure in the guise of an older Turkish writer, Ms. Agaoglu, who invites her for tea to her house. Ms. Agaoglu could not be more different from the narrator: she is tidy and self-contained, while the narrator is messy and chaotic, the Rosalind Krauss to her Jane Gallop. The older writer, who is obsessed with order and silence, explains to the narrator that, in order to truly become a writer, she must choose between having children and writing books: "She tells me, in a voice calm but firm, that to be able to stand on her feet as a woman novelist and to write freely and copiously, she chose not to have any children of her own" (Shafak 2013, 28). When she asks the narrator if she agrees with that statement, the younger writer finds that she is incapable of giving her an answer: immediately she starts listing the female authors she knows, only to find that there are just as many examples of women who have followed that path, as women who have not. Then she consults with the mini-harem within her but finds that each facet of her personality is too narrow-minded to allow her to make up her mind. When she emerges out of her mind, she realises that she is still unable to give Ms. Agaoglu an answer to her question. At the end of the memoir, when the narrator has gone through the cycle of birth, post-partum depression, and rebirth, she also manages to reach a form of reconciliation with her literary mother figure:

> "I think you did the right thing by becoming a mother in the end," she said, holding my hand in her hand, my eyes in her stare. I gently squeezed her hand, and offered humbly in return, "And I respect your decision not to become a mother so as to fully dedicate yourself to your writing."
>
> (Shafak 2013, 262)

Even if Heti and Shafak's narrators reach very different conclusions, they explore very similar topics: is an artist's life compatible with having children? Can you "have" a book the same way you would "have a child" and are babies and books the same? How did women before them manage to do both? And what happened to those who tried to forge their own path through the dilemma? Those two memoirs, along with others which I will be studying in due course, show that the lives of the women who wrestle with those questions do not need to end in tragedy: unlike Plath, Woolf and Lessing, Shafak and Heti do not kill themselves or abandon their children. They are both fortunate enough to live in societies, as different as 21st-century Turkey and Canada can be where it is acceptable for a woman either to choose to remain childless or to choose to be both a writer and a mother. The fact that both memoirs end on the resolution of an internal conflict carries tremendous hope for the women who will read their work in the decades to come.

Conclusion

What all the authors I have been studying are really wrestling with is, on the one hand, the internalised prescriptions of what is deemed proper for a woman in society and on the other, with the cultural representations of what an artist's life should be like. Very few male authors wonder aloud about whether they should have children or not, and if they do, they base their interrogation on very different reasons – I'm thinking here of Imre Kertész in *Kaddish for a Child Not Born* who writes of his decision not to father children as a result of his experience of deportation to the Nazi camps as well as the deeply sad memories he kept of his childhood (Huston 2004). For female writers, the question is one that imposes itself on them – whether they believe or not in the existence of a "biological clock" (see Glaser 2021). Yet torn between the figure of the Romantic artist, and his self-contained isolation, and the figure of the tragic female author who dedicated her whole life to her art, only to suffer the consequences, women who question themselves today need to find heroic figures to show them the way forward.

There are, of course, female writers, who have never felt that their creativity would be threatened by motherhood, like for instance, Ursula K. Le Guin, who, we learn in Julie Phillips's *The Baby on the Fire Escape* (Phillips 2022), managed to write over 20 novels and 100 short stories while caring for her three children. In her essay "The Fisherwoman's Daughter", she acknowledges that women face double standards in that, unlike male authors, they are required to choose between having children and writing books; a choice she never had to make herself thanks to the help of a supportive husband. She also believes that the injunction to make a choice between the two vocations is what eventually drove Virginia Woolf and Sylvia Plath to suicide (Le Guin 2011, 174). Yet by testifying to the fact that making that choice is not always necessary, Ursula K. Le Guin manages to break the cycle of doom that has afflicted female literary models: it is indeed possible to foster a functional relationship with one's family while at the same time refusing to give up on one's creative vision. As Julie Phillips summarises in the chapter of her book she devotes to Le Guin: "Where Lessing and Neel ditched the motherhood plot to raise children outside of traditional marriages, Le Guin claimed a space of her own within it" (Phillips 2022, 122). In fact, Phillips also shows, Le Guin simply did not understand the need for some writers to isolate themselves from other people in order to get their work done.

In a society where women can have a certain degree of control over their fertility, where they are not expected to bury their ambitions in their marriage, and where they can reasonably expect their husbands to shoulder some of the daily tasks associated with family life, female authors who also want to become mothers can decide to have it all and refuse to choose between two vocations which were long deemed to be irreconcilable. Yet what they are still missing is a tradition of mother writers to turn to for guidance. Those women who, in the middle of the 20th century, started claiming their status as authors were still under the influence of such figures as George Eliot, Jane Austen, the Brontës, as seen through the eyes of Virginia Woolf. They thus bought into the "books-or-babies" plot; in turn the female authors of the end of the 20th century kept on looking back to their 19th-century foremothers while also contemplating the fate of their direct ancestors, such as Doris Lessing and Sylvia Plath who both, in different ways, found it impossible to take on that challenge. Now it is time for a new generation of mother writers to pass on their knowledge and experience to their literary daughters and show them that they do not need to choose: they can engage in both careers, provided they have a room of their own, enough money to live on – as well as, I would add, a helpful husband and a reliable babysitter.

Notes

1 Although anthropologist Sarah Blaffer Hrdy would suggest that the main effect of medical contraception is that it has lowered the rate of infanticide, which used to be the main form of birth control (Hrdy 1999, 288).
2 See for instance Viviane Forrester's biography of Virginia Woolf, which revisits the commonly held belief that she had made a conscious decision not to have children (Forrester 2015).
3 See for example the 2012 essay by Anne-Marie Slaughter, "Why Women Still Can't Have It All" (Slaughter 2012).
4 For a discussion of the concept of "maternal ambivalence", see Chapter 5.

Works cited

Auerbach, Nina. 1985. *Romantic Imprisonment: Women and Other Glorified Outcasts*. Gender and Culture. New York: Columbia University Press.
Bourrier, Karen, and John Brosz. 2022. 'Women Writers Have Had Plenty of Babies. Here's the Data.' Slate, 25 September 2022. https://slate.com/culture/2022/09/women-writers-motherhood-history.html
Brain, Tracy. 2001. *The Other Sylvia Plath*. Longman Studies in Twentieth-Century Literature. New York: Longman.
———. ed. 2019. *Sylvia Plath in Context*. Cambridge: Cambridge University Press.

Braun, Alice. 2023. '"The Child's Cry/Melts into the Wall": Sylvia Plath and Maternal Ambivalence'. *E-Rea* 21 (1). https://doi.org/10.4000/erea.16624

Christodoulides, Nephie. 2005. *Out of the Cradle Endlessly Rocking: Motherhood in Sylvia Plath's Work*. Costerus 152. Amsterdam, NY: Rodopi.

Clark, Heather L. 2020. *Red Comet: The Short Life and Blazing Art of Sylvia Plath*. New York: Alfred A. Knopf.

Connolly, Cyril. (1948) 2008. *Enemies of Promise*. Chicago, IL: University of Chicago Press.

Crenshaw, Kimberle. 1989. 'Demarginalizing the Intersection of Race and Sex: A Black Feminist Critique of Antidiscrimination Doctrine, Feminist Theory, and Antiracist Politics'. *University of Chicago Legal Forum* Feminist Theory and Antiracist Politics, vol. 1: 139–67.

Currie, Mark. 2022. 'Maybe Baby: Uncertainty and Decision in Sheila Heti's Motherhood'. *Textual Practice* 36 (1): 116–34. https://doi.org/10.1080/0950236X.2020.1789207

Davey, Moyra. 2011. *Mother Reader: Essential Literature on Motherhood*. New York: Seven Stories Press.

Dederer, Claire. 2023. *Monsters: A Fan's Dilemma*. New York: Alfred A. Knopf.

Dobbs, Jeannine. 1977. '"Viciousness in the Kitchen": Sylvia Plath's Domestic Poetry'. *Modern Language Studies* 7 (2): 11–25. https://doi.org/10.2307/3194361

Fahlgren, Margaretha, and Anna Williams. 2023. 'Contested Motherhood in Autobiographical Writing: Rachel Cusk and Sheila Heti'. In *Narratives of Motherhood and Mothering in Fiction and Life Writing*, edited by Helena Wahlström Henriksson, Anna Williams, and Margaretha Fahlgren, 135–51. Palgrave Macmillan Studies in Family and Intimate Life. Cham: Springer International Publishing. https://doi.org/10.1007/978-3-031-17211-3

Flax, Jane. 1978. 'The Conflict between Nurturance and Autonomy in Mother-Daughter Relationships and within Feminism'. *Feminist Studies* 4 (2): 171. https://doi.org/10.2307/3177468

Flood, Alison. 2013. 'Zadie Smith Criticises Author Who Says More than One Child Limits Career'. *The Guardian*, 13 June 2013, sec. Books. www.theguardian.com/books/2013/jun/13/zadie-smith-one-child-career

Forrester, Viviane. 2015. *Virginia Woolf: A Portrait*. New York: Columbia University Press.

Fraiman, Susan. 2003. *Cool Men and the Second Sex*. Gender and Culture. New York: Columbia University Press.

Friedman, Susan Stanford. 1987. 'Creativity and the Childbirth Metaphor: Gender Difference in Literary Discourse'. *Feminist Studies* 13 (1): 49–82. https://doi.org/10.2307/3177835

Glaser, Eliane. 2021. *Motherhood: Feminism's Unfinished Business*. London: Fourth Estate Ltd.

Hallstein, D. Lynn O'Brien. 2010. *White Feminists and Contemporary Maternity: Purging Matrophobia*. New York: Palgrave Macmillan.

Heti, Sheila. 2018. *Motherhood*. London: Vintage.

Hirsch, Marianne. 1981. 'Mothers and Daughters'. *Signs: Journal of Women in Culture and Society* 7 (1): 200–222. https://doi.org/10.1086/493870
———. 1989. *The Mother/Daughter Plot: Narrative, Psychoanalysis, Feminism.* Bloomington, IN: Indiana University Press.
Hrdy, Sarah Blaffer. 1999. *Mother Nature: Natural Selection and the Female of the Species.* London: Chatto & Windus.
Huston, Nancy. 1990. *Journal de la création.* Arles: Actes Sud.
———. 2004. *Professeurs de désespoir.* Arles: Actes Sud.
Juhasz, Suzanne. 1978. *Naked and Fiery Forms: Modern American Poetry by Women a New Tradition.* New York: Octagon books.
Kristeva, Julia. 1981. 'Women's Time'. Translated by Alice Jardine. *Signs: Journal of Women in Culture and Society* 7 (1): 13–35. https://doi.org/10.1086/493855
Le Guin, Ursula K. 2011. 'The Fisherwoman's Daughter'. In *Mother Reader: Essential Literature on Motherhood*, edited by Moyra Davey, 161–86. New York: Seven Stories Press.
Mead, Rebecca. 2013. 'Writers and the Optimal-Child-Count Spectrum', 14 June 2013. www.newyorker.com/books/page-turner/writers-and-the-optimal-child-count-spectrum
Nelson, Maggie. 2015. *The Argonauts.* London: Melville House UK.
Olsen, Tillie. 1972. 'Women Who Are Writers in Our Century: One Out of Twelve'. *College English* 34 (1): 6–17. https://doi.org/10.2307/375214
O'Reilly, Andrea, ed. 2004. *From Motherhood to Mothering: The Legacy of Adrienne Rich's 'Of Woman Born'.* Albany, NY: State University of New York Press.
Phillips, Julie. 2022. *The Baby on the Fire Escape: Creativity, Motherhood, and the Mind-Baby Problem.* 1st ed. New York: W. W. Norton & Company.
Plath, Sylvia. 1963. *The Bell Jar.* London: Faber & Faber.
———. 1981. *The Collected Poems.* New York: Harper & Row.
Rich, Adrienne C. (1976) 1995. *Of Woman Born: Motherhood as Experience and Institution.* 2nd ed. Women's Studies. New York: Norton.
Sandler, Lauren. 2013. 'The Secret to Being Both a Successful Writer and a Mother: Have Just One Kid'. *The Atlantic*, 7 June 2013. www.theatlantic.com/sexes/archive/2013/06/the-secret-to-being-both-a-successful-writer-and-a-mother-have-just-one-kid/276642/
———. 2014. *One and Only: The Freedom of Having an Only Child, and the Joy of Being One.* New York: Simon & Schuster.
Schwartz, Murray M., and Christopher Bollas. 1976. 'The Absence at the Center: Sylvia Plath and Suicide'. *Criticism* 18 (2): 147–72.
Shafak, Elif. 2013. *Black Milk: On Motherhood and Writing.* Translated by Hande Zapsu. London: Penguin.
Shirm, Gretchen. 2022. 'Sheila Heti, Melanie Klein and Motherhood'. *Critique: Studies in Contemporary Fiction* 63 (3): 309–20. https://doi.org/10.1080/00111619.2021.2024128
Sinclair, Jennifer. 2005. 'Motherhood and the Temporal Logic of the Modern'. *Arena Journal* 24: 83–98.

Slaughter, Anne-Marie. 2012. 'Why Women Still Can't Have It All'. *The Atlantic*, 13 June 2012. https://www.theatlantic.com/magazine/archive/2012/07/why-women-still-cant-have-it-all/309020/.

Solnit, Rebecca. 2015. 'The Mother of All Questions'. *Harper's Magazine*, October 2015. https://harpers.org/archive/2015/10/the-mother-of-all-questions/

Spira, Andrew. 2020. *The Invention of the Self: Personal Identity in the Age of Art*. London: Bloomsbury Academic.

Stewart, G. 1979. 'Mother, Daughter, and the Birth of the Female Artist'. *Women's Studies* 6 (2): 127. https://doi.org/10.1080/00497878.1979.9978473

Sukenick, Lynn. 1973. 'Feeling and Reason in Doris Lessing's Fiction'. *Contemporary Literature* 14 (4): 515–35. https://doi.org/10.2307/1207470

Suleiman, Susan Rubin. (1979) 2011. 'Writing and Motherhood. The Mother Tongue'. In *Mother Reader: Essential Literature on Motherhood*, edited by Moyra Davey, 113–38. New York City: Seven Stories Press.

Taylor, David. 2016. 'The Modern Enemies of Promise'. *The Guardian*, 1 January 2016, sec. Books. www.theguardian.com/books/2016/jan/01/cyril-connolly-writers-modern-enemies-of-promise

Van Dyne, Susan R. 1993. *Revising Life: Sylvia Plath's Ariel Poems*. Chapel Hill, NC: The University of North Carolina Press.

Walker, Alice. (1972) 1994. 'In Search of Our Mothers' Gardens'. In *Within the Circle: An Anthology of African American Literary Criticism from the Harlem Renaissance to the Present*, edited by Angelyn Mitchell, 401–9. Durham, NC: Duke University Press. http://www.jstor.org/stable/10.2307/j.ctv1134fjj

———. (1979) 2011. 'One Child of One's Own: A Meaningful Digression within the Works'. In *Mother Reader: Essential Literature on Motherhood*, edited by Moyra Davey, 139–54. New York: Seven Stories Press.

Wolff, Janet. (1981) 1993. *The Social Production of Art*. 2nd ed. Communications and Culture. Basingstoke: Macmillan.

Woolf, Virginia. (1929) 2004. *A Room of One's Own*. Great Ideas. Harmondsworth: Penguin.

3 On pregnancy and childbirth

Introduction

In 2018, British author Jessie Greengrass published a novel entitled *Sight* in which she explored the history of X-ray vision through the eyes of a pregnant woman. In an article she wrote in *The Guardian* around the same time, she wondered why it was still so difficult to write about pregnancy, even to this day (Greengrass 2018). In the piece, entitled "Why Does Literature Ignore Pregnancy?", she looks at the reasons why pregnant bodies are so rarely represented in fiction. She quickly ends up confronted with a paradox: pregnancy and childbirth are not represented in the literary canon, because they are considered as essentially female experiences, which, up until the 20th century at least, were considered marginal in a field focused on men. Yet, she notices, when pregnancy and childbirth do get represented, it is very often through the eyes of men. Greengrass takes as an example the childbirth scene in *Madame Bovary*, which is dealt with over the course of two curt lines: "Think of Madame Bovary, whose labour is not only comically abrupt, but confirmed by her husband, as though she had somehow been absent herself". Greengrass concludes that pregnancy and childbirth, which involve transformation and push the body's boundaries to its limits, are experiences that should have a universal significance for humankind.

Many of the motherhood memoirs and autobiographical accounts of motherhood by female writers one may come across end up at some point asking the same question: that of why no one is talking about pregnancy and childbirth. Why isn't the experience of bringing forth a child, which is both so disruptive and transformative in a woman's life, not more central to literary representation? One does find instances of literary representation of pregnancy and childbirth in canon literature, with the most notable examples of Tolstoy, or Zola, among others, but very often, the lived experiences of women are appropriated by the male narrator in order to make a point about something else: a reflection on the contingency

DOI: 10.4324/9781003461388-4

of human life in the eyes of God, or a reminder of man's fundamentally animalistic condition (Poston 1978). Even when women started writing in their own voices, this would not necessarily mean that they would write about these experiences – if they had them at all – as they were still contaminated by the taboo of sexuality and the association with a certain sentimentality that female writers were trying to eschew in order to take a seat at a literary table still dominated by men. As Maria Kreppel remarks:

> Women in literature do not tell their own childbirth stories. Certainly, there are numerous birth scenes in recent fiction, but the manner of their presentation, when held up against fictional representations of other life experience, is disappointing. They are second-hand rather than immediate.
> (Kreppel 1984, 4)

Indeed, up until the middle of the 20th century, first-person accounts of pregnancy and childbirth were almost impossible to come by. The boom of the motherhood memoir, which I have mentioned in Chapter 1, has made the representations of those experiences more common, but for a long time, women who decided to explore them in a literary framework felt they were "going it alone", without the help of literary midwives, and this has a consequence on the way female authors have been framing their accounts, as they share the feeling they are breaking a taboo, forging new paths of representation for an event which has been central to many women's lives forever.

In this chapter I intend to explore the reasons why most female authors experiencing pregnancy and childbirth feel, as it were, locked out of the literary canon, and why they feel that these experiences must be put in writing. I specifically want to show that on top of being invisibilised, pregnancy and childbirth have been captured in literature by male points of view. This capture is replicated in the subordination of pregnant women to the medical institution, which has all but taken over the processes of pregnancy and childbirth, making women feel ignorant about their own bodily functions. For female authors to write about pregnancy and childbirth in the first person therefore means writing back at this double capture, making themselves the main protagonists of a narrative in which they are often considered as passive objects. Tess Cosslett also identifies this goal as essential to most literary accounts of childbirth:

> As a central, life-changing event for many women, childbirth needs to be made visible, written about, from a woman's perspective. Too often, the story has been taken away from women by the "audience perspective" accounts of fathers, or more influentially, doctors. A "medicalised" version of childbirth, in which women are objectified as machines for

producing babies, has become increasingly dominant in the twentieth century. This medical discourse has taken institutional shape in the routines of hospitalised birth. Medical versions of childbirth reduce the woman to an object: to restore her subjectivity is the aim of the women writers in this study.

(Cosslett 1994, 2)

The experiences of pregnancy and childbirth cause a major disturbance in the life of any woman, but I would like to show that it has a specific resonance in the life of a woman writer, as they confront her with the limits of the self, as well as the limits of writing. For different yet connected reasons that have to do with these experiences' inscription in a patriarchal framework, they are difficult to articulate and make sense of. This difficulty is made worse by the fact that, even to this day, women writers and women alike often struggle to find realistic representations, particularly of childbirth, which explains the popularity of internet forums and "mummy blogs", which have become unofficial repositories of communal experiences. But my point here is that representing the experiences of pregnancy and childbirth in literary texts is essential in order to break the silence and establish them as one of the common experiences of humanity.

The double capture

In this first part, I intend to show that the women writers who try to articulate their experiences of pregnancy and childbirth are faced with two issues. One is the difficulty to inscribe them within our common definition of what the self is. As we saw in Chapter 1, if we see the liberal self as the blueprint for subjectivity in the West, then how do we account for the splitting in two which is characteristic of pregnancy, and then childbirth? The second issue is related to the way these experiences have been increasingly medicalised over time. The discourse of obstetrics has become the main vantage point from which we have learned how to talk about being pregnant and giving birth. This evolution has a concrete influence on the way women give birth, and on the language they use to recount their experience. The challenge then is for women writers to find a way to put words on their lived experiences outside of the confines of the scientific discourse. These two issues may seem unrelated but are nevertheless connected by the deep hold of patriarchy over women's bodies and texts.

Problematic subjectivity

In her book *Being Born*, Alison Stone sets out to show that our existence is geared towards its finality and that, culturally, we define ourselves as "mere mortals", since our common destiny is to be dead at some point. Yet, for Stone, another element that binds humans together is their condition as "natals": we are all going to die, of course, but we also share the fact that, without an exception, we were all born – and born *from someone* (Stone 2019). The fact that we tend to forget this reality – no doubt linked to infantile amnesia – has implications in the way we frame the self as isolated rather than relational. We are alone when we experience the passage into non-being, yet birth is something that we experience along with someone else, that is the mother who brought us into the world. And even in the first few years after this event, we remain profoundly dependent on our mothers, or on the carers who are responsible for our survival. To consider ourselves as natals and not simply as "mortals" means changing the way we frame our whole sense of self: we are not isolated individuals who are purely in charge of our destinies: at some point in our lives, we existed in a co-dependent relationship with other human beings. Yet, Stone argues, we do not want to be reminded of that fact – we would rather perceive ourselves as independent and in charge, rather than recognise the fact that we once depended on a woman for our survival. In a culture that has been described by feminist Luce Irigaray as fundamentally "matricidal" (quoted in Stone 2019, 8–9), and which is predicated upon the disavowal of our maternal origins, this is something we do not wish to be reminded about.[1]

More specifically, the constant association between birth and death, the "womb-as-tomb" tradition, which runs through most of our philosophical culture, and which has been analysed by feminist philosophers such as Irigaray (1974) and Cavarero (1995) as testimony to the misogyny at the heart of Western metaphysics, informs our representations of birth as the beginning of mortality. The mother who gives life is supplanted by the mother as "maker of death", to quote from the piece by Claudia Dey (2018), and is erased in the process. In *The Blue Jay's Dance: A Birth Year*, Louise Erdrich wonders, somewhat provocatively, why the representation of women's labour, does not hold the same cultural currency as the death of Socrates (Erdrich 1995, 35). That, to me, is one of the first reasons why there are so few first-person accounts of pregnancy and childbirth in literature; although we can attribute this lack to cultural reasons (such as the association of birth with sexuality and female incarnation), there are deeper, philosophical reasons that underpin this erasure.

Another reason why pregnancy and childbirth are often left out of philosophical thought and literary expression has to do with the specific question that these experiences pose with regard to our conception of subjectivity. As Iris Marion Young notes: "We should not be surprised to learn that discourse on pregnancy omits subjectivity, for the specific experience of women has been absent from most of our culture's discourse about human experience and history" (Young 1984, 45). For Young and Tyler

(2000), the pregnant subject poses a threat to another major pillar of our culture, in that it disrupts our common definition of ontology: just like the baby is an essentially relational subject, the pregnant woman's subjectivity is not unique: she is split into two, she is not one or the other, but both all at once. Young continues: "The pregnant subject, I suggest, is decentred, split, or doubled in several ways. She experiences her body as herself and not herself" (Young 1984, 46). The pregnant woman's self is not contained and neatly defined, there is no clear boundary between the inner and the outer. Christine Battersby argues for a redefinition of ontology which would include the possibility for the self to split into two and bring forth another self into the world:

> Focusing on the female subject involves treating humans as non-autonomous, and instead thinking relationships of dependence (childhood/weaning/rearing) through which one attains selfhood. It also involves thinking the process of birthing as neither monstrous nor abnormal. Mothering, parenting and the fact of being born need to become fully integrated into what is entailed in being a human "person" or "self".
>
> (Battersby 1998, 2)

The possibility to give birth to another human being, Battersby argues, is one of the core features of the female subject-position and we need to reconsider our definition of the self as relational rather than simply isolated and self-contained. For Tyler and Young, our resistance to the acknowledgement of the possibility of a specific pregnant subjectivity is testimony to our fear of shattering the fantasy of the self as purely independent. Moreover, pregnancy is a transient form of subjectivity (women do not stay pregnant forever), Tyler explains, which is at odds with our definition of ontology to be stable and consistent. For her, this is the main explanation why "first-person narration and visual representations which bear witness to the 'unique temporality' [...] and transient subjectivity of pregnant existence from an embodied perspective, are largely absent from Western culture" (Tyler 2000, 292). For Cynthia Huff, the very definition of autobiography as centred around the "unitary thrust" of the male-defined ego is at odds with a life event such as childbirth, which has therefore been historically excluded from the range of experiences considered as "legitimate" by critics of autobiography (Huff 1991, 109) – at least up until the end of the 20th century, I would add.

The solution therefore is to open up the possibility for autobiographical accounts of pregnancy and childbirth to be part of our literary canon, and to make it a part of the universal human experience, as advocated by Greengrass. Of course, this is not without its challenges: as Tyler herself acknowledges, writing about pregnancy and childbirth can only be done using our existing language frameworks, which are influenced by patriarchal representations of the female body. Tyler begins her reflection with an autobiographical account of her participation in a philosophy seminar while heavily pregnant and her growing unease and sense of alienation from the rest of the audience who could not share in her intimate experience:

> The autobiographical writing which began this chapter attempted this *mattertalk*. Situated at the interfaces between philosophy and pregnancy, both real and imagined, it both fails and succeeds. Is it possible to express and represent a subjectivity which defies the category subject?
> (Tyler 2000, 298)[2]

The language of obstetrics

For Iris Marion Young the erasure of the pregnant woman's subjectivity is replicated in the way she is considered by the medical institution. Just like pregnancy is viewed as an anomaly in the context of classical ontology which defines the self as unique and undivided (consider the etymology of the term "individual"), it is viewed as a deviance from normal health (Young 1984, 46; Oakley 1979, 609), and therefore as a "dysfunctional", pathological state.

> I will argue that a woman's experience in pregnancy and birthing is often alienated because her condition tends to be defined as a disorder, because medical instruments objectify internal process in such a way that they devalue a woman's experience of those processes, and because the social relations and instrumentation of the medical setting reduce her control over her experience from her.
> (Young 1984, 55)

Women, she argues, have become alienated from their own experiences of pregnancy and childbirth, because they have been deprived by the medical institution of the words to describe them. In *Of Woman Born* Adrienne Rich sees the historical shift of knowledge from midwives to doctors, and the displacement of childbirth from the home to the hospital as one of the fundamental aspects of the "institutionalisation" of motherhood. Midwives, she argues, have been progressively sidelined to make way for the supremacy of the doctor, often male, over the health of the pregnant woman, which contributed to making childbirth a medical event, implying a particular set of skills and techniques. The knowledge of midwives was increasingly considered as dangerously close to witchcraft and became suspicious; as such it was rejected as part of the general fight against obscurantism which characterised the Modern period, while the introduction of medical technique in the knowledge around pregnancy and childbirth was considered as a form of progress. For Rich, this evolution was in fact the consequence of institutionalised misogyny, and she shows that pregnant women didn't necessarily fare well as a result. In the 17th century, the epidemic of puerperal fever coincided with the increase of births taking place in hospitals at a time when the principles of prophylaxis had yet to be implemented (Rich [1976] 1995, 139–42).

After Semmelweis developed his theories about asepsis around 1847, and convinced the medical world of the necessities of hygiene in the context of childbirth, hospitals became increasingly safe for women giving birth, and there is no doubt that the outcomes of childbirth for both women and their babies are today far less grim than they used to be. The advances in medical techniques have made childbirth safer, and recently even more comfortable for the women who are no longer condemned to suffer long, painful labours. Yet for Rich, the trade-off has been the supremacy of the medical gaze over women's experiences, along with the introduction of techniques and tools, among which the forceps, which, she claims, has allowed the male medical establishment to annex the experience of childbirth (Rich [1976] 1995, 167; see also Morel 2022; Donnison 1976). With the forceps, agency has been transferred from the woman giving birth to the male doctor delivering the child. It could also be argued that, although anaesthetics have introduced a great deal of comfort, it has also contributed to making women more passive.

For Paula Treichler, the obstetrical takeover of childbirth has been successful – not so much in making childbirth safer, but in creating a monopoly (Treichler 1990, 113). She argues that the "dialectic between risk and safety" which is used to justify the fact that most births now take place in hospitals has been the bedrock for the institutionalisation of pregnancy and childbirth. The problem, she concedes, isn't so much medicalisation *per se*, as she does recognise that it has made childbirth much safer, but the absence of alternatives to this takeover, as well as the ongoing, explicit, or subliminal persistence of the male imaginary in the figuring of the event. Even if recently, midwives have been reintroduced in the hospital, their practice remains under the control of doctors, who often get to say the final word. Although one could argue that the recent uptick in the number of home births is operating a shift in the balance of power between doctors, midwives, and mothers themselves. Midwifery, Rich and Treichler argue, has been associated with female knowledge, and therefore necessarily accessory and inferior to "official" medicine, constructed as more objective and male.

For Ann Oakley the control of the medical discourse over the experiences of pregnancy and childbirth is epitomised by the constitution of a body of knowledge and skills whose aim is to take precedence over not just midwifery but over the stories women have been sharing in order to prepare each other for what they were about to go through, particularly during childbirth. A lot of the obstetrical literature, she argues, warns against letting women access too much information on their own: the doctor must oversee what the pregnant woman knows (Oakley 1979, 612). For Oakley, pregnant women are not just considered by the medical institution as passive "baby containers", they are viewed as machines, computers that can be programmed and tweaked, which requires mastery over a particular set of skills that the pregnant woman should not have access to (Oakley 1979, 611). This analogy has been explored in a little-known novel from 1983 by UK novelist Elizabeth Baines, *Birth Machine* ([1983] 2013). It tells the story of a pregnant woman who unwittingly becomes the subject of a medical experiment, in which she realises her husband was complicit. She is repeatedly told by her husband she should not read any of the obstetrical literature and ends up undergoing an induction which she realises during labour was unnecessary. As Tess Cosslett suggests *"The Birth Machine* presents mechanised birth as part of a wider male technological conspiracy against women" (Cosslett 1994, 60).

For female writers to write about pregnancy and childbirth in the first person therefore means breaking the hold that the medical discourse has had over the representations of these experiences. But therein lies the difficulty: what are the words, the metaphors, that women can devise outside of the formerly constituted body of knowledge of obstetrics? How can they reclaim the outside gaze of the doctor-fixer and turn it inside to express their own realities? I have tried to demonstrate that women have been alienated from their own experiences by our traditional conceptions of ontology which do not consider pregnant women's specific subjectivity, and by the medical institution, which has denied agency and knowledge to women in order to replace them with the technical language of obstetrics. I will now be studying several accounts of pregnancy and childbirth by female authors to look at how they have been negotiating their way out of that double alienation, and how they can possibly reclaim the words to describe their experiences, both as writers and as mothers.

Pregnancy in literature

An encounter with ideology

The experiences of pregnancy and childbirth are often lumped together, but they are in fact two very different realities, and they pose different challenges in terms of literary representation. Because childbirth is an event, and a rather extreme one at that, it creates a moment in the narrative, a scene. With its own dramatic structure, and its protagonists, it often has a beginning and an ending, with many twists in between. Pregnancy on the other hand is a state, albeit a transient one – its temporality is both long and relatively short, marked by slow evolutions as well as revolutions. Another aspect of the experience of pregnancy is the realisation that a pregnant body is no longer one's own: it is shared with the unborn baby of course, but it also falls under the aegis of society's expectations as to what a mother should be. For female authors who recount their experience of motherhood, pregnancy is often the time when they encounter the power of ideology, in the form of medical prescriptions as materialised by the literature of "baby books" and pregnancy manuals. But as we will see, pregnancy can also be experienced as a transformation and a liberation from former constructions of the self.

In Rachel Cusk's *A Life's Work*, the narrator muses: "Motherhood is a career in conformity from which no amount of subterfuge can liberate the soul without violence; and pregnancy is its boot-camp" (Cusk 2001, 24). In this book, Cusk develops an array of metaphors revolving around totalitarian imagery which recurs whenever the narrator of the memoir is in contact with representatives of the medical institution. When she goes for her first ultrasound, she realises that her pregnancy has inscribed her within a system – she will now be "monitored", or "followed" by the medical institution. Her body is no longer hers alone but is considered first and foremost as a shelter for that most fragile of beings, the baby, for whom she is morally responsible if any harm should ever befall it. Soon, she realises that maternity is ruled by an authoritarian use of language:

> for modern pregnancy is governed by a regime breath-taking in the homogeneity of its propaganda, its insignia, its language. No Korean cheerleading team was ever ruled with so iron a rod as pregnant women in the English-speaking world. I long to receive some signal of subterfuge, some coded reference to a resistance. My sex has become an exiguous, long-laid, lovingly furnished trap into which I have inadvertently wandered and from which now there is no escape. I have been tagged, as if electronically, by pregnancy. My womanly movements are being closely monitored.
> (Cusk 2001, 30)

If, as Anne Oakley suggests, pregnant women are viewed like computers, then it also means they need to be programmed, and that is the role of pregnancy advice books (Oakley 1979, 612). The narrator of Cusk's memoir is terrorised by her reading of baby books, whose main pronouncements are listed as a series of absurd imperatives. "Like a bad parent, the literature of pregnancy bristles with threats and the promise of reprisal, with ghoulish hints at the consequences of thoughtless actions" (Cusk 2001, 35). The recommendations around food hint at the temple-like quality her body has now acquired: a pure shrine to the baby, it cannot bear to be desecrated or sullied: "*When you raise your fork to your lips*, reads one book on this subject, *look at it and think, Is this the best bite I can give my baby? If the answer is no, put your fork down*" (Cusk 2001, 35).

In 1940s Rhodesia, where Doris Lessing lived when she first became pregnant, women had what the narrator in Cusk's memoir didn't have: a community. "There is a companionship of women who are having their first babies that is like no other". This companionship was built partly upon a common defiance against doctors, and their ignorance of pregnant women's lived experience: "There was another bond then: an alliance against doctors" (Lessing 1994, 213). Lessing observes that, although science has evolved to validate some of the beliefs shared by women outside of the medical discourse, pregnant women's knowledge of their own bodies is still not considered on par with the official knowledge of obstetrics. She mentions for example the reaction of the unborn baby to different voices and to the presence of certain people around the mother:

> To such claims the doctors would say patronizingly you were imagining it, women did imagine things, you mustn't let your fancies run away with you. Now science has justified these old wives' tales. Have doctors stopped patronizing young women? I doubt it. Has any doctor said to a woman whom he has told is an old wife, with implication that she is hysterical, "I am sorry, we were wrong, you were right all the time"?
> (Lessing 1994, 214)

In Lessing's account, the women's bond is forged by a common rejection of doctors' orders. Their exchange of knowledge outside of the purview of the medical institution is a form of resistance against its hegemony.

Birth fears

As she realises that she is no longer herself, but the vessel of a "precious cargo", which she must do everything in her power to protect, the narrator in *A Life's Work* also realises that "the manner in which I will be broken open on arrival at our destination remains shrouded in mystery" (Cusk 2001, 40–41). While she had been reading pregnancy books in order to assuage her long-standing fear of childbirth, she realises that she is even more terrified than she used to be, which was probably the aim. For Susannah Sweetman, fear has always been a companion of birth, but the way that childbirth has been pathologised by the medical institution has only made matters worse. She explores the concept of "tokophobia", which refers to a seemingly irrational fear of childbirth, and sees it as a protest against the norms imposed over women's expected behaviour during pregnancy and childbirth, and against the hegemony of obstetrical expertise (Sweetman 2018, 22). For Sweetman, the only way to overcome those fears is for women to develop an alternative view of their pregnant bodies which they would no longer perceive as fragile, but also as strong and competent. I would argue that another way for women to avoid such terrors during pregnancy would be to allow stories to flow more freely between them. But try as she may, the narrator in Cusk's memoir is incapable of finding a realistic account of childbirth that she could use to ward off her fears. Instead, she is faced with a sinister "vow of silence" which precludes any form of projection into the event to come.

> I myself decide to broadcast my experiences at every opportunity, once I've had them; but the fact that I have never encountered such a disciple of truth, have neither heard, nor read during the course of my life a straightforward account of this most ubiquitous of happenings, suggests to me the presence of an additional horror surrounding the mystery: that somehow, during those tortured hours, some fundamental component of oneself is removed, so that afterwards although one looks and sounds more or less exactly as one did before, one is in fact a simulacrum, a brainwashed being programmed not to bear witness to the truth.
> (Cusk 2001, 24)

After the metaphors of prison and totalitarian imprisonment, the narrator in Cusk's memoir turns to the imagery of torture and imagines childbirth to be a mysterious tampering with the body, which can be in turn programmed and deprogrammed by the doing of some evil, unknown entity. But we do see that these imaginings are the direct result of her failure to find realistic first-person accounts of childbirth which would have no doubt allowed the narrator to place herself within a commonality of experience. In her autobiography, Lessing takes the opposite view and casts severe judgments on the influence the media has had on women's perceptions of the natural transformations of their bodies, whether it's menstruation, pregnancy, and menopause (Lessing 1994, 217). She remembers her pregnancy as a time when she was in complete control of her body, full of trust and hope for the future: "I was in a mood of triumphant accomplishment, and looking forward to the birth. I did not believe it would be as painful as they said, because I was so healthy and at ease with myself" (Lessing 1994, 216). Lessing absolutely refuses the catastrophising narrative that is used to frame the bodily experiences of women. She welcomes pregnancy as an occasion to be more fully herself, an expansion of her self rather than a limitation to her autonomy.

Natural birth

Giving back control of their own experiences of pregnancy and birth: such is the promise of the natural childbirth movement, which constructed itself as an alternative to the hegemony of the medical discourse. The concept itself was devised by a man, Grantly Dick-Read, who was the author of the international best-seller *Childbirth without Fear* ([1942] 2004). He encouraged women to give birth instinctively and as "naturally" as possible, without the use of intrusive medical practices, which, on its face, promises the liberation of pregnancy and childbirth from the strictures of patriarchal scientific discourse. Adrienne Rich herself took a rather dim view of the "alternative birth movement", which she considered as "a movement for the privileged", and which she accused of not delivering on its promise to free childbirth from the supremacy of doctors' knowledge (Rich [1976] 1995, xii). Furthermore, as Blewitt and Cosslett suggest, this seemingly alternative discourse still bears the mark of the patriarchal takeover of women's experiences and points of view and contributes to the essentialisation of women as "natural" mothers (Blewitt 2015, 17; Cosslett 1994, 2). The injunction for women to "trust their instincts" and to let "nature run its course" is also problematic in that it further deprives women of their agency and sets them up for failure.

Recent books aimed at deconstructing the contemporary debates around motherhood have been very critical of the way the discourse of "natural childbirth" has moved from periphery to centre and has become another form of mainstream ideology. Eliane Glaser, the author of *Motherhood: Feminism's Unfinished Business* takes a particularly negative view of "the idealisation of natural childbirth", which she feels is now "ubiquitous", from pregnancy books to antenatal classes (Glaser 2021, 34). She acknowledges that the natural childbirth movement first came as a useful challenge to the male-centred medical discourse, but it is now vying for the title of the official ideology of pregnancy, in other words, "the pendulum has now swung too far the other way" (Glaser 2021, 35). Lucy Jones, in *Matrescence*, also recognised the seductiveness of a discourse which would place female agency front and centre: instead of lying supine on a bed, birthing mothers were now encouraged to take control of their labour, choose, their positions and the overall modalities of their birth. But natural childbirth, she counters, overpromises; after a particularly difficult experience of childbirth, she realises that she had been "misled" (Jones 2023, 77).

In *A Life's work*, the narrator, for all her distrust of the "propaganda" of pregnancy, is ready to buy into the natural childbirth discourse, mainly in order to assuage her fears of medical intrusion. Yet she is under no illusion that this supposedly alternative theory is any less authoritarian than mainstream medical guidelines. She describes with great irony the philosophy of natural childbirth as based on that colonial and anti-feminist fantasy figure: the primitive woman who gives birth standing in a field before she carries on with her day as if to nothing, taking the ordeal in her stride:

> Pain, in other words, has been created by its expectation, and also by the fact that MEN make women lie on their backs and stay still during labour, when any primitive woman could tell you to stick with your sisters, stay on your feet, and keep MEN well out of it.
> (Cusk 2001, 28)

Later, she concludes:

> A sense of political outrage at the patriarchal medicalisation of birth, unfortunately, is not a sufficient qualification for going it alone. [...] Natural birth relies on the labouring woman following her instincts. I have certainly mislaid these instincts, if I ever had them.
> (Cusk 2001, 29)

The mere condemnation of the medical institution is not enough to create a viable alternative and ends up just adding more noise in the chorus of exhortations which assail the pregnant woman.

Pregnancy as transformation

For most women who write in the first person about the experience, pregnancy is characterised by a series of injunctions to conform. Yet in some rarer cases, pregnancy is perceived as a promise of transformation and even transgression. In 2015, Maggie Nelson published *The Argonauts*, a memoir in which she recounted the birth of her first son in the context of the family she has established with her queer husband, trans artist Harry Dodge and her stepson. As Ann Vickery notes, the memoir is structured around conventional narrative structures: the narrator meets her future husband, falls in love, gets married and has a child with him (Vickery 2020, 4). From that point of view, Vickery also notes, inscribing a queer family like Nelson's into heterosexual models is in itself transgressive. In Cusk's memoir, the narrator is grappling with a set of social norms which constrict pregnant women's bodies, all in the name of safety. She is aware that the ideology which frames these norms is rooted in a patriarchal view of women's role in pregnancy as essentially passive containers for their unborn children and which denies them any autonomy. Yet for Nelson to become pregnant in the context of a queer family amounts to a radical questioning of the ideological frame of family-making. Her position as a queer parent allows her to take an outsider's perspective on the traditional narrative of pregnancy and on the medical institution's hold over the experience. She does not feel as constricted by the recommendations of pregnancy advice books, as, the narrator summarily concludes, they were all written by men (Nelson 2015, 53–54).

Throughout the narrative, the narrator wonders if she is not buying into received norms of femininity and is worried, in other words, about being a "sell-out". In a culture that still defines family as heterosexual, she questions the possibility for queer families to exist alongside traditional families. One of the main issues she struggles with throughout is that of assimilation as opposed to difference: should queer families normalise themselves and enter the mould of traditional family-making, or should they claim a distinctive set of norms? Every step of the narrator's progress towards the constitution of her family is fraught and the result of an encounter with heteronormativity. She and her husband decide to get married in a hurry at a time when California was voting on Prop 8, which would rescind gay people's access to marriage. The event is recounted in a joyful tone as they navigate the wedding chapels of Los Angeles – the wedding is rushed, but happy, an act of resistance in the face of advancing reactionary forces (Nelson 2015, 30). Later, as they decide to get pregnant and realise they are going to need an IVF, she and her husband place their fate in the hands of the medical institution, yet once again the procedure does not feel intrusive or exploitative, and the nurses who help them along are presented as enabling and supportive. As Vickery notes, what this narrative of queer motherhood demonstrates is that traditional norms of family can be "expanded to accommodate difference" (Vickery 2020, 2).

From that point of view, then, the narrator in Nelson's memoir is not as worried about "losing her edge", becoming "uncool" to borrow from Fraiman's vocabulary and submitting to conformity, like for example Sheila Heti in *Motherhood*. In fact, becoming pregnant while queer also means disrupting the discourse of queerness as a flight from conformity, in which, Susan Fraiman has shown, conformity is essentially code for the maternal. Collins shows that in *The Argonauts*, the narrator's engagement with Fraiman's analyses (Nelson 2015, 94) on the binary between maternal reaction on the one hand and queer revolution on the other, which Fraiman shows holds sway over discussion of gender in academic and intellectual circles, means that she is also wary of another set of norms which would place her on the side of stasis, passivity and conformism (Collins 2019, 312):

> Within such a stark binary schema, what remains unthinkable is queer pregnancy, queerness *within* the cycles of reproduction, queer women

with biological children whether from hooking, marriage, or artificial insemination – or, for that matter, queer men with kids genetically their own.

(Fraiman 2003, 132)

By defending the possibility of a queer pregnancy, the narrator in *The Argonauts* is also breaking that binary and inventing new ways of being a queer woman:

> What about my pregnancy – is that inherently heteronormative? Or is the presumed opposition of queerness and procreation (or, to put a finer edge on it, maternity) more a reactionary embrace of how things have shaken down for queers than the mark of some ontological truth? As more queers have kids, will the presumed opposition simply wither away? Will you miss it?
>
> (Nelson 2015, 16)

The narrator does not view her pregnancy as a hindrance to her freedom or as a limit to her autonomy – on the contrary, she views it as an experience of queer transformation, as suggested by the parallel she draws with her husband's body transformations as he embarks on a course of testosterone. From that decentred point of view, she is able to interrogate the association which is often made between maternity and conformity and defends a radical view of pregnancy as a form of queering of the body:

> Is there something inherently queer about pregnancy itself, insofar as it profoundly alters one's "normal" state, and occasions a radical intimacy with – and radical alienation from – one's body? How can an experience so profoundly strange and wild and transformative also symbolize or enact the ultimate conformity? Or is this just another disqualification of anything tied too closely to the female animal from the privileged term (in this case, nonconformity, or radicality)?
>
> (Nelson 2015, 16)

By assuming that position, Nelson carries out the project articulated by Imogen Tyler: "… it is time to make a pregnant self, to reclaim pregnancy as a transient subjectivity by reframing pregnant women as the active subjects of their own gestation" (Tyler 2000, 292). In *The Argonauts*, pregnancy is not a time of passive submission to ideology, it is the occasion for a radical interrogation of what being pregnant means: through the various marginal references, the narrator enters a dialogue with psychoanalysts, queer and feminist thinkers and stakes her claims as "that wild oxymoron, a pregnant woman who thinks" (Nelson 2015, 113). By engaging more particularly with gay and queer critics, she inscribes her experience of pregnancy within the framework of a "queer praxis": the shattering of the self which is experienced by the pregnant woman is akin to the gay experience of same-sex encounters theorised by such thinkers as Leo Bersani or Lee Edelman (Collins 2019, 316).

By contrasting different accounts of pregnancy in writers such as Lessing, Cusk, or Nelson, I have tried to demonstrate that, as a special moment in a woman's life, it can be experienced, and therefore represented, in very different ways. For those three authors, being pregnant means confronting society's expectations with regard to women's bodies and their roles as mothers, which is why it can be experienced as a struggle with ideological constructs, whether it be doctors' orders, natural childbirth manuals or the rules of heteronormativity. Yet what is common to those narratives is the necessity for pregnant women to form part of a collective, to exchange knowledge, in other words, to stick together. Failing that, they are condemned to remain passive under the rule of conflicting discourses, which causes them to experience pregnancy as alienating. I am in particular struck by the fact that none of the female authors mentioned here turned to their mothers for guidance. I believe that those literary narratives of pregnancy as well as childbirth are essential to recreating a network of female-centred knowledge which could counter hegemonic discourses on the subject.

Childbirth in literature

Because it is an event – and a rather extreme one at that – rather than a process, the issues raised by the representation of childbirth in literary texts are quite different from those raised by pregnancy. Like Jessie Greengrass, Carol Poston wonders: "Given that birth is such an overwhelming experience, why do we find it so rarely described in literature?" (Poston 1978, 20). This impression is partly contradicted by reality: there are indeed examples of pregnant and birthing women in literature, as early as in *Tristram Shandy*, and later in Tolstoy, Zola, and Joyce. Poston specifically looks at Zola's novel *La Terre*, in which childbirth is described as a savage and barbaric event, the woman being reduced to an animal through the running comparison of her labour with that of a cow. She argues that, in most instances she has come across: "although the experience has been woman's, the language has been men's" (Poston 1978, 20). The way pregnancy and childbirth are represented in literature, especially up to the 20th century, are prime examples of the way the female experience has been framed within male scripts and male poetics: pregnant and birthing women are objects of representation, sometimes they are used as narrative devices, but they are never the masters of their own experiences.

When women do try to depict their own experiences from a personal point of view, they find that they need to reckon with the fact that most births today take place in the context of the hospital. As we have seen earlier, it is the result of the pathologising of the experience, but it also inscribes the event in an environment usually associated with death and illness. The hospital is also a place ruled by the language of the medical institution, which keeps control over the very words used to frame childbirth. Very often the female authors who try to describe their experience struggle to articulate it in a language outside of the domain of obstetrics, a discipline which reigns supreme in the maternity ward. For Maria Kreppel, the takeover of the medical discourse via the emerging science of obstetrics further established the authority of the outsider's point of view on childbirth, be it the doctor's or the husband's. As she goes back in time to find examples of childbirth scenes as early as the 18th century, she chooses to look at the scene of the main protagonist's birth in *Tristram Shandy*:

> Tristram's birthing not only highlights the latest eighteenth-century obstetrical technique, but it also exemplifies the fictionalizing of childbirth. In novels, childbirth is almost always an observed event told through the eyes of doctor or attendant or father or, in this case, the child itself.
>
> (Kreppel 1984, 2)

Today even if women tend to be more in charge of their experience of childbirth and have far more access to knowledge, thanks in part to the availability of resources on the Internet, they are still faced with the challenge of telling their truths in their own words.

The childbirth metaphor

Another hurdle female authors have to face when attempting to give an account of childbirth in a literary context is the fact that the experience has been appropriated by the male literary tradition. Susan Stanford Friedman shows how a corollary to the cultural representation of the artist as an isolated genius which emerged with Romanticism, was the appropriation of childbirth as a metaphor for artistic creativity. This metaphor, far from recentring the experience of women, further entrenches the division between creation and procreation.

> The male comparison of creativity with woman's procreativity equates the two as if both were valued equally, whereas they are not. This elevation of procreativity seemingly idealizes woman and thereby obscures

woman's real lack of authority to create art as well as babies. As an appropriation of women's (pro)creativity, the male metaphor subtly helps to perpetuate the confinement of women to procreation.

(Friedman 1987, 64)

By depicting themselves as "birthing" their artistic work, male artists therefore make it impossible for female authors to write about their experience of bringing forth both children and books in a non-metaphorical way. This is why the taboo on the representation of female authors' procreativity is at the origin of the split between motherhood and creativity which has run deeply throughout most of literary history.

Yet as Nancy Huston has shown, female artists can, and should, reclaim this metaphor as their own. In *Journal de la création*, which could be translated as "A diary of creation", she makes a conscious choice of conflating creation and procreation, the first being a variation of the second: "This will be my *Diary of creation*. A diary of my pregnancy, but also a reflection on the other type of creation – meaning art – and on the links possible and impossible between the two" (Huston 1990, 12 translation mine). As she progresses through her reflection, she reaches the following conclusion:

> Women, even as they ardently desire to become authors, are less convinced of their right and their capacity to do so. For the good reason that, in all the stories that speak of creation, they find themselves not on the side of the *auctor* (author, authority), but on the side of the *mater* (mother, matter).
>
> (Huston 1990, 29 translation mine)

Speaking *as a* pregnant woman on issues of creation and procreation is in itself a way of defying the ban on first-person representations of pregnancy and childbirth.

Another effect of the opposition between creation and procreation has been the prevalence of the outsider's point of view on the representation of childbirth in literature. Up until the motherhood memoir boom and the emergence of first-person narratives of motherhood, childbirth, when it was represented at all, was described from the point of view of a man, who was watching, or listening from another room, like for instance Levin in *Anna Karenina*, in the famous scene of Kitty's delivery. In that, literature only acts as a reflection of the cultural values of its time: childbirth was associated with sexuality and with the animal nature of man, and as such, it was deemed improper for literary representation. Just like women were confined to their bedroom, and later to a hospital room, childbirth as a literary event was put under erasure or elided – or else it was told from a clinical point of view, but a common aspect of the childbirth scenes up until the middle of the 20th century was that the interiority of the woman giving birth was inaccessible as a vantage-point with authority on the event.

Finally, even as female authors started to speak in their own voice and to describe their reality, they were soon faced with yet another paradox: if pregnancy and childbirth are experiences of splitting and sometimes shattering of the self, how is it possible to put them into writing? In addition, if what is at stake is the possibility for female authors to reclaim their lived experience from the capture of male representations of pregnancy and childbirth, who gets to recount these events if there is no single voice left? Who is in charge of doing the telling? By looking at several examples of childbirth scenes, I will try to answer those questions, which are located at the intersection of philosophy, culture, and literature. Although, as we will see, the taboo on the representation of childbirth in literature has been lifted and, as an event, it is no longer confined to the realm of the unspeakable, we will see that to put it in writing still means engaging with the ineffable.

Watching herself giving birth

With writers such as Doris Lessing or Sylvia Plath, childbirth began to be represented as an event central to a woman's life and central to the plot: as Tess Cosslett notes, even the place given to childbirth in a narrative is meaningful in itself: "To structure a novel around such an event was an innovation; to make childbirth a central subject was transgressive and shocking in itself" (Cosslett 1989, 265). While the childbirth scene in autobiographical novels like *A Proper Marriage* (Lessing 1954) and *The Bell Jar* (Plath 1963), which both tell the story of a young woman's journey into autonomy and adulthood, may not be central to the narrative, it definitely constitutes a climax. Yet what these two scenes also share is that they are told in the third person, from the point of view of an onlooker, even though they were both written by women who had experienced childbirth. For Carol Poston, those accounts, although female-authored, have been contaminated, as it were, by the prevalence of the outsider's perspective which still held sway over literary representations of childbirth (Poston 1978, 23).

A Proper Marriage, by Doris Lessing, tells of the formative years of Martha Quest, a young bride in 1950s South Rhodesia (now Zimbabwe), who becomes pregnant against her will at a time when she is trying to liberate herself from her colonial, petit-bourgeois background. As she lies in her hospital bed, helpless and racked with pain, she feels her self being split into two, which she experiences not as transformative or liberating, but as the shattering of the construction of herself as a free spirit:

> She was now lying almost naked, her great tight knotted belly sticking up in a purple lump, watching with fascination how it contracted and strained, while she kept alert the determination not to lose control of the process; while she was lit with curiosity as to the strange vagaries of time and, above all, and increasingly, almost to the point of weeping fury, that all her concentration, all her self-consciousness, could not succeed in creating the state of either pain or painlessness while its opposite was in her. It was a complete failure of her, the free spirit: how was it possible not to remember something that had passed ten seconds before, and would recur so soon?
>
> (Lessing 1954, 190)

Try as she may, Martha is failing to keep control on her perceptions of time and space, which results in a failure of the unified self:

> There were two Marthas, and there was nothing to bridge them. Failure. Complete failure. She was helpless with rage. She heard the pain-gripped Martha cry out, "Oh God, oh God!" and she was curious at the ancient being in her that cried out to God. Damned liar, coward, idiot! said Martha to herself from across the gulf. It only needs that you should call out "Mother!" And behold, Martha, that free spirit, understood from the exquisite shore of complete, empty non-sensation that she had been groaning out "Mother, Mother, Mother!" Without a flicker of feeling in any part of her body, she felt the tears of failure roll down her face; and looked up through them to see the pink nurse looking down at her with unmistakable disappointment.
>
> (Lessing 1954, 191)

As Sherah Wells and Tess Cosslett remark about that scene, the "free spirit" Martha believed herself to be is defeated by the disorienting experience of pain (Cosslett 1994, 139; Wells 2011, 5). Even worse than that, as she tries to call out to a higher entity for help and comfort, she finds herself calling not just to God but to her mother, that abhorrent figure Martha had tried so hard to keep at bay. Her reaction is yet another manifestation of the matrophobia, or hatred of one's mother, which informs Martha's creation of her identity. The novel, which was written only a few years after de Beauvoir's *The Second Sex* is testimony to the matrophobia which reigned among the post-war generation of female writers. In Martha's case, giving birth means becoming "mother-like", that is becoming "like her mother", something she entirely rejects, and which manifests itself in a violent shattering of her sense of self.

Some 40 years later, Lessing would write her autobiography, whose first volume, *Under My Skin* recounts the events represented in *A Proper Marriage*. When she gets to the point when she gives birth to her first son, she chooses to gloss over the event and refers her readers to her novel:

> I did not get into the labour ward until early morning and there I was deposited on a high bed and left. I was in great pain. This is described in *A Proper Marriage* – well more or less, it will do.
> (Lessing 1994, 218)

The flippant tone with which she disposes of the details of the scene is notable here. Instead of giving us her own, first-person account of childbirth, she prefers to leave her readers with the earlier, third-person account, which is given autobiographical authority. Her insistence, throughout this passage, that she was young and healthy, and that the delivery was perfectly normal, fails to hide the fact that there is a hole where the experience should be, a hole which she does not wish to pry into for fear of being reminded of the particular trauma of pain:

> Sometimes women say, It is not true you forget labour pains. But I think you remember you did have bad pain, but not the pain itself: you forget the intensity of the pains in between each pain. Real remembering is – if even for a flash, even a moment – being back in the experience itself. You remember pain with pain, love with love, one's real best self with one's best self.
> (Lessing 1994, 218)

If the number of iterations of the word "pain" is any indication, the autobiographical narrator chooses to foreclose the memory of childbirth for fear of reliving that traumatic experience, some 40 years later. But more deeply than that, I believe that the autobiographical narrator refuses to revisit an event which caused such a profound splitting of her sense of self, an experience which is at odds with the very strongly defined and delineated self that Lessing has been constructing in the three volumes of her autobiography. For authors like Lessing and Plath, who wrote at a time when women writers were still trying to establish their position as authors in their own right, in a literary tradition still dominated by men, experimenting with the self was not something to be taken lightly.

Interestingly enough, the hospital where Martha gives birth is run by nurses – the doctor is an unobtrusive figure whose silhouette appears fleetingly, but his role is definitely not central. The patriarchal power of the medical institution is here wielded by the nurses and the matrons: they tut-tut at Martha's anguished cries and keep enjoining her to behave "like a good girl" (Wells 2011, 3). They rush in and out of her room, completely oblivious to Martha's pain and anguish. The only humanity she encounters comes from a "native" cleaning lady who enters her room unbeknownst to the medical staff – who, it is implied, would probably have disapproved – to try and soothe the young woman.

> As a fresh pain came, she said, "Let the baby come, let the baby come, let the baby come." It was a croon, an old nurse's song. Martha trembled with exhaustion, and tensed herself, but the woman smiled down and sang, "Yes, missus, yes, let it come, let it come".
> (Lessing 1954, 192)

The Black cleaning lady appears in the narrative as far more humane than the nurses who are associated with cogs in a large patriarchal machine. She also seems to have insight into some mysterious, ancestral knowledge that is inaccessible to Martha and the nurses, who are blinded by their reliance on a scientific discourse that makes childbirth inhuman and mechanical. I would suggest here along with Tess Cosslett that this stereotypical representation of the subaltern carries the risk of essentialising her difference (Cosslett 1994, 32).

Sylvia Plath, like Lessing, was deeply ambivalent about her role as a mother and viewed childbirth as an event which endangered her autonomy from her mother as well as her husband. Plath's autobiographical novel *The Bell Jar* can in many ways be compared to Lessing's *Children of Violence* novels: like Martha Quest, Esther Greenwood is a young woman struggling to assert her autonomy as a woman and as an artist in a patriarchal society that would have her settle down with a husband and become a housewife. The childbirth scene in the novel is comparable to the scene in *A Proper Marriage* in that it is described in the third person from the point of view of Esther, who is visiting her boyfriend Buddy in the hospital where he works as an intern. At the time, Sylvia Plath had given birth to her daughter and had therefore experienced childbirth first-hand. Yet in her novel, she decides to represent the experience from the point of view of a younger autobiographical self. Not only is she choosing to adopt an outsider's point of view, but she also stands next to Buddy and his fellow medical students, placing herself on the side of the medical institution. One of the students expresses concern and discomfort at knowing that a woman is watching among them, as if she were usurping a point of view she should not be entitled to: "'You oughtn't to see this,' Will Muttered in my ear. 'You'll never want to have a baby if you do. They oughtn't to let women watch. It'll be the end of the human race'" (Plath 1963, 61).

The transgression here is that a woman should be allowed to watch this event unfold as if she were a man, yet the effect is that the narrator feels profoundly alienated from what she is witnessing.

> The woman's stomach stuck up so high I couldn't see her face or the upper part of her body at all. She seemed to have nothing but an enormous spider-fat stomach and two little ugly spindly legs propped in the high stirrups, and all the time the baby was being born she never stopped making this unhuman whooing noise.
>
> (Plath 1963, 62)

From Esther's point of view, the woman giving birth is the helpless victim of some form of unspeakable violence, and the medical apparatus evokes "some awful torture table, with these metal stirrups sticking up mid-air at one end and all sorts of instruments and wires and tubes I couldn't make out properly at the other" (Plath 1963, 61). Esther herself experiences a shattering of her self: from where she is standing, she is watching the scene unfold from the point of view of medical students, for whom childbirth is essentially a question of practice, but unlike them, she cannot help but empathise with the woman whose body is mutilated by the episiotomy, and whose identity is negated by the patronising attitudes of the doctors. When the woman is presented her baby, she seems completely defeated: she does not answer or raise her head, as if she were not actually present.

Esther is also outraged at discovering that the doctors intend to tamper with the woman's memory of the event.

> Later Buddy told me the woman was on a drug that would make her forget she'd had any pain [...].
> I thought it sounded just like the sort of drug a man would invent. Here was a woman in terrible pain, obviously feeling every bit of it or she wouldn't groan like that, and she would go straight home and start another baby, because the drug would make her forget how bad the pain had been, when all this time, in some secret part of her, that long, blind, doorless and windowless corridor of pain was waiting to open up and shut her in again.
>
> (Plath 1963, 61–62)

Esther denounces here the fact that the medical institution can, at will, deprogram and later reprogram a mother into docile acceptance of her fate. There seems to be a male conspiracy against the community of women, intent on precluding any exchange of knowledge between them so that they don't rebel against their condition and precipitate "the end of the human race". In her article "Delivery: The Cultural Re-presentation of Childbirth", Cynthia Huff looks at letters sent by women to the US publication "Ladies' Home Journal" in the 1950s, around the time when Sylvia Plath was a young woman herself. Huff explains that an anonymous letter by a nurse working in the maternity ward of a hospital denouncing the awful conditions in which young mothers were treated, prompted a "flood of letters" to the editor, especially from other women who would go on to recount their own tales of mistreatment and cruelty. They all told of their feelings of being put through an "assembly-line", like so many machines to be attended to by the callous and indifferent doctors. For Huff, this spontaneous outpouring of personal narratives was testimony to a collective desire on the part of women to express themselves on the subject of childbirth, spurred by the reading of other women's stories (Huff 1991, 115). This hunger for a shared corpus of stories is analysed as a result of the treatment of women by the medical institution: they refused to remain silent, their speech stifled by the patriarchal discourse of obstetrics.

In *The Bell Jar*, the woman giving birth is made monstrous by her helplessness, an insect stuck on her back, pinned to her hospital bed by the pain and by the male medical gaze. It feels as if Esther is projecting on this faceless body the horror she feels at her female condition, and at the threat of such a terrible loss of autonomy. This description somehow fits with the common sentiment felt among mid-20th-century women at seeing their efforts at autonomy be ruined by the material reality of pregnancy and childbirth, a view that can be found especially among writers belonging to first-wave feminism, like Simone de Beauvoir for example. Imogen Tyler notes that unlike feminist philosophers like Young or Battersby who saw pregnancy as an alternative to classic ontology, Simone de Beauvoir still considered pregnant women as essentially passive subjects, mired in the immanent, material reality of their bodies (Beauvoir [1949] 2012; Tyler 2000, 294). For Carol Poston, Plath's representation of childbirth is a prime example of the anger and resentment at "an animal process which takes woman out of her 'rational' selfhood and places her in the hands of male attendants" (Poston 1978, 24). For Marilyn Yalom, Esther's phobia of motherhood is to be understood within the cultural context of pre-Roe v. Wade 1960s USA, at a time when motherhood was not a choice but constituted a threat to young women's independence as becoming pregnant often meant an entry into housewife status (Yalom 1985, 20). The self who watches the other woman give birth is a self who is trying to remain autonomous by "abjecting" the reality of childbirth, and motherhood in general. Yet the fact that this scene was written by a woman who had given birth herself should give us an indication of the ambivalence Plath felt towards her own condition as a young mother at the time she wrote the novel.

From the third to the first person

With the 1970s, the advent of second-wave feminism, and its insistence on the personal as political, the focus started to shift from the outsider's point of view to the lived experience of the mother, with the notable example of Jane Lazarre's *The Mother Knot*, which opens on a depiction of the birth of the narrator's second child. In terms of narrative economy, starting a motherhood memoir with a childbirth scene is quite significant and implies the central role of the event in a mother's life as it marks the beginning of her career. Moreover, Lazarre decides to counter the chronological order by starting her memoir with the birth of her second child, not the first. This birth is both a beginning and an ending, it marks the conclusion to the period of confusion the narrator experienced in the first years with her child as she learnt to become a mother, but it also ushers in a new model of motherhood: she is a "different person" (Lazarre [1976] 1997, 7), and she now knows what to expect from the experience ahead of her. Equipped with the knowledge she did not have before and stripped of the illusions she had fostered during her first pregnancy, she is now ready to embark on the next stage of her mothering.

That does not mean that her experience of birth is any less painful or frightening. Like Lessing, the narrator in Lazarre's memoir had approached her first birth with the naivety of the young and healthy (Lazarre [1976] 1997, 3), yet at the time when she is getting ready to renew the experience, she is wiser, and as a result, "terrified". As her labour drags on, she tries to navigate her escalating pain by following the techniques she learnt in her natural childbirth classes, as well as the recommendations of her doctors: voices from each chapel course through her mind, but nothing seems to work: "They gave me Pitocin to speed up contractions, which, my feminist sisters had warned me, made the pains more intense and less controllable. But who cared. At least they would be over faster. I wanted it to be over" (Lazarre [1976] 1997, 5). As much as she wants to be in control of her labour and decide the terms of her birth, the narrator realises that alone and engulfed in pain, she is reaching the border of her sanity. This is made manifest by a form of depersonalisation: she hears screaming, and she knows it is coming from her, yet she does not seem to have control over it. Eventually as she starts to make peace with the possibility she might be dying, her second child is born. This narrative of childbirth is probably one of the first first-person accounts of childbirth given by a female author in English: it is remarkable in its attempt to forge a path for self-expression outside of the words of the medical institution.

In Rachel Cusk's motherhood memoir, *A Life's Work*, written 25 years later (2001), the narrator also remembers the sense of her self being split into body and mind. This is made even worse by the fact that she needs to undergo a C-section, which renders her completely passive and places the event under the control of the medical institution. Also under the influence of the principles of natural childbirth, the narrator had decided to give birth at home. Yet as her due date nears, she realises that she will need to give birth in the hospital after all, as a home birth would be too dangerous. At this time, she realises that all resistance is indeed futile: "I am told I must now remain in hospital. Rebelliously, desperately, I discharge myself and go home. The next day I come back and surrender" (Cusk 2001, 45). Later, as she is wheeled into the operating theatre for her C-section, she is reminded of representations she has come across of "execution chambers": like in Lazarre's account, the narrator is unsure whether she is going to give birth or meet death. The hospital is represented as a place that is fundamentally hostile and even dangerous: she is robbed of her agency and is made passive by the anaesthetics, which cut her lower half from the rest of her body. Like Lessing, this impression is compounded by her loss of control of space and time:

> I can see my own face reflected in the broad lamp above me. I look at the clock and see that only ten minutes have passed since I left the ward. What's happening? I say. My voice sounds preternatural coming out of my dead body. I fear suddenly that I have been forgotten, that I am going to be left dismantled, a talking head on a table. I fear that my soul is being uncaged and allowed to fly away. Nobody replies to my question.
>
> (Cusk 2001, 48)

In Cusk's memoir, childbirth is recounted in the first person, but the narrator's point of view is that of a baffled participant. She can witness the doctors and the nurses coming in and out of the room, but it all fails to make sense. Her question "What's happening?" does not find an answer from the medical staff and hints at the black void at the heart of her experience: someone knows what is happening, but the narrator does not have access to that knowledge. What is striking in this narrative of childbirth is the role of the medical staff around the narrator: they are faceless shadows poking and prodding at her body, but there is no exchange between her and them, no meaning being shared. The narrator feels cut off from the terms of what is happening to her: the meaning of her experience has been confiscated by the medical staff and made inaccessible.

Once again, a comparison with Maggie Nelson's text is interesting: in *The Argonauts*, childbirth is a victory, just like pregnancy had been an act of defiance against reactionary, heteronormative narratives. The "I" who gives birth is active, not passive, and the medical staff are presented as enablers, not faceless evil characters:

They say I can push. I push. I feel him come out, all of him, all at once. I also feel the shit that had been bedevilling me all through pregnancy and labor come out too. My first feeling is that I could run a thousand miles, I feel amazing, total and complete relief, like everything that was wrong is now right.

(Nelson 2015, 165)

Even the release of faeces which creates so much shame and anxiety in pregnant women, is experienced as part of a triumph of the body over the social and medical norms which would represent the birthing body as pathological and abject. The active presence of the narrator's partner Harry is also noteworthy, as in most childbirth scenes, fathers and partners tend to recede in the background, when they are not completely absent. Not only is Harry experiencing the birth with the narrator, but he is also given a voice and a point of view of the events unfolding: his voice is interlaced with that of his partner's as he muses on his own broken family history. A parallel can be drawn with Jane Lazarre's account of childbirth in *The Mother Knot*, in which the narrator absents herself from the scene to reflect on her husband's childhood (Lazarre [1976] 1997, 3–4). The fact that the narrator's husband should be Black in a time when interracial marriages were still relatively rare makes his presence alongside his white partner a victory against racism, just like the presence of a trans husband beside his wife is in itself a defiance of heteronormative definitions of what a family should be.

First-person narratives of childbirth in autobiographical accounts have become more common in recent years – see for example Anne Enright in *Making Babies: Stumbling into Motherhood* (2012), Andrea Buchanan in *Mother Shock: Tales from the First year and Beyond – Loving Every (Other) Minute of it* (2003), or Chitra Ramaswamy in *Expecting: The Inner Life of Pregnancy* (2016), among others. But these accounts were all written in the last 20 years, as part of the boom of motherhood memoirs. Could the very fact that this experience should be written in the first person be construed as a way for female authors to reclaim the childbirth metaphor? In fact, very few narratives I have come across actually describe childbirth metaphorically – if anything, childbirth is an encounter with the limits of the self and with the possibility of death, and it is often a struggle against the patriarchal medical institution. The mode of writing is often linear and metonymic rather than metaphoric. Could this be because something in childbirth resists sense-making and literary articulation?

Conclusion

Taking a historical look at the place which has been given to the experiences of pregnancy and childbirth in literary texts allows us to see how the place of motherhood has come to evolve in the literary canon. From a near-total absence in texts up to the 20th century to its foregrounding in complex, first-person narratives in the 21st century, pregnancy and childbirth are indeed beginning to gain visibility, to the point of becoming part of the common stock of human experience. Women can now turn to literature in order to find realistic depictions of what they are going through when they become pregnant, even though there is still some way to go before they can choose to explore the type of childbirth experience they want to have. Having access to varied accounts by women from different backgrounds, they can now make their own choices. I would also add that the evolution of the representation of pregnancy and childbirth in literature goes hand in hand with the autonomy left to women as part of the medical discourse. Now that more women become gynaecologists and obstetricians, there is arguably more respect for women's bodies and desires in the medical discourse around pregnancy and childbirth, although, once again, as Glaser (2021) and Jones (2023) have argued, the old orthodoxies are hard to shake off.

As a coda, I would add that, while one is indeed surprised at the paucity of examples of literary representations of pregnancy and childbirth in prose, there is a wealth of poetic texts on the subject, and particularly in the case of childbirth, which is a frequent topic of texts by women poets. This may sound counterintuitive, as many poets have lamented the lack of poems on the topic of motherhood. In her book *Writing Like a Woman*, US poet Alicia Ostriker remembers writing a long poet about pregnancy and starts to wonder:

> One morning, when it was about two-thirds done, I realized that I had never in my life read a poem about pregnancy and birth. Why not? I had read hundreds of poems about love, hundreds of poems about death. These were, of course, universal themes. But wasn't birth universal?
> (Ostriker 1983, 127)

British poet Liz Berry, author of *The Republic of Motherhood* (2018), also testifies to the impression of being failed by the literary tradition when she first became pregnant: "But when I looked at poems, the place that had always comforted me, that experience was hard to find. It made me feel very lost" (The British Library, n.d.). Another British poet, Rachel Bower, author of *Moon Milk* (2018a) writes in an article about her desire to inscribe herself in a literary tradition:

> Where, for example, could I find my own lived experiences of growing, birthing, and caring for a child in the history of literature? Where were the poems (or short stories or novels) about shame and loss, about

unbearable love, and unimaginable boredom, about the intersection between birth and death?

(Bower 2018b)

There is in fact a tradition, at least in poetry, of writing about pregnancy and motherhood, as the publication of several anthologies can attest (Gilbert, Gubar, and O'Hehir 1995; Otten 1993; Clanchy 2012). Yet it is telling that those three authors had never become aware of this tradition when they first became pregnant. In the introduction to her anthology, Charlotte Otten notes that women have always written about their experiences of pregnancy and birth, but these writings were confined to their journals, or to letters written to each other; poetry was out of the question (Otten 1993, xv; see also Huff 1991). Yet it took the publication of Anne Sexton's poem "In Celebration of my Uterus" (1969), for the taboo of procreation in poetry to be broken. Sexton's poem belongs to a tradition of poetry, which began in the 1960s, intent on bringing to the foreground specifically female experiences such as pregnancy and childbirth and on inscribing those themes within the lyric mode of self-expression, on a par with male poets' chosen themes. There is also another famous poem by Sharon Olds, "The Language of the Brag" (1980) in which childbirth specifically is presented here as a feat of self-expression by women, an enlargement rather than a shattering of the self, in the tradition of such American poets as Walt Whitman and Allen Ginsberg, who both experimented with the limits of the self and claimed access to a universal embrace of the human condition. Tharp and McCallum see this poem as a "watershed moment", "a challenge to a culture that has routinely used the language of birth for everyone and everything except the actual event" (Tharp and MacCallum-Whitcomb 2000, 2).

In "The Stranger Guest: The Literature of Pregnancy and New Motherhood", Lily Gurton-Wachter draws a parallel between the experiences of war and motherhood, which, she claims, are both framed in terms of trauma and alienation. As she taught a class on war literature while pregnant, she realised that canonical literature still very much made war the central human experience, when the experience of birth and new motherhood are relegated to the margins of female-only reality (Gurton-Wachter 2016). The same could be said about romantic love, which has taken a disproportionate place in the range of emotions expressed in poetry and in literature in general. Under the supremacy of romantic love, the feelings a mother may express for her child are perceived to be simple, mawkish, and lacking in any interest whatsoever. This is when we should remember that, as natals, we were all "of woman born", which means that we all lived inside someone's womb, and we all went through the trauma of birth alongside our mothers. As a shared experience of our common humanity, it would only be fair to make it a legitimate topic of poetic, and more widely, of literary representation.

Notes

1 The figure of the "virgin birth", that of Jesus, and before him, the birth of Pallas Athena, the Greek goddess of wisdom, who came out of Jupiter's body in a full set of armour speak to this fantasy of disincarnated birth.
2 It does strike one that many of the critical works I have come across on the topic of childbirth begin with the author's account of her own experience of pregnancy and childbirth (Poston 1978; Young 1984; Tyler 2000).

Works cited

Baines, Elizabeth. (1983) 2013. *Birth Machine*. 3rd ed. Cromer: Salt Publishing.
Battersby, Christine. 1998. *The Phenomenal Woman: Feminist Metaphysics and the Patterns of Identity*. London: Routledge.
Berry, Liz. 2018. *The Republic of Motherhood*. London: Chatto & Windus.
Blewitt, Sarah Emily. 2015. *Hidden Mothers and Poetic Pregnancy in Women's Writing (1818–Present Day)*. Cardiff: Cardiff University Press.
Bower, Rachel. 2018a. *Moon Milk*. Scarborough: Valley Press.
———. 2018b. 'Writing Birth: On the Poetry of Motherhood'. *Wild Court* (blog). 14 November 2018. https://wildcourt.co.uk/features/1869/
Buchanan, Andrea. 2003. *Mother Shock: Tales from the First Year and Beyond-- Loving Every (Other) Minute of It*. New York: Seal Press.
Cavarero, Adriana. 1995. *In Spite of Plato: A Feminist Rewriting of Ancient Philosophy*. London: Routledge.
Clanchy, Kate, ed. 2012. *The Picador Book of Birth Poems*. London: Picador.
Collins, Katie. 2019. 'The Morbidity of Maternity: Radical Receptivity in Maggie Nelson's *The Argonauts*'. *Criticism* 61 (3): 311–34. https://doi.org/10.13110/criticism.61.3.0311
Cosslett, Tess. 1989. 'Childbirth from the Woman's Point of View in British Women's Fiction: Enid Bagnold's *The Squire* and A. S. Byatt's *Still Life*'. *Tulsa Studies in Women's Literature* 8 (2): 263–86. https://doi.org/10.2307/463738
———. 1994. *Women Writing Childbirth: Modern Discourses of Motherhood*. Manchester: Manchester University Press.
Cusk, Rachel. 2001. *A Life's Work: On Becoming a Mother*. New York: Picador.
de Beauvoir, Simone. (1949) 2012. *Le deuxième sexe I: Les faits et les mythes*. Paris: Gallimard.
Dey, Claudia. 2018. 'Mothers as Makers of Death'. *The Paris Review*, 14 August 2018. www.theparisreview.org/blog/2018/08/14/mothers-as-makers-of-death/
Dick-Read, Grantly. (1942) 2004. *Childbirth without Fear: The Principles and Practice of Natural Childbirth*. London: Pinter & Martin Publishers.
Donnison, Jean. 1976. 'Medical Woman and Lady Midwives'. *Women's Studies* 3 (3): 229–50. https://doi.org/10.1080/00497878.1976.9978394

Enright, Anne. 2012. *Making Babies: Stumbling into Motherhood*. New York: W. W. Norton & Company.
Erdrich, Louise. 1995. *The Blue Jay's Dance: A Birth Year*. New York: HarperCollins.
Fraiman, Susan. 2003. *Cool Men and the Second Sex*. Gender and Culture. New York: Columbia University Press.
Friedman, Susan Stanford. 1987. 'Creativity and the Childbirth Metaphor: Gender Difference in Literary Discourse'. *Feminist Studies* 13 (1): 49–82. https://doi.org/10.2307/3177835
Gilbert, Sandra M., Susan Gubar, and Diana O'Hehir, eds. 1995. *MotherSongs: Poems for, by, and about Mothers*. 1st ed. New York: W. W. Norton & Company.
Glaser, Eliane. 2021. *Motherhood: Feminism's Unfinished Business*. London: Fourth Estate Ltd.
Greengrass, Jessie. 2018. 'Why Does Literature Ignore Pregnancy?' *The Guardian*, 22 February 2018. www.theguardian.com/books/booksblog/2018/feb/22/why-does-literature-ignore-pregnancy
Gurton-Wachter, Lily. 2016. 'The Stranger Guest: The Literature of Pregnancy and New Motherhood'. *Los Angeles Review of Books*, 29 July 2016. https://lareviewofbooks.org/article/stranger-guest-literature-pregnancy-new-motherhood/
Huff, Cynthia. 1991. 'Delivery: The Cultural Re-presentation of Childbirth'. *Prose Studies* 14 (2): 108–21. https://doi.org/10.1080/01440359108586435
Huston, Nancy. 1990. *Journal de la création*. Arles: Actes Sud.
Irigaray, Luce. 1974. *Speculum de l'autre Femme*. Paris: Éditions de Minuit.
Jones, Lucy. 2023. *Matrescence: On the Metamorphosis of Pregnancy, Childbirth and Motherhood*. London: Allen Lane.
Kreppel, Maria. 1984. 'Books I've Read: Crosscurrents in Obstetrics and Literary Childbirth'. *Atlantis: Critical Studies in Gender, Culture & Social Justice* 10 (1): 1–11.
Lazarre, Jane. (1976) 1997. *The Mother Knot*. Durham, NC: Duke University Press.
Lessing, Doris. 1954. *A Proper Marriage*. New ed. Children of Violence, Doris Lessing; Book 2. London: Flamingo.
———. 1994. *Under My Skin: Volume One of My Autobiography to 1949*. New York: Harper Perennial.
Morel, Marie-France. 2022. *Accompagner l'accouchement d'hier à aujourd'hui. La main ou l'outil?* 1001 bébés. Toulouse: Érès.
Nelson, Maggie. 2015. *The Argonauts*. London: Melville House UK.
Oakley, Ann. 1979. 'A Case of Maternity: Paradigms of Women as Maternity Cases'. *Signs: Journal of Women in Culture and Society* 4 (4): 607–31. https://doi.org/10.1086/493653
Ostriker, Alicia. 1983. *Writing Like a Woman*. Ann Arbor, MI: University of Michigan Press.
Otten, Charlotte F., ed. 1993. *The Virago Book of Birth Poetry*. London: Virago.
Plath, Sylvia. 1963. *The Bell Jar*. London: Faber & Faber.
Poston, Carol H. 1978. 'Childbirth in Literature'. *Feminist Studies* 4 (2): 18–31. https://doi.org/10.2307/3177434
Ramaswamy, Chitra. 2016. *Expecting: The Inner Life of Pregnancy*. Glasgow: Saraband.

Rich, Adrienne C. (1976) 1995. *Of Woman Born: Motherhood as Experience and Institution*. 2nd ed. Women's Studies. New York: Norton.

Stone, Alison. 2019. *Being Born: Birth and Philosophy*. Oxford University Press. https://doi.org/10.1093/oso/9780198845782.001.0001

Sweetman, Susannah. 2018. 'Birth Fear and the Subjugation of Women's Strength: Towards a Broader Conceptualization of Femininity in Birth'. In *Motherhood in Literature and Culture: Interdisciplinary Perspectives from Europe*, edited by Gill Rye, Victoria Browne, Adalgisa Giorgio, Emily Jeremiah, and Abigail Lee Six, 17–32. New York; London: Routledge, Taylor & Francis Group.

Tharp, Julie Ann, and Susan MacCallum-Whitcomb, eds. 2000. *This Giving Birth: Pregnancy and Childbirth in American Women's Writing*. Bowling Green, OH: Bowling Green State University Popular Press.

The British Library. n.d. 'Liz Berry "The Republic of Motherhood"'. Accessed 9 July 2019. https://soundcloud.com/the-british-library/liz-berry-the-republic-of-motherhood

Treichler, Paula A. 1990. 'Feminism, Medicine, and the Meaning of Childbirth'. In *Body/Politics: Women and the Discourses of Science*, edited by Mary Jacobus, Evelyn Fox Keller, and Sally Shuttleworth, 113–38. New York; London: Routledge.

Tyler, Imogen. 2000. 'Reframing Pregnant Embodiment'. In *Transformations: Thinking Through Feminism*, edited by Sarah Ahmed, Jane Kilby, Celia Lury, Maureen McNeill, and Beverley Skeggs, 288–302. London: Routledge.

Vickery, Ann. 2020. 'Revaluing Memoir and Rebuilding Mothership in Maggie Nelson's The Argonauts'. *Australian Literary Studies* 35 (1): 1–13. https://doi.org/10.20314/als.ad45a0d006

Wells, Sherah. 2011. 'The Self Which Surfaces: Competing Maternal Discourses in A Proper Marriage'. *Doris Lessing Studies* 30 (1): 7–12.

Yalom, Marilyn. 1985. *Maternity, Mortality, and the Literature of Madness*. Pennsylvania State University Press.

Young, Iris Marion. 1984. 'Pregnant Embodiment: Subjectivity and Alienation'. *The Journal of Medicine and Philosophy* 9: 45–62. https://doi.org/10.1093/jmp/9.1.45

4 Mother writing

Introduction

At the beginning of *A Life's Work: On Becoming a Mother*, Rachel Cusk's memoir of early motherhood, the narrator experiences a strong feeling of alienation and struggles with the impression of being exiled from her own life. Seeking solace in the world of poetry she comes across Samuel Taylor Coleridge's poem "Frost at Midnight" and stumbles upon the following lines: "The inmates of my cottage, all at rest, / Have left me to that solitude, which suits / Abstruser musings: save that at my side / My cradled infant slumbers peacefully". She realises that "like many childless people I had never noticed the baby". How could Coleridge – how could anyone – think of writing a poem with a baby in the room, even if that baby is perfectly quiet, or asleep? "I begin to see my predicament as the result of some deep failure of sensibility, some meanness of soul" (Cusk 2001). I have already mentioned the deep cultural imprint Romantic poets, or to be more precise, the public persona and ethos of Romantic poets, have had on our conception of what being an artist implies. Judging from their private lives, it would be fair to say that most Romantic poets did not particularly distinguish themselves in their involvement in domestic matters and in the care of children. The baby in Coleridge's poem seems to be more of a decorative item, as she is barely mentioned elsewhere in the poem, an element of the general atmosphere of the poem, rather than a flesh-and-bone infant, who would probably be tossing around in her cot, if not waking up for a night feed, at which point we imagine her being swiftly carried to her mother's arms.

Coleridge was the prime example of the early-19th-century Romantic poet who was gifted the power of "apprehending the Image", to borrow from Frank Kermode's terms, and who in search of the Image, "has to pay a heavy price in suffering, to risk his immortal soul, and to be alone, not only to be separate from all others but to have not even one friend" (Kermode 2002). This representation of the poet is very much at odds

DOI: 10.4324/9781003461388-5

with the figure of the mother writer who has put her child to bed and is finally free to explore her artistic imagination for a few uninterrupted hours. Coleridge himself was particularly sensitive to the risk of being interrupted: the vision in his poem "Kubla Khan" comes to an abrupt halt when someone knocks at his door, the infamous "person from Porlock" who single-handedly ruins the poet's epiphany. There has of course been some speculation as to the identity of the mysterious person from Porlock, but as Julie Phillips concludes in her "Porlock Day Manifesto":

> Coleridge's biographers have never been able to put a name to the Person from Porlock. They speculate that this village nuisance never existed. Coleridge made up the interloper as an excuse for not having gone on. In a sense, the Person *is* the poem's ending, and the return to reality is its logical conclusion.
>
> (Phillips 2017)

The person from Porlock, Phillips contends, has become the epitome of philistinism or of the intrusion of the banal in the sublime. Most women who write, she continues, have several little persons from Porlock at home, constantly interrupting them by knocking at their doors, with a question, an anecdote, or simply because they want to play.

This chapter will be focused on the material conditions of the female author who attempts to continue writing once she has become a mother. How does she reconcile her vocation with the all-encompassing task of caring for a small child? How does she stake her claim to specific time away from her duties as a mother, as well as to the mental space necessary for her to explore her imagination? What are the cultural taboos she will need to break in order to affirm her desire to write as well as mother? As we shall see, there is a wide range of different situations, and some female authors seem to fare better than others, finding no real material hurdle or existential difficulty in juggling their vocation as writers and their roles as mothers.

In the preface to *Double Lives: Writing and Motherhood*, another anthology of creative writing by mothers, Marni Jackson gives a hint as to why there seems to be so little writing on the topic of early motherhood, which is that women are exhausted and stretched thin to the point that they simply do not have the material time to sit down and work (Cowan, Lam, and Stonehouse 2008, xiii). The issue of time is, once again, essential: the mother's schedule is forever challenged by her child's demands, and she finds that the only time she can finally have to herself is when she manages to put her down to sleep. This is of course mostly true of mothers with very young children. As they grow older, their mother often finds that she can leave them in the care of their partner, or that they can occupy themselves for short periods of time while they go about with their writing lives. But that can only last for a time: children do not stay long outside of their mother's orbit. Very soon they'll get bored of whatever they were doing and come back clamouring for their mother's attention. In *A Life's Work*, the narrator realises with some dismay that her children are not like "children in novels, playing long imaginative games that don't involve you" (Cusk 2001, 132), but need to be attended to, distracted and engaged with, when she wishes nothing more than to be left alone. In the introduction to their anthology, Cowan, Tinwei Lam, and Stonehouse write of the war waged by children on their mother's attention: while the desire to write and to have children are both creative drives, the latter often makes the former impossible: "Imagine a child's cry from another room in the midst of a writer's long-awaited, hard-earned moment of quiet or at the start of a crucial but fleeting epiphany" (Cowan, Lam, and Stonehouse 2008, xvii).

As the previous quote suggests, writing is not only a matter of making the appropriate time to write but also about finding that mental space in which the author's thoughts are free to roam, and reconnecting with her imaginary landscape. In her book *All Joy and No Fun: The Paradox of Modern Parenthood*, Jennifer Senior points at one specific aspect of living with small children: "the early years of family life don't offer up many activities that lend themselves to what psychologists call 'flow'" (Senior 2014, 28). "Flow" is a state described by psychologist Mihaly Csikszentmihalyi as a long stretch of uninterrupted, focused activity, whether it be athletic, or creative. Time seems to flow smoothly and rapidly as we engage in a meaningful, sometimes even pleasurable task that requires all our attention. Flow, Senior argues, is impossible to achieve with children around:

> To be in flow, one must pay close and focused attention. Yet very young children are wired for discovery, for sweeping in lots of stimuli. And if they can't be in flow, chances are you'll have a hard time slipping into flow yourself – in the same way that athletes have a much harder time finding their groove if their teammates are distracted.
>
> (Senior 2014, 32)

So how do writers manage to keep writing once they become mothers? Very often they wait until their children are asleep, or wake up very early, curtailing their own need for sleep. In an article entitled "The Heartbreaking Ingenuity of the Mother-Writer", author Olivia Campbell looks at the hurdles young mothers need to overcome in order to claim some time to write, and she finds that many of them also need to contend with the traditional representation of the (often male) writer who locks himself in a cabin, Salinger-style, away from the trivialities of everyday life, in order to write his masterpiece.

> We have this heady image of authors penning their books while sitting peacefully at oversized hardwood desks overlooking vistas of lush trees or skyscrapers. But if you've read a book penned by a woman with young children recently, there's a significant chance it was written while hiding, losing sleep, or using inventive distractions.
>
> (Campbell 2021)

She gives several testimonies from other mother writers who have had to write during their children's naps, hidden in their cars, in the bathroom, or even under a blanket in order to escape their children's demands for their time and attention. Interestingly enough, she says, some women find that their writing has benefited from this constraint upon their time, while others have all but crumbled under the demands from their families. Children alone should not be blamed for their mothers' failure at fulfilling their vocation as writers; for Campbell, the problem originates in our society's idealisation of the role of mothers as single carers for their family, as well as a "minimization of women's writing as a hobby". In the introduction to her anthology of writing by mothers, Carolyn Jess-Cooke reaches a similar conclusion:

> When it comes to writing, the question of "finding time" relates to the act of writing as something a woman with kids shouldn't ordinarily set as a priority. [...] Writing is frivolous, perhaps indulgent, subversive, and even selfish, when done by women, and serious and perfectly normal when done by men.
>
> (Jess-Cooke 2017, 13)

These questions actually open up more avenues of thought: is there a specific form of "mother writing"? Does the writing by mothers adapt to the new constraints on their time and mental space to take on a new form determined by their circumstances? To take that point further, does the writing produced by women who are also mothers differ in significant ways from the writing produced by men and non-mothers? Is there a distinct imaginary accessible only to mothers? The answers to those questions vary widely, depending on the author, with some finding it impossible to reconcile their vocation and their role and allowing their voice, at least for a time, to trail into silence, while others find that they can tap into their experience of motherhood to explore new forms of creativity. Once again, I would like to show the dilemma of the mother writer is one that takes its roots in our cultural representations of motherhood, and the notion that it is antithetical with authorship. Being a mother involves a compulsory selflessness, while we allow author figures to be self-involved in the name of their artistic vocations. In order for women to authorise themselves – that is, allow themselves to be authors – I suggest we need to deconstruct this fake binary. I will look specifically at authors who have explored a form of creativity within the constraints and interruptions incurred by their roles as carers to their families.

Mother shock

Crossing the border

Recent scholarly books have explored the possibility that motherhood may be conceived of as an existential crisis. Lucy Jones uses the concept of "matrescence" in order to describe the deep sense of transformation experienced by young mothers, one that is akin to the crisis teenagers go through in adolescence (Jones 2023). For Claire Arnold-Baker, motherhood is best described as an "existential crisis" which completely reshapes the mother's sense of identity, as well as her sense of belonging to time and place (Arnold-Baker 2020). For several authors who write of their experience of motherhood, becoming a mother feels like being displaced, even banished to a foreign country. This foreign country is a place that is devoid of all the landmarks and coordinates they were used to and represents alienation and displacement from the reality hitherto experienced. I believe that the spatial metaphors are important here because they express the mother writers' mourning not just of their own selves but also of their mental spaces, where they could explore their imagination as an inner space to which they cannot have access to once the child has arrived in their lives. That new land in which they have arrived is hostile and bare but is it also a prison from which they cannot escape and where there is no place to hide. The question then is to know whether this country can be explored or whether it should be fled from at the earliest possibility, whether motherhood is a new vantage point from which the mother-writer can write, or whether she should get back to her old self/country as soon as her children have grown enough to take care of themselves.

In the memoir written by Andrea Buchanan, *Mother Shock: Tales from the First Year and Beyond—Loving Every (Other) Minute of It*, the running metaphor used to describe the experience of motherhood is the passage into a foreign country, of which the mother does not even speak the language (Buchanan 2003). This change of country, and implicitly of cultural references and landmarks, is all the more unsettling as it happens while the subject physically remains in her surroundings, creating an impression of *unheimlich* – a displacement from the home which still happens in the home.

Among the recent poetry written on the topic of motherhood, Liz Berry's (2018) *The Republic of Motherhood* opens with an eponymous poem which describes the reality of motherhood as a passage in a foreign state. The country entered by the poet is a dystopian dictatorship in which she is stripped of her clothes as well as her individuality and condemned to forced labour along with legions of other faceless women. The totalitarian metaphor here attempts to render the shock of losing control over one's life and one's sense of time. In her memoir, Rachel Cusk uses very similar language to describe her own experience of motherhood: words like "prison", "regime", "dictatorial", and "torture camp" all participate in the painting of a picture of early motherhood as a radical loss of dignity and freedom.[1] The narrator is condemned to watching the world from the bars of a prison she herself has locked herself into, or alternatively, from across the border of a totalitarian regime, from which she can catch a glimpse of the old country she used to inhabit. At some point in the memoir, the narrator talks about her plan to attend a concert with a friend, leaving her baby in the care of her mother-in-law. Instead of enjoying the concert, she finds herself constantly phoning home in order to make sure the baby is all right without her:

> In the street outside the traffic honks and roars. People mill around me, passing out into the London night. They are not only ignorant of the strife-torn region in which now I live; they are as remote from it as if it lay on the other side of the world.
>
> (Cusk 2001, 88)

The home a prison

The feeling of being displaced, or even banished, means that the writer who becomes a mother has been expelled from one space and deported into another, has been stripped of one status, and labelled with another. Their home itself, which used to be a writer's home, is now a mother's home, that place where mothers have historically been relegated in order to care for their children. During the Industrial Revolution, the home became the locus for the domestic, a safe haven from the necessities of work and productivity, but for some women, the home actually became a prison where they had to renounce their aspirations for independence (Bueskens 2018). But even beyond the cultural and political injunction to stay at home, 20th-century as well as 21st-century women realise that their aspirations to freedom often stop at the nursery door. Therefore, in Cusk's or in Lazarre's memoirs, the home becomes a prison camp to which they are banished. In the introduction to her memoir, Cusk explains:

> Motherhood, for me, was a sort of compound fenced off from the rest of the world. I was forever plotting my escape from it, and when I found myself pregnant again when Albertine was six months old I greeted my old cell with the cheerless acceptance of a convict intercepted at large.
> (Cusk 2001, 12)

There is an apparent paradox in being banished into one's home, but the displacement is mainly symbolic. What some mother writers do actually lament is the fact of having been robbed of their symbolic position as writers but also locked out of their personal imaginary space. From that perspective, writing means escaping the prison cell, being free to roam the open fields of the imagination. As Adrienne Rich explains in *Of Woman Born: Motherhood as Experience and Institution*, writing is incompatible with mothering, it is a separate space altogether: "For me, poetry was where I lived as no-one's mother, where I existed as myself" (Rich [1976] 1995, 31).

Similarly, the narrator in Jane Lazarre's *The Mother Knot* describes motherhood as a form of entrapment, often referring to herself as a prisoner in her own home (Lazarre [1976] 1997). She nevertheless catches her first glimpse of freedom when she goes out to attend a mother's group, in which other women allow themselves to tell each other about the reality of their experience, away from the oppressive clichés which force women to remain silent about their difficulties. As one woman, Anna, decides to share with the other women the uncomfortable truths she has discovered about motherhood, the narrator realises with relief:

> And with that statement something fell off, crumbled, disintegrated within me – the wall which had kept me alone, the prison cell, the solitary confinement, and the terrible possibility that even in this universally feminine experience, I would still be, at least to myself, horribly odd – all these were cracked by the familiarity of Anna's words and began to fall away.
> (Lazarre [1976] 1997, 68)

Eventually, the narrator in *The Mother Knot* manages to escape her prison-home, by attending support groups (an experience which the narrator in Cusk's memoir finds profoundly alienating), and by seeking refuge in the library, which is the only place where she can find comfort in her situation as prisoner: "I curled up in the black leather chair in the corner of the library, moving comfortably in my prison suit, which, freed at last from the stiff jail-house uniformity, was beginning to take on a shape of its own" (Lazarre [1976] 1997, 138). What the narrator is able to find there is the elusive mental space she needs as a writer and has been denied by her new reality as a mother.

From that point of view, Doireann Ní Ghriofa's poetic memoir *A Ghost in the Throat*, can be read as a chronicle of the escapist fantasy of a poet longing to find a creative room of her own. It evokes the daily life of a poet who is also a mother of four, the domestic drudgery of caring for her children and her husband, as well as the disruption introduced by the traumatic birth of her last child. Each day the narrator starts a list of tasks she needs to perform and ticks them off one by one in order to give a semblance of structure to her life: "As I clean, my labour makes of itself an invisibility. If each day is a cluttered page, then I spend my hours scrubbing its letters. In this, my work is a deletion of a presence" (Ní Ghriofa 2020, 28). Over time, the narrator becomes obsessed, or rather haunted, by an Irish 18th-century poem called "Caoineadh Airt Uí Laoghaire" by Eibhlín Dubh Ní Chonaill. The poem and her author become a companion for the narrator in Ní Ghriofa's book, who finds refuge in the text written by an author about whose life almost nothing has remained beyond the poem which she wrote. As she sets about translating the work in English, the narrator resorts to the metaphor of the house, as if the text was composed of so many rooms she needed to tend to:

> In Italian, the word stanza means "room". If there are times when I feel ill-equipped and daunted by the expertise of those who have walked these rooms before me, I reassure myself that I am simply homemaking, and this thought steadies me, because tending to a room is a form of labour I know that I can attempt as well as anyone.
> (Ní Ghriofa 2020, 31)

The house metaphor serves to give the poet the legitimacy to take on a poetic task that she did not feel authorised to carry out as a mother and a housewife. The narrator is aware that there is a streak of escapism in her attempts to track the author of her beloved poem, yet her attempts at recovering the facts of Eibhlín Dubh Ní Chonaill's life echo her own desire to escape erasure – the erasure of her voice and of herself altogether.

If motherhood is a prison, who is the jailor? Should we blame the baby? For Adrienne Rich, it is the institution of motherhood which imprisons women in their own bodies and their homes (Rich [1976] 1995, 13), forcing them to believe that their aspiration to independence must take second place to their roles as mothers. Rich also explains how the construction of the home as a single unit, with the individual home or flat, has cut women away from the community of other mothers, which historically has been crucial to allowing mothers to keep some form of independence

(Hrdy 1999). I also believe that the feeling of displacement which recurs in many memoirs of motherhood has to do with a loss of bearings, and a rearrangement of the familiar incurred by the arrival of the baby. Just like space, time is also reconfigured dramatically.

Time and self

Once they are past the shock of birth and have settled into their lives with a baby at home, many authors who write on the topic of motherhood talk about a relationship with time which is completely altered by the baby's needs: in short, the baby's time becomes the mother's time. In *Ongoingness*, a memoir on the author's obsession with diary writing, Sarah Manguso documents the rupture which appeared in her relationship to time after the birth of her baby. Whereas diary writing had before been a way to hang on to time and control its flow, with the baby's arrival in her life, the narrator is forced to let go of her grip and let the baby's needs dictate the structure of her day:

> I used to exist against the continuity of time. Then I became the baby's continuity, a background of ongoing time for him to live against. I was the warmth and milk that was always there for him, the agent of comfort that was always there for him.
>
> (Manguso 2019, 59)

Concretely, this control over the mother's time also implies a control over her body and her ability to interact with others as the baby's needs are so urgent and intense, that they leave little to no place for her mother's desires. Like Manguso, the narrator in Rachel Cusk's memoir *A Life's Work* experiences the dissolution of time as a lapse into savagery:

> Caring for her is like being responsible for the weather, or for the grass growing: my privileged relationship with time has changed, and though these tasks are not yet arduous they already constitute a sort of serfdom, a slavery, in that I am not free to go. It is a humbling change. It represents, too, a reckoning of my former freedom, my distance from duty.
>
> (Cusk 2001, 135)

Both writers experience the loss of their control over time as an assault on their freedom. One morning, the narrator wakes up at 9.30 to her baby's furious crying after a night disrupted by feedings. She observes: "Other people have gone to work, to school, while we slept: the world is at its desk. We are in the housewifely slurry of everything that is both too late and too early, of madness and morning television" (Cusk 2001, 68). Her time is the time of housewives and mad people, it is no longer structured or meaningful. Similarly, the desk she is being kept away from by her mothering duties is the metonym for productive, socially rewarded work, the antithesis of the type of work she is performing at home alone with her baby. Yet this work is "the hardest work I have ever done" (Cusk 2001, 213).

All of a sudden, the mothers who write of their experience are thrown into a completely different conception of time, one that Lisa Baraitser would call "maternal time" (Baraitser 2008, 75). Borrowing from the work of philosopher Julia Kristeva (Kristeva 1981), and sociologist Karen Davies (Davies 1990), Baraitser defines maternal time as a time that is cyclical, structured around the necessities of caregiving; that is, fundamentally different from the time experienced by men, whose time is geared towards the future and structured by the limit between work and leisure. Women like the narrators in Manguso or Cusk's books previously subscribed to that second representation of time: like men, they also sat at a desk and engaged in some sort of productive activity. Becoming a mother means a shift towards that repetitive, cyclical time which is specific to women's experience. For a writer, therefore, being a mother means having to let go of the illusion that she was as free and self-contained as a man. The narrator in Cusk's memoir finds that she has "split in two", between the "person" she once was and the mother. At some point, she tries to glue together the different parts of her life by taking the baby to a park with her friend, but she finds that she cannot reconcile her two selves:

> To be a mother I must leave the telephone unanswered, work undone, arrangements unmet. To be myself I must let the baby cry, must forestall the hunger, or leave her for evenings out, must forget her in order to think about other things. To succeed at being one means to fail at being the other.
>
> (Cusk 2001, 62)

The sense of dislocation of time is intrinsically linked with the feeling of dissolution of the self experienced by the mother writer. She is no longer free to organise her own time, which now depends on the necessities of caring for her baby.

A maternal aesthetic?

Maternal subjectivity

So far, I have taken a materialist view of the specificity of maternal writing, mostly by identifying the concrete hurdles mother writers have to face in the practice of their craft and in the relationship with their creativity.

Yet if we go beyond the question of the material constraints on writing experienced by mother writers, would it be possible to identify a specific form of writing by mothers? Could we even go as far as to claim there is a distinct form of maternal aesthetic, an *écriture maternelle*, to be considered as an offshoot of *écriture féminine*? The answer to those questions cannot be a straight yes or no, but examining this possibility depends on where one would locate this specificity (in the mother's body, in her psyche, or in her circumstances) and how it would manifest (could we identify a separate maternal aesthetic, or simply a commonality of themes and structures) across different texts written by mothers. Assuming that mothers write in a specific way would mean that they possess some distinct qualities that non-mothers do not.

The concept of *écriture féminine* came from a particular phase of second-wave feminism which we could roughly identify as "difference feminism". For authors like Hélène Cixous, Luce Irigaray, or Julia Kristeva, dismantling the hold of patriarchy means countering it with specifically female worldviews and values. *Écriture féminine* gives women the possibility to express their own reality, it is a writing that aims to liberate women's bodies from the taboos imposed on them by the logic of phallogocentrism. In the case of Julia Kristeva, the alternative to symbolic language is to be found in the semiotic, the pre-verbal moment of language in which children are immersed before they break with their mothers to enter the realm of the Symbolic. In Chapter 1, I looked at those theories and the lasting influence they have had on writing about motherhood. My conclusion is that positing the existence of an *écriture féminine*, and by extension of an *écriture maternelle*, runs the risk of essentialising women into the "other" to reason, as well as locking them into their bodily realities. Yet as many feminist critics such as Christine Battersby (Battersby 1998) or Iris Marion Young (Young 1984), have shown, there is a specificity to female subjectivity, and one that hinges upon the possibility for women to experience motherhood.

Would it be possible therefore to articulate a specific maternal position, and its impact on mothers' writing, without essentialising mothers into a marginal position? The experience of motherhood, as I have shown in Chapters 1 and 2, is one that questions and deconstructs our traditional representation of the self. If we agree that our conception of the individual as unique, independent, and self-possessed is culturally defined, then the existence of a specific form of maternal subjectivity does not need to be considered as a minority position, but as another way of envisaging the relationship between self and others, that is endowed with its own specific and equal value. Philosopher Alison Stone argues that:

> in the West the self has often been understood in opposition to the maternal body, such that one must break away from the mother and

maternal care-givers on whom one depends in infancy and childhood to become a full participant in the spiritual, political, or cultural values of one's community.

(Stone 2013, 1)

For Stone, the way out of essentialising positions is to redefine Western liberal conceptions of subjectivity to allow for a different conception of the self, which would not be as centred around self-containment and separatedness but would rather allow for the self to be defined in terms of relationality. If we agree that the experience of motherhood both displaces and opens up our notion of subjectivity, could we argue that it has an impact on the way mothers write, and especially when they write about themselves?

The definition of a specific "maternal subjectivity", according to Karin Voth Harman, who wrote the entry on "Motherhood and Life Writing" in the *Encyclopaedia of Life Writing*, is at the heart of much of the self-life writing produced by mothers (Harman 2001). In other words, she argues that what has emerged from the volume of feminist writing on motherhood since the 1980s and 1990s is a redefinition of traditional conceptions of subjectivity, one that is based on relationality rather than separatedness. In her essay "Troublesome practices: Mothering, Literature and Ethics", Emily Jeremiah gives an overview of the debates about the existence of a form of "maternal writing" in literary criticism:

> I will not argue that mothers can and should write literature, but that mothering and literary production both profoundly relational practices – can be linked and deployed as challenges to traditional western ideals of rationality and individuality, in subversive and ethically compelling ways.
>
> (Jeremiah 2002, 2)

Jeremiah starts from the premise that mother writers have authorised themselves to write, now that the taboo on women being both at once is slowly being lifted. She is interested in the practice of mother writing itself, and in the possibility that the association between mothering and literary production could subvert traditional, that is male-defined, representations of subjectivity. Writing by mothers, she believes "involves a questioning of traditional masculinist ideas concerning (authorial) autonomy and authority, and it suggests new directions for feminist conceptions of relationality and of knowledge production" (Jeremiah 2002, 2).

Jeremiah identifies three main historical phases in the conception of the relationship between literary production and mothering. The first is what she calls "Images of Mothers criticism", which consists in replacing the representation of mothers within the frame of literary representation. The second approach is posited upon Virginia Woolf's claim that "we think back through our mothers if we are women" and consists of identifying a matrilineal literary tradition. The final approach is one that aims at identifying a maternal subjectivity constructed by way of the writing itself. Jeremiah is fully aware that this claim could be considered as essentialising and that it could lock mother writers in a position of marginality. This is especially true, as we have seen in Chapter 1, of the work by French feminists such as Kristeva, Cixous, and Irigaray. Jeremiah recognises that at some point in the emergence of maternal studies as a field, a form of "strategic essentialism" was necessary in order to shed light on the figure of the writing mother. Yet her contention is that the specificity of motherhood should not be conceived of as a biological reality but should instead be located in a sociohistorical context, which in our case, is that of Western capitalism. Giving a voice to writers who write from a perspective as mothers is a way to put forward an alternative view of society, one that would emphasise relationality rather than separation, nurturance rather than competition (Jeremiah 2002, 5).

Suzanne Juhasz's reflections on the issue of maternal subjectivity are helpful to work our way out of the risk of essentialism. Instead of identifying maternal subjectivity as a subject position from which writing can be produced, she offers to address the issue the other way around. "Writing from a maternal perspective", she argues, "can construct maternal subjectivity in a linguistic form" (Juhasz 2003, 395). Motherhood is, in her view, a complex subject position, one that is built upon relationality. The mother finds herself at the crossroads between different subject positions as a mother to her children, daughter to her mother, and often wife or partner. The real difficulty, therefore, is to find a voice that would account for this multiplicity of viewpoints and relationships. Writing *as* a mother would therefore mean picking up the different threads of one's existence and giving them some sort of sense: "I am proposing that mother-writing can work to construct, or even create maternal subjectivity by bringing together in the same textual space the aggregate of identities that mothers possess and establishing a viable relationship, or 'grammar,' among them" (Juhasz 2003, 400). In other words, maternal subjectivity is not the starting point of maternal writing, but its endpoint: from that point of view, writing participates in the attempt to make sense of the plurality of positions and to recreate a coherent self from the mess of multiple affiliations. From that point of view, maternal writing can be conceived of as a specific form of work, a weaving of threads which results in the creation of a text, in the etymological sense of the word.

Doireann Ní Ghríofa' *A Ghost in the Throat* is probably a good example of the type of text that has its source in the desire to sing in one's voice among the multiplicity of demands and relationships. The memoir begins with a repetition of the formula "This is a female text", which makes it sound like a manifesto: "This is a female text, composed while folding someone else's clothes. My mind holds it close, and it grows, tender and slow, while my hands perform innumerable chores" (Ní Ghriofa 2020, 7). The conditions in which the text was composed give us a hint as to why the narrator wants us to read her text as a "female text": far from our usual representation of the artist sitting away in a locked room, the narrator claims later in the text she wrote on her phone, usually while doing housework or looking after her children; in other words, it was a text written while caring for others. There is a constant parallel between her work as a mother and her work as an author, particularly through the theme of donation which runs through the memoir: the narrator sees the work she performs in pumping her milk in order for it to be donated to premature infants as a preparation for the work she would later do in order to revive the life of Eibhlín Dubh Ní Chonaill. Donating her milk to others is seen as similar work to donating her time and her words to a woman poet whose life has been erased. This text is a female text, and I would even add a "maternal text", because it is constructed as an attempt to make sense of a woman's experience as a mother, a wife, and a poet and also because it practices a specific form of attention to others. By weaving her story with Eibhlín Dubh Ní Chonaill's poem and life story, by opening her own text to a text that was written centuries prior to her own, she is also participating in the creation of a matrilinear tradition of writing by women.

Maternal work

In Ní Ghriofa's work, motherhood is not an identity; it is a corporeal experience and a practice. Ann Snitow who, like Emily Jeremiah, tried to draw a chronology of the debates on the role of motherhood within feminism, identified the work of Sara Ruddick as a turning point. Much of the feminist writings of the 1960s and 1970s were dedicated to deconstructing the mechanisms of gender-based oppression, among which motherhood held a central position (Snitow 1992). When Adrienne Rich's *Of Woman Born* had already started to introduce some nuance, particularly by introducing the distinction between motherhood as an institution and mothering as practice (O'Reilly 2004), it was Sara Ruddick who would push the point to its logical conclusion by showing that mothering is a specific type of work. In what Snitow calls an "important threshold article" (Snitow 1992, 39), Ruddick argued that motherhood is not an identity but a practice, a specific form of work (Ruddick 1980). She would later develop this idea in a book (Ruddick 1995), whose main contention is that mothering (and not "being a mother") is a form of relationship, an engagement with the world which is informed by one's labour of caring for a child. This idea to me is central: if there is anything that is specific about the literary production of mothers, it does not have to do with their *being* mothers but with their *work* as parents. Unlike *écriture féminine*, which 1970s French feminists located in the women's psychic and bodily identities (Jones 1981), maternal thinking derives from a specific relational practice, a form of engagement with, and attention to another. For Ruddick, "maternal thinking" is a product of the female experience, yet one which is not grounded in anatomy or even biology, it is a result of the construction of the female as motherly:

> I do not wish to deny any more than I wish to affirm some biological bases of maternal thinking. The "biological body" (in part a cultural artefact) *may* foster certain features of maternal practice, sensibility and thought. Neither our own ambivalence to our women's bodies nor the bigoted, repressive uses which many men, colonizers, and racists have made of biology, should blind us to our body's possibilities. In concentrating on what mothers do rather than upon what we are, I postpone biological questions until we have the moral and political perceptions to answer them justly.
>
> (Ruddick 1995, 346)

In the conclusion to Cusk's *A Life's Work*, the narrator reflects on the "work" she had to perform so that a mother would be made out of her, "the hardest work I have ever done" (Cusk 2001, 212). The very title of the book expresses a similar idea: becoming a mother is for the narrator "a life's work", the work of a lifetime, in the sense of the hardest, most important work she'll ever do but also a work that supersedes all other forms of work, which supposes that it could even be more significant than her work as a writer. Like Ruddick, the narrator sees motherhood as "not a condition but a job", from which she manages to get more and more breaks as her daughter grows up and she finds more time for herself: "My daughter is more and more a part of this freedom, something new that is being added, drop by daily drop, to the sum of what I am" (Cusk 2001, 214). Maternal subjectivity, therefore, is not only the product of the bodily experience of carrying a child and bringing her into the world, it is also shaped by the relationships a mother will foster with her children, and the experience of herself as being depended upon for love and caring. As she is walking alone around Oxford Street the narrator in Cusk's memoir realises that she is unable to partake in the activities she used to enjoy, such as shopping for clothes, precisely because she no longer views herself as self-contained:

> I lack the desire for myself that would teach me what to choose; I lack the sense of stardom in my own life that would urge me to adorn myself. I am backstage, attendant. I have the curious feeling that I no longer exist in synchronicity with time, but at a certain delay, like someone on the end of a transatlantic phone call. This, I think, is what it is to be a mother.
>
> (Cusk 2001, 215)

The narrator is no longer a star in her own world, her attachment to another human being has displaced her from the centre of her own life: for Cusk's narrator, this is the one defining aspect of her experience of being a mother. No longer a separate individual, the narrator finds that she is also what her daughter has given her: "We are an admixture, an experiment" (Cusk 2001, 214). Just like the narrator in *A Life's Work* eventually manages to pick up the loose threads of her life as the demands from her mothering work become less demanding, the narrator in Ní Ghriofa's memoir starts to make sense of her journey when she learns that she will no longer have children. She credits her imaginary companionship with the poet from the past for a renewed interest in the world around her and for the possibility to exist as her own self:

> Before my life collided with hers, so many of my hours were spent skittering between the twin demands of milk and lists that I hadn't noticed how blurred the furze had grown around me. Now I delight in the yellow petals jigging in the breeze, in every thorn-tip, and even in the bare gaps between them.
>
> (Ní Ghriofa 2020, 202)

In Ní Ghriofa's account, motherhood is a journey in which the self learns to open itself to other voices: it is a form of attention and attendance to others' needs, a donation of one's time and one's body.

Motherhood as genre

While I'm sceptical about the existence of a form of maternal writing, or of maternal aesthetic as distinct poetics, I nevertheless believe that we can somehow delineate a specific way of being in the world associated with the experience of motherhood, which in turn can influence the way women will be writing of themselves in relation to their lives as mothers. I'm interested in particular in the claim made by literary critic Sarah Blackwood, who invites us to consider motherhood not as a topic of writing but as a genre in itself. Motherhood, she claims, is not a topic the reader may choose to find interest in or not; it is an experience which in turn structures the writing of mother-writers. The proposition that motherhood can be thought of as a genre is distinct from the claim that there should be such a thing as a specific form of maternal writing, because it does not consider motherhood as an identity but as a practice, which requires that we should consider the material conditions of writing while being a mother:

> Call it the Maggie Nelson, or Jenny Offill, effect, two writers who fused form (short, epigrammatic passages) with content (motherhood is nothing but a collection of short bursts of focus set inside the oceanic nothingness of time passing) in new surprisingly effective ways.
> (Blackwood 2018)

In other words, when they become mothers, female writers find that their experience of time, as well as place, has changed, along with their place in the world and their relationship with others. I would like to look at the ways this will influence their choice of themes as well as form.

Deciding to view motherhood itself as a genre means identifying specific elements which mark writing by mothers as opposed to writing by non-mothers. And as we will see, it does not mean that this specificity derives from a biological reality. As Nina Auerbach famously asked in her essay "Artists and Mothers: A False Alliance": "Do our wombs silently dictate when we write?" (Auerbach 1985). To that question, I would answer no, they do not. But the day-to-day interactions with a small child, the constant interruptions, the lack of space, as well as the patronising gaze of society upon mothers, those certainly do. My approach here is more materialist than essentialist: as we will see, women who write with a child in the other room will probably write differently from men who lock themselves up in their offices while they count on their partners to take care of their daily lives. I would also like to show that the sheer volume of writing by mothers *as* mothers has encouraged a liberation among mother writers, who can find the strength to write about their own experience drawing on the existence of a literary community of women who have experienced the same reality. In the effort to establish motherhood as a genre, I would also like to try and delineate the major themes and structural issues that recur in writing by mothers who choose to recount their experiences.

"A writing structured by its own constraint"

In *A Room of One's Own*, Virginia Woolf tries to lay out the foundations for what could be a specific form of writing by women. Their novels, she contends, must be "adapted to the body", and they also need to be "shorter, more concentrated than those of men [...] For interruptions there will always be" (Woolf [1929] 2004, 135). Similarly, for philosopher Lisa Baraitser, interruption is at the heart of the experience of motherhood. The maternal subject, she argues "is a subject of interruption", and this has an effect on her relationship with time itself (Baraitser 2008, 74). What fundamentally changes is the amount of control a mother has on her own time, as it is constantly interrupted by the child's demands, and this is even truer for the mother writer, whose activity requires long stretches of uninterrupted time on her own. For Baraitser, "motherhood lends itself to anecdote rather than the grand narrative of 'mother-writing' due to the constant attack on narrative that the child performs" (Baraitser 2008, 15). Once she has become a mother, the time a woman can dedicate to her writing is therefore organised around her relationship with her child and especially when that child is not old enough to understand that her mother does not want to be disturbed. As soon as the baby is born, she will require her mother's presence almost constantly so that she can be fed, cleaned, and soothed, which leaves her mother little leeway as to the organisation of the time she will manage to keep for her writing. Some mother writers manage to accommodate their writing around their caregiving, while others feel torn between their mothering duties and their desire to write, which is a source of anxiety and resentment. In some cases, the mother writer feels that she is never going to be able to write another line as the lack of time is compounded by the lack of sleep and the inability to concentrate, which generates existential anguish.

But is it really impossible to write within the constraints of motherhood? As we have seen in the previous chapters, many authors have gone on writing, "because of, not in spite of" their becoming mothers, to borrow from the distinction made by Alice Walker (Walker [1976] 2011). How do mother writers, work around, or work with the interruptions? Baraitser also brings up the figure of the person from Porlock, more specifically the way British poet Stevie Smith has resurrected him (assuming that person is a "he") in her poem "Thoughts about the Person from Porlock". Smith suggests that Coleridge probably wanted the interruption if only to provide him with an excuse not to finish the poem. According to Lisa Baraitser, a woman may find that she is also longing for that interruption provided by the arrival – intrusion? – of the child in her life to open up new ways of relating with others and new avenues of creativity:

> And perhaps we also long for a child purely as a longing for interruption, for something that will break up our egoistic relation with

ourselves, open out our thinking, allow us a moment's respite from a consciousness and subjectivity that is experienced as burdensome.

(Baraitser 2008)

She argues that interruption is a defining phenomenon in the experience of motherhood, which displaces the centre of subjectivity from the self to the relation between the self and the baby and reconfigures the maternal subject's relationship to time itself.

In her motherhood memoir *Le Bébé*, French author Marie Darrieussecq details the sense of bafflement, which characterised the early period with her baby. She claims that for the first few weeks, she discovered she had lost even the very desire to write about her experience as a mother. Yet she does not resent this interruption in her writing life, she welcomes it as a necessary interruption and describes how writing emerges gradually. She is aware that she is required to make a choice between motherhood and her career as a writer, a choice which she refuses to make:

> I have been asked about what I would do if I had to choose between the baby and writing. And the baby, would he be asked, with the same perversity, to say who he prefers, between his daddy and his mummy?
>
> There are conflicts which generate writing, in one's immediate surroundings and beyond; but this question I'm being asked is the one, whether it is uttered or kept silent, that all women must contend with: which do they prefer, huh, between their children and their work[2]?
>
> (Darrieussecq 2002, 80–81)

The narrator says she is aware that the time she is spending with the baby is bound to remain brief. Her passing despair is cut short by news that her baby is going to be taken care of in a day-care centre. Like Lazarre, the possibility to place the care of the baby in the hands of another, if only for a few hours a day, is essential to the mother's sense that she will get her life back eventually. In France, compared with other Western countries, childcare remains relatively cheap and accessible. Hence, the narrator decides to allow herself to enjoy the experience to the full, to "get inebriated by this time with the baby" (Darrieussecq 2002, 13). The book is slim and does not aim to give an all-encompassing account of what it feels like to be a mother; rather, it is made of small touches of impression, snippets of feelings represented in short paragraphs separated by asterisks. Darrieussecq's writing intends to physically replicate on the page the experience of motherhood and specifically the paucity of time left to the writing mother who is constantly interrupted: "*A writing structured by its own constraint*, the clichés find their echo, the baby's cries cut up these pages, from asterisk to asterisk" (Darrieussecq 2002, 34). What

Darrieussecq suggests is that the experience of being with a baby brings forth a new form of writing which aims at making visible the material realities of motherhood.

In her collection of personal essays *100 Essays I Don't Have Time to Write: On Umbrellas and Sword Fights, Parades and Dogs, Fire Alarms, Children, and Theater*, Sarah Ruhl explores thoughts about drama along with her experience of being a mother. The essays are short, never more than three or four pages long. A key to this choice can be found in the very first essay, "On interruptions", which evokes the struggles of mothers who are trying to write when their children are around. In the essay, Ruhl does not just describe what it feels like to be interrupted by a small child, she allows the text to be interrupted by him:

> The child's need, so pressing, so consuming, for the mother to be there, to be present, and the pressing need of the writer to be half-there, to be there but thinking of other things caught me –
>
> Sorry. In the act of writing that sentence, my son, William, who is now two, came running into my office crying and asking for a fake knife to cut his fake fruit.
>
> (Ruhl 2014, 3)

The essays are short quite simply because they have been written around the interruptions from the author's three children. Similarly, Cusk reflects on the structure of her narrative in *A Life's Work* and explains why she was unable to write a linear account of her first year as a mother: "It describes a period in which time seemed to go round in circles rather than in any chronological order, and so which I have tried to capture in themes rather than by the forgotten procession of its days" (Cusk 2001, 18). Similarly, Anne Enright writes small thematic chapters that all aim to describe her experience of mothering without following a chronological order (Enright 2012) (see Frye 2010 on that topic). Elif Shafak also notes that it was impossible for her to write chronologically about her experience, particularly of postpartum depression. It is interesting to note that most accounts of pregnancy follow a strict chronological order, as it is an experience of growth and gradual modification which is counted in months and weeks, while the first months with a baby are often a time of confusion and loss of bearings.

Another major work by a mother-writer is *Dept. of Speculation*, by Jenny Offill (Offill 2014). It is made of a loose adultery plot, interspersed with fragmentary reflections, in part on the difficulty of being creative while mothering. The novel is made of short fragments put together collage-like, and for scholar Wojciech Drąg, it can be read as an example of what Sharon Spencer calls the "architectonic novel" (Drąg 2017). Drąg's analysis of the novel's form is indeed very convincing, but he does not really consider the possibility that its fragmentary nature may be constrained by the difficulty of finding enough time to write continuously.

Naptime writing

In *Le Bébé*, Darrieussecq describes the experience of spending time with a baby thus: "It's a repetitive and disjointed experience, and when the baby sleeps, life resumes, but when he is awake, it's his life which dominates" (Darrieussecq 2002, 12). The issue of sleep – whether it's the mother's or the baby's – is a particularly fraught subject: motherhood memoirs all describe the exhaustion of the first sleepless months, but as Darrieussecq suggests, the baby's capacity to sleep is the condition for her mother's freedom, a promise that she can finally be herself, if only for a few hours. The narrator in Cusk's memoir describes her shame at trying to enjoy a short time to herself when she tries – and fails to put the baby down for her nap: "I feel as if I have been discovered in some terrible infidelity. My thoughts of freedom cover themselves and scatter and I am filled with fury and shame" (Cusk 2001, 70). In short, the mother's ability to write, or even think about writing, depends on her child's being asleep, which means that the time she will have to herself will be necessarily short and precarious. In her preface to the anthology *Doubles Lives*, author Marni Jackson remembers her first years as a mother:

> I was too ground down to do the sort of deep, sustained, solitary work that a novel requires. So instead, I began to write about what was keeping me from writing. I would go through those intense, soul-fraying mornings that every new mother goes through, race to my desk when he finally slept, and try to give them some sort of shape and weight and meaning by writing them down. I felt I had simultaneously found myself and been erased.
> (Cowan, Lam, and Stonehouse 2008, xiii)

In the novel *Night Waking* by Sarah Moss, the main character Anna is an academic who spends her summer on a remote island with her family and finds herself shouldering the burden of caring for her children while her husband spends most of the day outside working on his research. Yet Anna, like her husband, is an academic, and she is supposed to work on a big project, which is made impossible by the constant demands from her children. The novel chronicles Anna's desperate, yet comical attempts to get her younger son to sleep, which he adamantly refuses, in order to at least foster the illusion that she is working on her project (Moss 2011). Although the novel is not a memoir, it is written from the point of view of a first-person character and provides a perfect illustration of what trying to work with young children amounts to, in terms of frustration and sometimes despair. According to Emily Jeremiah, the novel explores the possibility of resistance and recovery. Quoting Lisa Baraitser, Jeremiah makes the case that the constant interruptions and the extreme fatigue Anna has to contend with are also a source of creativity and reinvention (Jeremiah 2018, 207).

For other writers, such as Maggie Nelson, believing that the chosen form of a piece of writing is dictated by the author's experience of motherhood is essentialising. In an interview she gave around the time when *The Argonauts* was published, she comments on all the assumptions that are made by journalists and commentators about her writing and particularly her choice of the fragmented form. She exclaims: "I didn't go to the fragmented form because of naptime!" (Nelson 2017). Nelson is also very critical of the narrative which would require women to "rise up from the ashes" in order to be able to formulate their experience, particularly of childbirth: "There's a continuity of person!". Marie Darrieussecq is also suspicious of the discourse that would make motherhood a woman-specific experience. In *Le Bébé*, the narrator claims: "There is no such thing as feminine writing, of course; there may be feminine themes. Some men actually know how to take them on" before she quotes a passage from *Ulysses* featuring a mother taking care of a small child (Darrieussecq 2002, 50). In several interviews Darrieussecq gave around the time of the publication of her memoir, she explains that her experience of being a mother made her keenly aware of gender inequality, mostly in the fact that she was expected to be the sole carer of her child and therefore to renounce her writing vocation. For her, the conflict between motherhood and creativity is artificial and one that is solely created by the social injunctions made on mothers. Yet, in line with de Beauvoir's vision of motherhood, Darrieussecq believes that women are complicit in their own alienation. They choose to be the sole carer of their child because it gives them an illusory sense of power: "It's convenient for mothers, because it's a power that they have, but it's a power that's only short-lived, it's a deception, just smoke and mirrors, the price is too high" (Barraband and Gassmann 2005, 15). The specificity of maternal texts, therefore, should not be sought in their form, but rather in the main tropes they mobilise in order to account for the experience of motherhood.

Matrifocal texts

The practice of mothering, it can be argued, affects maternal writing in its form and its structure, but it also has a more fundamental impact, specifically on the themes chosen and on the purposes of those texts. One concept I find useful here, in that it allows us to root the difference of maternal writing in practice rather than in essence, is that of "matrifocal texts", a term which was coined by Elizabeth Podnieks. In the introduction to her 2010 book *Textual Mothers, Maternal Texts: Motherhood in Contemporary Women's Literatures*, she suggests that matrifocal texts are designed as a way to reclaim the mother's voice, and to move away from the tradition of "daughter-centric"[3] texts (Podnieks and O'Reilly 2010). Like Suzanne Juhasz, she believes that matrifocal texts allow women to gain control over the narrative of their own lived realities (Podnieks and O'Reilly 2010, 7) and to give a shape to an experience that feels both fragmented and confusing. Specifically, women who write from a matrifocal perspective seek to rip away what Susan Maushart called "the mask of motherhood" (Maushart 1999), and to reclaim the experience of motherhood from the patriarchal discourses that usually surround it.

Texts by Adrienne Rich, Jane Lazarre, or Rachel Cusk, to cite the authors of the most outstanding texts, all inscribe their narratives within a critique of the patriarchal discourses which constrain their experience. By analysing the patronising discourse of obstetrics, the moralising commandments of pregnancy books or the injunctions to stay at home and renounce their professional and/or literary careers, these texts all attempt to give visibility to an experience which had hitherto remained confined to the domestic. Each of these three texts opens with an introduction which states its purpose. For Rich, it consists of "examin[ing] motherhood—my own included—in a social context, as embedded in a political institution: in feminist terms" (Rich [1976] 1995, ix). For Lazarre, the aim of writing *The Mother Knot* is to dismantle "the ubiquitous Western myth of placid, fulfilling maternity" (Lazarre [1976] 1997, xxi) and remove the statue of the "good mother" from its pedestal. Rachel Cusk shies away from making an equally political statement in her own introduction and claims a humbler goal: "I have merely written down what I thought of the experience of having a child in a way that I hope other people can identify with" (Cusk 2001, 14). This sentiment is reaffirmed in an article Cusk wrote after her memoir was published, in the light of the comments that were made by readers and in the media: in "I Was Only Being Honest", Cusk realises that it was precisely the honesty she had adhered to in *A Life's Work* which had triggered such massively negative reactions (Cusk 2008). By writing of her experience without taking care to embellish or sentimentalise the details, she had definitely broken a taboo, and she paid the price for it. For Elizabeth Podnieks, the "unmasking of motherhood" which she sees as a common goal of matrifocal texts is an effort aimed at rejecting the patriarchal scripts of female submissiveness and acceptance:

> Read as a genre in and of itself as part of a tradition of writings about motherhood, matrifocal literatures are sites of textual liberation, where

women self-consciously and outspokenly chart, confront, debate, and celebrate maternal feelings, practices, bodies and identities.

(Podnieks 2020, 176)

The motherhood memoir

The best entry point into a study of the commonalities between different texts written by mothers as maternal texts is the genre of the "motherhood memoir". In Chapter 1, we already looked at some of its main defining features and at the conditions under which it was able to emerge as a genre in its own right. The memoir can be defined as a form of self-life writing in which the author brings forth an account of her experience as a mother. Unlike the autobiographical project, it does not aim to give an overview of the author's life but rather focuses on one salient aspect of it (Rak 2004). Several authors have purported to study the motherhood memoir as a genre in itself: Brenda O. Daly and Maureen T. Reddy in *Narrating Mothers: Theorizing Maternal Subjectivities* (1991), Justine Dymond and Nicole Willey in *Motherhood Memoirs: Mothers Creating/Writing Lives* (2013), Joanne Frye in "Narrating Maternal Subjectivity: Memoirs from Motherhood" (2010), and Heather Hewett in "Motherhood Memoirs" (2020). Hewett gives the following definition of the genre of the motherhood memoir:

> The subgenre provides a portal to a range of issues related to the landscapes of contemporary parenting, including the existence of both shifting and static understandings of gender and gendered roles within families; clashes between cultural expectations, structures of power, and current parenting practices among majority, minority, and marginalized populations; the question of whose stories are told, whose stories aren't told, and what forms these stories take; and finally, who reads (and doesn't read) motherhood memoirs and how various audiences make meaning out of maternal autobiographical writing.
>
> (Hewett 2020, 191)

For all those authors, motherhood memoirs all engage in the sort of writing Elizabeth Podnieks describes as "matrifocal", in that they all try to establish some form of personal truth in the face of the ideological discourses that usually surround motherhood, as well as babies. As Marie Darrieussecq argues in her own motherhood memoir: "The baby is wrapped in discourses which are as thick as swaddling clothes" (Darrieussecq 2002, 34). In all of the memoirs which fall under the umbrella of the motherhood memoir, the narrator often expresses her shock at discovering the reality of motherhood, as she realises how unprepared she had been for the experience. This is present in the very title of some books: *Mother Shock: Tales from the First Year and Beyond--Loving Every (Other) Minute of It* by Andrea Buchanan (2003), *Making Babies: Stumbling into Motherhood* by Anne Enright (2012), *And Now We Have Everything: On Motherhood Before I Was Ready* by Meaghan O'Connell (2018). Many of them (Lazarre, Cusk, Shafak to name but a few) look back on their pre-motherhood selves and wonder at their naïve beliefs they could carry on with their lives as normal, namely, that they would continue to write as they did before they had their children. As we will see in the next chapter, a common feature is also the experience of conflicting feelings and a form of ambivalence, which clashes with society's commonly held view that mothers must experience pure, unadulterated joy in the company of their children.

For many of the authors who are trying to identify the similarities between texts which pertain to the category of the motherhood memoir, the question of subjectivity is paramount. We have seen earlier that one of the defining aspects of the experience of motherhood was its impact on the definition of subjectivity (Battersby 1998; Baraitser 2008; Stone 2013) and particularly in representations of the experience of pregnancy (Young 1984). As the mother's body learns to accept the presence of another human being within herself, and as she needs to engage in a close relationship with him/her during the baby's early infancy and beyond, her subjectivity necessarily shifts away from the usual definition of the self as unique and self-sufficient, redefining itself as relational and enmeshed with the subjectivities of her children (Chodorow 1978). For Justine Dymond and Nicole Willey, the motherhood memoir is a site where the traditional conceptions of subjectivity can be renegotiated. Similarly, for Joanne Frye, "the outline of maternal subjectivity that emerges is a self who is multiple, who critiques the notion of selflessness while tracing out the actual *process* of developing a loving maternal bond and thus acknowledging an interpersonal self" (Frye 2010, 197). In other words, writing the motherhood memoir is an attempt by its author to pick up the strands of her subjectivity which have become frayed and messy in order to weave them back into a coherent narrative. Very often it means acknowledging that the self is multiple, and that it can welcome different coexisting instances. The most dramatic example is the presence of the "thumbelinas" in Elif Shafak's *Black Ink: On Motherhood and Writing* (Shafak 2013),[4] which all represent different aspects of the narrator's personality.

However, other motherhood memoirs represent the impression felt by mothers that their self is splitting. In Jane Lazarre's memoir, *The Mother Knot*, the narrator frequently engages with other instances of herself, such as "the girlwoman" or "the dark lady". In order to be a mother to her child, she has had to "banish" the creative but also the most childish part of herself:

> For if she was present when the baby needed me, she was of necessity pushed aside, sent to go hungry. She who had been my life, whom I knew I had to nourish daily in order to be fed in return, hid for weeks, hoarding her gentleness and her strength, placing no gifts in my outstretched hands.
>
> (Lazarre [1976] 1997, 28)

Similarly, the narrator in Cusk's memoir *A Life's Work* discovers that she has split in two and that the two instances of herself (the mother and the person she was before she became one) flow in two different directions (Cusk 2001, 62).

Brenda Daly and Maureen Reddy argue that the form of self which emerges in maternal texts is a self which must be thought of as "communal" or undifferentiated, that is, which expands beyond the delineation of the self as enclosed upon itself – although they do agree that this undifferentiation would be difficult to signify in writing. One of the most exemplary texts written from the point of view of a communal self would be Annie Ernaux's *Les Années*, as it describes the decades of the author's life from the point of view not of the narrator herself but of the political community in which she inscribes herself, including the "I" into a communal "we" (Ernaux 2009). In the case of the motherhood memoir, this attempt at expanding the self beyond the confines of the individual usually translates into a desire to write not just for oneself but for the community of mothers out there who will be reading it, in the hope that they will find comfort in knowing that they are not alone in their experience of the hardships of motherhood. That purpose is analysed by Heather Hewett in her piece "You Are Not Alone: The Personal, the Political, and the 'New' Mommy Lit" (2005), for whom Rich, Lazarre, Cusk, as well as the authors of lighter fiction such as Alison Pearson's *I Don't Know How She Does It* (2010) or Gill Sims's *Why Mummy Drinks* (2017), all attempt in different ways to connect with other mothers in order to make them feel they are understood. Many of those memoirs focus on the material difficulties of being a mother and a writer at the same time, but some of them also consider the possibility that motherhood may act as a spur to creativity rather than a hindrance.

Motherhood as source of creativity

In her article "Writing and Motherhood: The Mother Tongue", Susan Suleiman argues that the main objective of distinguishing a form of maternal writing is to allow mothers to break the silence and especially to dismantle the belief that mothers are to be written about but cannot be the subjects of their own discourses (Suleiman [1979] 2011). As she embarks on an overview of the writing produced up to the end of the 1970s, when her article was originally published, she identifies two major themes: "I see them clustered into two large groups: opposition and integration, motherhood as obstacle or source of conflict and motherhood as link, as source of connection to work and world" (Suleiman [1979] 2011, 121). And if one looks at the writing produced on the topic of motherhood in a time which is prior to the boom of motherhood writing that took place in the 2000s, one can definitely identify two major directions. On one side, one may encounter the likes of Rich and Lazarre, for whom being a mother comes in the way of being an artist and impedes literary creation, and on the other side are writers such as US poet Alicia Ostriker, who militantly defend a creativity rooted in the experience of motherhood. In her poem "Propaganda Poem: Maybe for Some Young Mamas", the poetic voice stages herself reading her pregnancy poetry to a "so-called 'feminist' classroom" full of de-Beauvoir-reading feminist students who reject motherhood as alienating and patriarchal. The poet engages in a discussion with the young women trying to convince them that, on the contrary, giving birth to a baby is not only compatible with living a feminist life, but it can also be a tremendous source of creativity (Ostriker [1980] 2009, 44). The use of the word "propaganda" in the title, along with the agonistic form of the poem, carries the implication that an ideological battle needs to be fought against prejudices that have been internalised by women themselves.

In an article entitled "A Wild Surmise: Motherhood and Poetry", Ostriker gives the reader a different account of her encounter with feminist scholars to whom she gave a reading of her collection *Once More Out of Darkness*:

> On one occasion when I read it to a graduate class in Women and Literature at Rutgers, arguing that writing and motherhood were not necessarily mutually exclusive enterprises, someone remarked that it was one thing to write about pregnancy, where you could be symbolic and spiritual, but quite impossible to use the squalling brats as poetic material after you had them, messing around underfoot, killing your schedule.
>
> (Ostriker 1983, 129)

For Ostriker, the reason for this intense pushback from other women is the predominance of male themes in poetry. We are used to reading about romantic love and sexual desire, as well as war and death, but very rarely do we read poetry about birth, she contends, even though this affirmation would soon be contradicted by a number of anthologies on the poetry of motherhood. She concludes:

> As our knowledge begins to accumulate, we can imagine what it would signify to all women, and men, to live in a culture where childbirth and mothering occupied the kind of position that sex and romantic love have occupied in literature and art for the last five hundred years, or the kind of position that warfare has occupied since literature began.
> (Ostriker 1983, 131)

It is indeed interesting that Ostriker should take this debate to the field of poetry. Because it has been construed as the most supreme form of literary expression, and also because our current representation of the artist has been forged based on the figure of the Romantic poet (see Chapter 1), poetry was for a long time considered as antithetical to the pursuit of motherhood, grounded in the messy, banal realities of taking care of small children. Pushing for a better representation of childbirth and early motherhood and to have them stand as subjects of poetry which are equally worthy of interest is one major way to change the narrative on the relationship between motherhood and creativity.

Irish poet Eavan Boland has also made this topic the centre of her autobiographical reflections, both in *Object Lessons* (1995) and *A Journey with Two Maps* (2012). In both books, which, I would claim, pertain to the genre of autotheory, Boland explores the cultural and historical contexts in which she forged her poetic voice. She notably explains how the poetic tradition in Ireland is heir to two major influences: on the one hand, bardic Irish song and on the other British Romantic poetry. In both poetic traditions, she explains, women are treated as screens onto which male fantasies can be projected. For these two reasons, she realises: "By luck or by its absence, I had been born in a country where and a time when the word woman and the word poet inhabited two separate kingdoms of experience and expression" (Boland 1995, 114). She realises that in order to think of herself as a real poet, worthy of self-expression, she needs to deconstruct the image of the poet as an isolated genius: "My solitude was an illusion. No poet, however young or disaffected, writes alone" (Boland 1995, 103). In *A Journey with Two Maps*, Boland pushes the reflection further by tackling the issue of the subject of poetry: "I found that without knowing it I had learned to write poetry, at least in part, by subscribing to a hierarchy of poetic subjects" (Boland 2012, 63). Like Alicia Ostriker, Eavan Boland pleads for a new conception of poetic expression which would include the more mundane aspects of the poet's life and particularly her relationship with her children:

Standing in a room in the winter half-light before the wonder of a new child is aesthetics. Hesitating at the meaning of subject matter as fit for poetry is aesthetics. Searching back to the prompts and resistances involved in becoming a poet – the reading, the writing – is also aesthetics. I came to believe there is no meaning to an art form with its grand designs unless it allows the humane to shape the invented, the way gravity is said to bend starlight.

(Boland 2012, 75)

Conclusion

In this chapter, I have tried to explore the possibility that the experience of motherhood may have an impact on the writing produced by authors who are also mothers. This impact is visible in different aspects, which I would gather under three main categories: form, politics, and subjectivity. What I have found is that while women certainly do not write from their wombs, they do however write from within a very particular context. Unable to enjoy long stretches of uninterrupted time, and somehow deprived of their mental space, both necessary to write, some writers renounce altogether, and there is probably a study to be made of those authors who gave up on their vocation once they became mothers. Yet those authors who continue to write must do so in the time and space they manage to retain, even in the early days of their babies' lives. This necessarily has an impact on the form and the length of their writing, as evidenced by the recurring choice of the short and fragmented form. Beyond the material circumstances of the writer, I have tried to demonstrate that for those authors who write *as* mothers (and a number of authors who are also mothers do not do that), the experience of motherhood has an impact on the very substance of their writing. Because it reshapes their relationship to time and space, as well as their definition of subjectivity, the way they write is affected on a deeper level.

To many writers, the experience of motherhood is also a brutal encounter with the reality of patriarchy. For the authors of motherhood memoirs, one of the main stated aims of writing is to share their experience in order for other mothers to be able to identify with it. Their writing therefore purports to become part of a community of writing to which other writers and non-writers alike may be able to refer to in order to break out of the isolation created by guilt, which as we saw especially in the first chapter, is one of the main affects experienced as a constituent of the event of motherhood. Yet although authors of motherhood memoirs often claim to write for other women, we have also seen that they write for themselves, as these narratives are an attempt to make sense of their new lives as mothers and to rebuild a new form of subjectivity.

Beyond the motherhood memoir, I have tried to see if there were specificities to the category of the maternal text. To borrow from the words of Sara Ruddick, motherhood is a practice which can be defined as a specific form of attention. If there is anything that stands out from the writing produced by mother writers, or maternal text, it is the perception of the self's interdependence with others. This necessarily implies a redefinition of the author as a figure in her own writing: no longer the master of her own time, she must learn to write within the interruptions, to navigate between the demands that are made of her energy and care. If she cannot lock herself in a room of her own, she must at least leave the door ajar and learn to welcome the little persons from Porlock who no doubt will come knocking throughout her day.

Notes

1 I wrote an article specifically on the subject of totalitarian imagery in Cusk's *A Life's Work*: Braun, Alice. 2017. ' "A Compound Fenced off from the Rest of the World": Motherhood as the Stripping of One's Self in Rachel Cusk's *A Life's Work: On Becoming a Mother*'. Études Britanniques Contemporaines. Revue de La Société D'études Anglaises Contemporaines, no. 53 (December).
2 The translations of Darrieussecq's work are mine.
3 For the definition of "daughter-centric" texts, see Chapter 1.
4 For a discussion of Elif Shafak's memoir, see Chapter 2.

Works cited

Arnold-Baker, Claire, ed. 2020. *The Existential Crisis of Motherhood*. Cham: Palgrave Macmillan.
Auerbach, Nina. 1985. 'Artists and Mothers: A False Alliance'. In *Romantic Imprisonment: Women and Other Glorified Outcasts*, 171–83. Gender and Culture. New York: Columbia University Press.
Baraitser, Lisa. 2008. Maternal Encounters: The Ethics of Interruption. London: Routledge. https://doi.org/10.4324/9780203030127
Barraband, Maryvonne, and Xavier Gassmann. 2005. 'Entretien avec Marie Darrieussecq'. *La lettre de l'enfance et de l'adolescence* 59 (1): 9. https://doi.org/10.3917/lett.059.0009
Battersby, Christine. 1998. *The Phenomenal Woman: Feminist Metaphysics and the Patterns of Identity*. London: Routledge.
Berry, Liz. 2018. *The Republic of Motherhood*. London: Chatto & Windus.
Blackwood, Sarah. 2018. 'Is Motherhood a Genre?' *BLARB*, 20 May 2018. https://blog.lareviewofbooks.org/essays/motherhood-genre/
Boland, Eavan. 1995. *Object Lessons: The Life of the Woman and the Poet in Our Time*. New York: Norton.
———. 2012. *A Journey with Two Maps: Becoming a Woman Poet*. Manchester: Carcanet.

Buchanan, Andrea. 2003. *Mother Shock: Tales from the First Year and Beyond--Loving Every (Other) Minute of It.* New York: Seal Press.
Bueskens, Petra. 2018. *Modern Motherhood and Women's Dual Identities: Rewriting the Sexual Contract.* Abingdon; New York: Routledge.
Campbell, Olivia. 2021. 'The Heartbreaking Ingenuity of the Mother-Writer'. *Literary Hub*, 3 September 2021. https://lithub.com/the-heartbreaking-ingenuity-of-the-mother-writer/
Chodorow, Nancy J. 1978. *The Reproduction of Mothering: Psychoanalysis and the Sociology of Gender.* Oakland, CA: University of California Press.
Cowan, Shannon, Fiona Tinwei Lam, and Cathy Stonehouse. 2008. *Double Lives: Writing and Motherhood.* Montreal: McGill-Queen's University Press.
Cusk, Rachel. 2001. *A Life's Work: On Becoming a Mother.* New York: Picador.
———. 2008. 'I Was Only Being Honest'. *The Guardian*, 21 March 2008, sec. Books. www.theguardian.com/books/2008/mar/21/biography.women
Daly, Brenda O., and Maureen T. Reddy, eds. 1991. *Narrating Mothers: Theorizing Maternal Subjectivities.* Knoxville, TN: University of Tennessee Press.
Darrieussecq, Marie. 2002. *Le Bébé.* Paris: P.O.L.
Davies, Karen. 1990. *Women, Time, and the Weaving of the Strands of Everyday Life.* Aldershot; Brookfield, WI; Avebury: Gower Publishing Company
Drąg, Wojciech. 2017. 'Jenny Offill's Dept. of Speculation and the Revival of Fragmentary Writing'. *Miscelánea: A Journal of English and American Studies* 56 (December): 57–72. https://doi.org/10.26754/ojs_misc/mj.20176787
Dymond, Justine, and Nicole Willey, eds. 2013. *Motherhood Memoirs: Mothers Creating/Writing Lives.* Bradford: Demeter Press.
Enright, Anne. 2012. *Making Babies: Stumbling into Motherhood.* New York: W. W. Norton & Company.
Ernaux, Annie. 2009. *Les années.* Paris: Gallimard.
Frye, Joanne S. 2010. 'Narrating Maternal Subjectivity: Memoirs from Motherhood'. In *Textual Mothers, Maternal Texts: Motherhood in Contemporary Women's Literatures*, edited by Elizabeth Podnieks and Andrea O'Reilly, 187–201. Waterloo: Wilfrid Laurier University Press.
Harman, Karin Voth. 2001. 'Motherhood and Life Writing'. In *Encyclopedia of Life Writing: Autobiographical and Biographical Forms*, edited by Margaret Jolly, 617–18. London; Chicago, IL: Fitzroy Dearborn.
Hewett, Heather. 2005. 'You Are Not Alone: The Personal, the Political, and the "New" Mommy Lit'. In *Chick Lit: The New Woman's Fiction*, edited by Suzanne Ferriss and Mallory Young, 119–40. New York: Routledge. https://doi.org/10.4324/9780203036211
———. 2020. 'Motherhood Memoirs'. In *The Routledge Companion to Motherhood*, edited by Lynn O'Brien Hallstein, Melinda Vandenbeld Giles, and Andrea O'Reilly, 191–201. Abingdon; New York: Routledge.
Hrdy, Sarah Blaffer. 1999. *Mother Nature: Natural Selection and the Female of the Species.* London: Chatto & Windus.
Jeremiah, Emily. 2002. 'Troublesome Practices: Mothering, Literature and Ethics'. *Journal of the Motherhood Initiative for Research and Community Involvement* 4 (2): 7–16.

———. 2018. 'Broken Nights, Shattered Selves: Maternal Ambivalence and the Ethics of Interruption in Sarah Moss's Novel Night Waking'. In *Motherhood in Literature and Culture: Interdisciplinary Perspectives from Europe*, edited by Gill Rye, Victoria Browne, Adalgisa Giorgio, Emily Jeremiah, and Abigail Lee Six, 197–208. New York; London: Routledge.
Jess-Cooke, Carolyn, ed. 2017. *Writing Motherhood: A Creative Anthology*. Bridgend: Seren.
Jones, Ann Rosalind. 1981. 'Writing the Body: Toward an Understanding of "l'Ecriture Feminine"'. *Feminist Studies* 7 (2): 247–63. https://doi.org/10.2307/3177523
Jones, Lucy. 2023. *Matrescence: On the Metamorphosis of Pregnancy, Childbirth and Motherhood*. London: Allen Lane.
Juhasz, Suzanne. 2003. 'Mother-Writing and the Narrative of Maternal Subjectivity'. *Studies in Gender and Sexuality* 4 (4): 395–425. https://doi.org/10.1080/15240650409349236
Kermode, Frank. 2002. *Romantic Image*. London; New York: Routledge.
Kristeva, Julia. 1981. 'Women's Time'. Translated by Alice Jardine. *Signs: Journal of Women in Culture and Society* 7 (1): 13–35. https://doi.org/10.1086/493855
Lazarre, Jane. (1976) 1997. *The Mother Knot*. Durham, NC: Duke University Press.
Manguso, Sarah. 2019. *Ongoingness/ 300 Arguments*. London: Picador.
Maushart, Susan. 1999. *The Mask of Motherhood: How Becoming a Mother Changes Everything and Why We Pretend It Doesn't*. New York: New Press New York.
Moss, Sarah. 2011. *Night Waking*. London: Granta Books.
Nelson, Maggie. 2017. Maggie Nelson on Writing, Pregnancy, and Matrophobia. *YouTube*. www.youtube.com/watch?v=w_PcDssfq1g
Ní Ghríofa, Doireann. 2020. *A Ghost in the Throat*. Dublin: Tramp Press.
O'Connell, Meaghan. 2018. *And Now We Have Everything: On Motherhood Before I Was Ready*. 1st ed. New York: Little, Brown and Company.
Offill, Jenny. 2014. *Dept. of Speculation*. London: Granta.
O'Reilly, Andrea, ed. 2004. *From Motherhood to Mothering: The Legacy of Adrienne Rich's 'Of Woman Born'*. Albany, NY: State university of New York press.
Ostriker, Alicia. (1980) 2009. *The Mother/Child Papers*. Reissue édition. Pittsburgh, PA: University of Pittsburgh Press.
———. 1983. *Writing Like a Woman*. Ann Arbor, MI: University of Michigan Press.
Pearson, Allison. 2010. *I Don't Know How She Does It*. New York: Vintage Digital.
Phillips, Julie. 2017. 'A Porlock Day Manifesto'. 10 May 2017. http://4columns.org/phillips-julie/a-porlock-day-manifesto
Podnieks, Elizabeth. 2020. 'Matrifocal Voices in Literature'. In *The Routledge Companion to Motherhood*, edited by Lynn O'Brien Hallstein, Melinda Vandenbeld Giles, and Andrea O'Reilly, 176–90. Abingdon; New York, NY: Routledge.

Podnieks, Elizabeth, and Andrea O'Reilly, eds. 2010. *Textual Mothers, Maternal Texts: Motherhood in Contemporary Women's Literatures*. Waterloo: Wilfrid Laurier university press.
Rak, Julie. 2004. 'Are Memoirs Autobiography? A Consideration of Genre and Public Identity'. *Genre* 37 (3–4): 483–504. https://doi.org/10.1215/00166 928-37-3-4-483.
Rich, Adrienne C. (1976) 1995. *Of Woman Born: Motherhood as Experience and Institution*. 2nd ed. Women's Studies. New York: Norton.
Ruddick, Sara. 1980. 'Maternal Thinking'. *Feminist Studies* 6 (2): 342–67. https://doi.org/10.2307/3177749
———. 1995. *Maternal Thinking: Toward a Politics of Peace*. Boston, MA: Beacon Press.
Ruhl, Sarah. 2014. *100 Essays I Don't Have Time to Write: On Umbrellas and Sword Fights, Parades and Dogs, Fire Alarms, Children, and Theater*. New York: Farrar, Straus and Giroux.
Senior, Jennifer. 2014. *All Joy and No Fun: The Paradox of Modern Parenthood*. New York: Harper Collins.
Shafak, Elif. 2013. *Black Milk: On Motherhood and Writing*. Translated by Hande Zapsu. London: Penguin.
Sims, Gill. 2017. *Why Mummy Drinks*. New York: HarperCollins.
Snitow, Ann. 1992. 'Feminism and Motherhood: An American Reading'. *Feminist Review* 40 (1): 32–51. https://doi.org/10.1057/fr.1992.4
Stone, Alison. 2013. Feminism, Psychoanalysis, and Maternal Subjectivity. London: Routledge. https://doi.org/10.4324/9780203182932
Suleiman, Susan Rubin. (1979) 2011. 'Writing and Motherhood. The Mother Tongue'. In *Mother Reader: Essential Literature on Motherhood*, edited by Moyra Davey, 113–38. New York City: Seven Stories Press.
Walker, Alice. (1976) 2011. 'A Writer Because of, Not in Spite of, Her Children'. In *Mother Reader: Essential Literature on Motherhood*, edited by Moyra Davey, 99–102. New York: Seven Stories Press.
Woolf, Virginia. (1929) 2004. *A Room of One's Own*. Great Ideas. Harmondsworth: Penguin.
Young, Iris Marion. 1984. 'Pregnant Embodiment: Subjectivity and Alienation'. *The Journal of Medicine and Philosophy* 9: 45–62. https://doi.org/10.1093/jmp/9.1.45

5 Bad mothers

Introduction

In 2011, Joan Didion published *Blue Nights*, a memoir in which she engaged with her grief over the successive deaths of her husband and adoptive daughter (Didion 2011). In the book Didion tries to make sense of her late daughter's life, as well as her struggles with mental illness and alcohol addiction, and she also reminisces about how her daughter was integrated into the lives of her high-powered, celebrity author parents (Joan Didion herself and the journalist John Gregory Dunne). The narrator frequently wonders whether she was a good parent to her child or if she somehow was responsible for the inner turmoil her daughter seemed to have suffered from all her life. Unlike many mother writers who have written about pursuing their artistic life while also being a parent, Didion did not consider the presence of her adoptive daughter an impediment to her career as an international reporter, for reasons that probably had to do with her material conditions as a wealthy and famous author. Beyond the fact that Didion and her husband had enough money to ensure that their daughter would be properly taken care of when they were away, there is a sense in the text, that Quintana came second, even third, to the two major concerns in her mother's life: her career as a writer and her marriage. Boris Kachka, in *New York Magazine*, uses interviews and testimonies from people who had known the family to reveal that Didion's daughter had been struggling with manic depression and alcoholism, something that is not revealed in so many words in Didion's account (Kachka 2011). Caitlin Flanagan, in *The Atlantic*, is even more straightforward in her denunciation of Didion's neglect of her own daughter and asks the question of where Quintana was when her mother was working on one of her big projects: "Not with her mother" (Flanagan 2012). Rachel Cusk, who also wrote a review of *Blue Nights* for *The Guardian*, was not interested in the details of Quintana's life and possible illnesses. Instead, she is troubled by the style of the memoir, which is remarkably solipsistic, "a kind of

DOI: 10.4324/9781003461388-6

parental attention-seeking that again and again drives Didion's sentences away from their subject and back to herself" (Cusk 2011). Indeed, most of the anecdotes about Quintana's life are occasions for her mother to reminisce about her past achievements.

Was Joan Didion a bad mother? And what would be her worst crime? Failing to leave her daughter enough space in her life as a writer, or in her writing itself? In *Blue Nights*, Didion herself admits that when Quintana made a list of her mother's sayings, she included the mention "Shush I'm working", which was seized upon as the main proof of Didion's neglect of her daughter, whom she seems to have ranked second to her writing vocation. In the *Atlantic* piece that she wrote on the benefits of having just one child,[1] Lauren Sandler hits back at Caitlin Flanagan and flies to Didion's rescue: "What's wrong with 'shush I'm working?'" (Sandler 2013). Joan Didion, as well as Susan Sontag, are held by Sandler as exemplars of the coexistence of artistic freedom and motherhood – that coexistence, she reminds us, was only made possible by the fact that both were mothers to single children. Whatever we think of Joan Didion's qualities as a parent, and however much we may want to speculate on whether her daughter might have fared better in life had her mother not been such a renowned and dedicated artist (and I have certainly been tempted to do just that), I'm interested in understanding why we are so fascinated by female literary figures who we believe have failed their mission as parents.

From a much more light-hearted and comical point of view, US author Ayelet Waldman has explored the reasons why we feel the need to cast moral judgment on women's parenting skills in *Bad Mother: A Chronicle of Maternal Crimes, Minor Calamities, and Occasional Moments of Grace* (Waldman 2009). Throughout the book, she refers to the figure of the Bad Mother with capital letters, in order to show that she is a fantasy, a screen on which we project our own fears and insecurities, as children of mothers, but also as mothers ourselves. In the first chapter of her memoir, she examines her own track record of passing judgment on the mothers around her, until she found herself in the proverbial dock and was made to go through a very public moral trial. What was her crime? In 2005 she wrote an article for *The New York Times* in which she confessed to feeling more love for her husband, writer Michael Chabon, than for her children (Waldman 2005). Nationwide outrage ensued and Waldman ended up invited on Oprah Winfrey's talk show to discuss her views, to an unbelieving and sometimes hostile audience. The fact that so many negative reactions came from women allowed her to understand that women themselves were responsible for much of the shaming of other women when it came to motherhood: "Still, the blare of condemnation that drowns out so much of civil discourse on the subject of mothering and child rearing originates not from some patriarchal grand inquisitor's office but, in large part, from individual women", or in other words, "The Bad Mother cops with the most aggressive arrest records are women" (Waldman 2009, 9).

The existence of the Bad Mother, Waldman continues, supposes the existence of her opposite, the Good Mother, who is just as much a creature of fiction as her negative double. She explains that she conducted an informal poll of the women around her to try and delineate the main characteristics of the Bad Mother, and came to realise that, for most mothers, the Bad Mother is what they are not, or would like to be. This in itself is fitting with the fact that the one characteristic that comes back in the depictions of what Good Motherhood would be, is self-abnegation:

> Her children's needs come first; their health and happiness are her primary concern. They occupy all her thoughts, her day is constructed around them, and anything and everything she does is for their sakes. Her own needs, ambitions, and desires are relevant only in relation to theirs. If a Good Mother takes care of herself, it is only to the extent that she doesn't hurt her children.
>
> (Waldman 2009, 10)

To come back to the case of Joan Didion, this was first and foremost what she was on trial for: placing her own needs – as a woman and as a writer –before her daughter's. Yet no one thought to submit her husband, the adoptive father of Quintana, to the same amount of scrutiny. In fact, Waldman realises that most people find it much easier to define what a good father is: he simply shows up, or stays around the children, but he is definitely not held to the same high standards (Waldman 2009, 11). Joan Didion is not alone in the category of female authors who have transgressed the rules of Good Motherhood and who have been suspected of neglecting their children for the sake of their art. Julie Phillips has devoted a whole book, *The Baby on the Fire Escape: Creativity, Motherhood and the Mind-Baby Problem*, to the stories of creative women who have struggled with how to reconcile their artistic vocation with their roles as mothers: all of them, she suggests, had to flout in one way or another the rules of acceptable motherhood in order to claim their right to self-expression, which some of them placed above their duties to their children (Phillips 2022). One of those women is British author Doris Lessing, who, as a literary figure, is forever associated with her decision to abandon her children when they were barely toddlers. It could be argued that Sylvia Plath is another one of those authors who has been coded as a Bad Mother, for when she committed suicide at 30, she left behind two young children of the same age as Lessing's. Both those authors have been the subject of endless speculation, their life stories probed and searched for signs that could explain decisions which have been perceived as morally abhorrent. Although Plath and Lessing made very different choices, they both broke strongly held taboos for similar reasons, which had to do with the fact that they could no longer reconcile their vocation as artists with their roles as mothers.

Plath and Lessing have cast a long shadow over the writers who are also mothers, their lives serving either as a cautionary tale or as a source of inspiration. Many of the authors who have written about their experience of motherhood revisit their stories at one point or another. Lessing, Plath, as well as Didion, are the original "art monsters", to borrow a term that has been gaining a lot of traction in the last recent years, and which has been used to interrogate the double standards to which male and female authors have been held in the eyes of the public. Yet I would like to show that female authors who have also been mothers to their children have also run the risk of being labelled as monsters because of their willingness to discuss the darker sides of the experience of motherhood, thereby daring to disrupt the usual narrative about motherhood as a source of unadulterated bliss, which still held sway in the middle of the 20th century. The real transgression was to discuss the possibility that mothers may experience ambivalent feelings towards their children. Though, as we have seen with the proliferation of motherhood memoirs, it has now become acceptable to openly discuss complex feelings such as ambiguity and resentment, it took the disruptive testimony of several literary mothers to allow their literary daughters to fully express the whole gamut of their real emotions with regard to their children. This discussion warrants a look into the concept of "maternal ambivalence", which has by now become widely discussed in the field of maternal studies.

Mother writers and the art monsters

The art monster

There has been a flourish of publications in recent years interrogating the notion of the art monster, which was originally coined by US author Jenny Offill. In the novel *Dept. of Speculation*, which was already discussed in the previous chapter, the narrator, who is also a writer, reflects on her new life as a wife and a mother: "My plan was to never get married. I was going to be an art monster instead" (Offill 2014, 8). The origins of this pronouncement can be found in an interview she gave to the *Literary Review* in 2010, entitled "Is There Anything Literary about Motherhood?". Offill explains how, once she became a mother, she found it particularly difficult to continue writing:

> The demands of a small child are directly opposed to the state of mind you need to write. When Faulkner talked about how a writer becomes

a serious novelist, he said, "An artist is a creature driven by demons. He is completely immoral".

(Morris 2010)

Once again, what Offill is pointing at is that being a mother and a being writer feel like two contradictory enterprises, first for material reasons that have to do with the needs of the child, but also for symbolic reasons: women who want to stake their claims as authors are still struggling with the totemic figures of the "monstrous" male artist who is ready to relinquish morality in order to pursue his vision. Yet the likes of Faulkner were never chastised for their self-professed "immorality", as it was perceived as a necessary condition to the making of their art. Like many other male authors entirely devoted to their vocation, Faulkner was able to count on his wife Estelle, who stuck to their marriage even though she was resentful of his emotional distance.

US feminist authors Claire Dederer and Lauren Elkin both released books dealing with that specific topic in 2023: *Monsters: A Fan's Dilemma* (2023) and *Art Monsters* (2023). Both books came in the wake of a series of scandals, all gathered under the social media hashtag #metoo, which involved several well-known male celebrities and cultural figures, all accused of having sexually preyed upon women, and sometimes even men. What this cultural movement revealed primarily was that the excesses, sometimes even crimes, of certain male artists, which for a long time had been tolerated in the name of freedom, the artist's sovereignty, or a right to transgression, had suddenly become inexcusable. Claire Dederer writes of her discomfort at watching once beloved films by Woody Allen or Roman Polanski after it was revealed that they had both had relationships with much younger girls. She realises that cultural history is full of male artistic figures whose life choices could be considered morally questionable in that they had hurt the people around them, using their artistic vocation as a shield against criticism. Pablo Picasso and Ernest Hemingway are the prime examples of figures who have been absolved of their morally abhorrent ways in the name of their "genius". In the chapter devoted to Valerie Solanas and Sylvia Plath, who both tried to lash out at the perceived violence of men around them, Dederer lays out the cultural fundaments of our tolerance of abuse by male artists:

> The violence of male artists has a story. The story is this: He is subject to forces that are beyond this control. Sometimes these forces get out of hand, and he slips up and commits a crime. That's unfortunate, but we understand that these forces are the same forces that make his art great.
>
> (Dederer 2023, 211)

She contends that we have been primed to consume the artistic production of male artists whose moral failings we choose to ignore:

> I knew that critics have been arguing the biographical fallacy for decades – the work of the New Critics, Americans writing mostly in the first half of the twentieth century, did a lot to promulgate the idea that the work ought to be fastidiously divorced from its maker.
> (Dederer 2023, 39)

The point made by Dederer is not that more male authors should be pilloried for their moral failings, large and small, but rather that we have allowed a discourse to take hold which would have it that artistic genius must be pursued at all costs, and that artists can and should be held to different standards than the rest of the population. Yet the status of artistic genius is very often a position of great privilege, as Virginia Woolf argued in *A Room of Ones' Own* (Woolf [1929] 2004), and the pursuit of a life entirely dedicated to one's art often means relying on the labour and/or money of another, often the artist's wife or companion. Nancy Huston (2004) and Kate Zambreno (2014) have both explored the fact that most of the male authors we consider today as "geniuses" depended on their wives for inspiration, but also for their daily sustenance (see also Elkin 2023, 78). The fact that the women who have helped those great artists produce their art have often completely disappeared from literary history is very telling of the fact that we perceive artists as isolated agents, untethered from relationships, and therefore absolved from any responsibility to the people around them.

For Dederer, the one moral flaw we tend to forgive in male artists is their selfishness; it is actually even expected of artists to be selfish in order to produce their art: "A book is made out of small selfishness. The selfishness of shutting the door against your family. The selfishness of ignoring the pram in the hall. The selfishness of forgetting the real world to create a new one" (Dederer 2023, 162). Rebecca Solnit, who wrote about Dederer's first piece on the art made by monstrous men (Dederer 2017), also wonders: "maybe there's a special kind of Bohemian-dude selfishness, which the idea of the genius—the person who is more special and important than other—encourages" (Solnit 2017).

Selfishness is a character trait which is not tolerated in a mother. The fact that Joan Didion may have figuratively shut the door on her daughter's needs has been judged not as a necessary condition to her writing but as a moral failing on her part, one which places her on art monster territory. Yet female art monsters do not get the same kind of leniency usually reserved for male authors. Elkin and Dederer have identified three main female art monsters, namely Doris Lessing, Sylvia Plath, and Anne Sexton, whose lives have been marred by scandal, moral condemnation, madness, and suicide. The three of them have gone down in history as mothers who have failed in their mission as mothers, which is the highest crime a woman can commit: Doris Lessing famously abandoned her children, Sylvia Plath killed herself when her children were bare toddlers, and Anne Sexton severely abused her children and eventually took her own life as well. Countless studies and biographies have been written about them, and their lives have been probed and dissected, and become the object of endless speculation. Their work is often judged in the light of the facts of their troubled lives, which is something that also happens in the case of male artists, albeit to a lesser degree.

The male art monster is an easy enough figure to identify. He believes himself to be above the usual categories of morality, which he transcends in the name of his artistic vocation. He evolves seemingly untethered from relationships with the people around him yet depends on their devotion in order to be able to produce his art. Who is the female art monster then? She aspires to the same freedom as her male counterpart and places her duty to her art above her commitment to her children. The art monster is a useful figure in order to interrogate the gender biases at work in how we receive and judge the lives and the works of male and female artists. The female art monsters are usually judged far more harshly for their life choices than their male counterparts. In Chapter 2, we saw that contemporary authors who write about motherhood are often eager to inscribe themselves in a tradition of other mother writers and turn to their "literary foremothers" for guidance. The female art monster is different from the "literary foremother", in that she is not to be looked up to as a source of inspiration or a role model. Her life is a cautionary tale, but it is often apprehended with empathy and sometimes even tenderness. Many mother writers have revisited the life story of Sylvia Plath in order to understand what could have driven a talented young poet to abandon her two children (Boland 2012; Huston 1990; Shafak 2013). In their accounts, the figure of Sylvia Plath is not that of a monster, but rather of a martyr, whose life had become so intolerable she could not even find comfort in her art. How can we account for the existence of the bad mother writer? Is she only selfish? Or has she been driven mad?

"Bad Mothers" vs. "Mad Mothers"

I borrow this distinction from the work of Sarah LaChance Adams. Like Adrienne Rich in the last chapter of *Of Woman Born* ("Violence: The Heart of Maternal Darkness"), she convokes one of the most striking examples of infanticide, as they regularly spring up in the news. The existence of those appalling figures, the mothers who kill their own children function as modern-day Medeas: we use their tragic figures as a way to exorcise our own fears, which is that some mothers may feel anything other than pure love and tenderness for their offspring and may on the contrary be driven to gruesome violence against them. We are often quick to pathologise them and to reassure ourselves that they were driven to such extremes by mental illness, but as LaChance Adams reminds us, things are often more complicated than they seem (LaChance Adams 2014, 4). In fact, we would like to believe that there is a fundamental difference between the common "bad mother", who will fail in her maternal duties, and the "mad mother" who will go as far as destroying her children. Maintaining a clear boundary between the two allows us to "abject" the infanticidal mother beyond the boundaries of "normal" behaviour, but the relationship between the two is often more continuous than is comfortable for us to admit. For Rich, it is simply too easy to turn to psychiatry to explain why some mothers may kill their own children; in fact these acts can be interpreted as a reaction against the violence of the institution of motherhood (Rich [1976] 1995, 277).

For psychoanalyst Marilyn Yalom, the incidence of madness among female artists is higher than among the rest of the population, with patriarchal oppression acting as a major factor (see Gilbert and Gubar [1979] 2000). She also believes that the experience of maternity (as distinct from the institution of motherhood) often acts as a catalyst for mental breakdown among this category of women, whose artistic tendencies make them prone to mental illness (Yalom 1985, 5). She specifically looks at the lives of poets such as Sylvia Plath and Anne Sexton, whose life stories have placed them somewhere between the bad and the mad mother categories. Her main thesis is that their experience of maternity (which she distinguishes from the institution of motherhood) drove them to madness precisely because they were writers prior to their becoming mothers. What is it then that makes mother writers more susceptible to madness than the rest of mothers? Is it the interruption of their creative flow, the invasion of their mental space, as we saw in Chapter 4? This is in keeping with the tradition of the mad female artist for whom Charlotte Perkins Gilman's Jane in "The Yellow Wallpaper" has become an archetype ([1892] 2015). In this iconic short story, the narrator's postpartum psychosis is directly linked with her doctor-husband's orders that she be forbidden from touching her pen (see Johnson 1989).

British author Polly Clark has written in *The Guardian* of her experience with postnatal depression, which she attributes to "a dangerously well-developed sense of self". She does not say whether this has to do with her profession as a writer, but she does acknowledge that madness was for her the only way out as her sense of self was crumbling (Clark 2017). The questions which remain to be answered are to know whether female authors are indeed more likely to experience a form of madness once they become mothers (in the form of postnatal depression or psychosis), as Yalom seems to suggest, but if this is true, what would be the ultimate reason? Would it have to do with the fact that motherhood is perceived as incompatible with one's vocation as an artist, and would require women to renounce their creativity? Or is it because female authors suffer from a form of mental fragility which would make them more vulnerable to the trauma of welcoming a child into their lives?

In *A Room of One's Own*, Virginia Woolf makes a very similar claim when she suggests that madness and suicide were the only reasonable outcomes for a woman with a gift for writing born at the same time as Shakespeare (Woolf [1929] 2004, 110). Yet Woolf's thesis does not rest on any psychological pre-givens which would condemn the fictional Judith Shakespeare to such a tragic fate; rather she attributes it to the cultural and material conditions in which she would have had to live, and to the lack of permission given to women writers over the course of history. Even if the institution of motherhood has survived the progress made by women in the 20th century, particularly by taking new forms (with attachment theory and intensive parenting for example), we have found ample proof that female writers can claim to be authors in their own right, even once they have become mothers. It is true that authors such as Anne Sexton or Sylvia Plath still had to contend with the hold of patriarchy on motherhood, on top of their own mental struggles, but the number of female writers who have been able to negotiate the transition into motherhood and have later managed to write about it indicates that the lapse into madness is not the only fate they are bound to meet. Thankfully, not all mother writers have become mad or have been driven to suicide. Some of them have instead chosen to write their truth, even if it meant having to submit themselves to be judged, as in the case of Doris Lessing.

Doris Lessing and the "intelligent young woman"

Other female art monsters do not rouse the same feelings of compassion but instead are considered in a manner that is ambiguous and cautious. Chief among these is Doris Lessing, who is notorious, not only for having abandoned her two children but for having seemingly felt little remorse over the deed. The scene, which is recounted in both her autobiographical novel *A Proper Marriage* (Lessing 1954) and in her autobiography (Lessing 1994), features an idealistic bright young woman who decides that being a mother is incompatible with her future as both a writer and a communist activist. In her own book, Claire Dederer admits that she cannot help but cast judgment on Lessing's choice, while she also wonders if she would have been so quick to judge had the offender been a man

(Dederer 2023, 196). For British author Lara Feigel, who engaged in a dialogue with Lessing's work in order to make sense of her own aspiration to freedom as a mother writer, accepting that Lessing had to abandon her children in order to fully become herself is a necessary condition in order to accept her work as a whole as an endless quest for freedom.

> When I first decided to turn my preoccupation with Lessing into a book, I knew that the moment would come when I had to confront her leaving her children. It quickly became tiresome how many people mentioned it. Often, it was the first thing they said. "Wasn't she a monster? Didn't she leave her children? Could you do that?" I wanted to stand up for her, and found there were various ways of doing it. I could point to all the men who'd abandoned children along the way, and whom we didn't generally judge as monsters. Augustus John, Lucian Freud, John Rodker, Michael Hoffman.
>
> (Feigel 2018a, 67)

Feigel argues that it is possibly even more difficult for a mother to be a writer than it would be for a mother who has any other occupation, precisely because the activity of writing involves retreating into a private space from which one's family may be, at least temporarily, excluded. It is easier to slip in and out of one's role as a lawyer or a nurse than it is when one is a writer, which requires access to a specific mental space in which the child is often seen as an intruder. Eighty years after Lessing made the decision to abandon her children, the narrator in Feigel's memoir confesses that she still feels uncomfortable about leaving her family, even for a few days, in order to get her writing done: "there is such a taboo in mothers abandoning their children that it's there in every departure, even if it's only for a few days" (Feigel 2018a, 91). Feigel sees Lessing as an inspiring figure because she refused to let that one fateful choice define her: mainly, it was something she had to do, and her career certainly would have been very different had she remained a housewife in Rhodesia (now Zimbabwe).

I believe that Lessing has left such a strong mark on the imaginations of mother writers (and women writers in general) not just because she abandoned her own children, but because she apparently found her decision justified. In her autobiography, *Under My Skin*, she made the claim, now endlessly quoted, that "There is no boredom like that of an intelligent young woman who spends all day with a very small child" (Lessing 1994, 236). The truly controversial part in this quote is the way Lessing distinguishes herself from other mothers: the fact that she is an intelligent young woman stuck with a small child she is forever pushing in a pram instead of writing novels or handing out Communist pamphlets is the real scandal here. The implication, as we are made to understand, is that there could be a certain class of young women who are simply not made for traditional practices of mothering, and that they, in the name of their intelligence, should not be subjected to the same expectations as other women. The view held by Lessing may seem to us abhorrent, along with some of her other views on the family in general, but what is really monstrous here is that she is willing to express it out loud without fear of the consequences. Other writers were made to pay a heavy price for voicing similar concerns.

Rachel Cusk and the curse of honesty

For Lauren Elkin, the female art monster is not just the artist whose moral failings we feel entitled to judge: she is also someone who is willing to push the limits of what we find acceptable for a woman to express. In other words, she is going to say the unsayable and admit to feelings which may create a sense of discomfort in that they displace our representations of what femininity and motherhood, should imply. Like Chris Kraus, who in *I Love Dick*, pushed the boundaries of female self-expression by representing an extreme example of unrequited love and self-inflicted shame (Kraus 2016), the real monstrosity lies in the attempt to reveal the more unsavoury aspects of female experience:

> The artists I'm thinking of in this category blur the line between author and subject, pushing at the boundaries of narcissism to make the personal a universally relevant category. They help us to take the monster out of the realm of morality, into some more subtle, harder-to-define ethics that is also an aesthetics, in the sense that I give it here: a way of feeling that art alone can produce. This monstrous art strives to understand or express something about what it is to be embodied and socialised as female; it is feminist, not feminine.
>
> (Elkin 2023, 64–65)

This desire to push the boundaries of the acceptable comes with a heavy price tag when the artist is also a mother, as Rachel Cusk found out upon the release of her memoir *A Life's Work*, which, as she claims in the introduction, is an attempt to take an honest look at her experience of motherhood, in its most confusing aspects. The outpour of vitriol and outrage from reviewers and readers alike was so staggering that she was invited on a popular radio show to explain herself. Seven years after the book was published, Cusk reflected back on this sequence in a *Guardian* piece entitled "I Was Only Being Honest". She quotes several of the most negative reviews, which blasted her negative outlook on motherhood and, in some cases, accused her of outright child neglect (Cusk 2008). As she goes on to explain, Cusk felt shamed not as a writer, but as a mother, as if simply writing about her conflicting feelings was tantamount to child abuse. And that, she explains, is because the reviewers were not judging the book as readers but as mothers. In fact, the reactions themselves provided an illustration of what Cusk was trying to portray in her book: the ideology of motherhood as foisted upon mothers by pregnancy and childcare manuals, the routine public shaming that would take place in toddler groups and parks (see also Hanson 2013).

Surprisingly, Cusk's book was not the first to have looked at motherhood in a less-than-positive light. Before her, Adrienne Rich and Jane Lazarre had published memoirs which also depicted mothers feeling ambivalent about their children, and these did not create such an uproar. What kind of taboo had Cusk transgressed? For the sociologist Orna Donath, regret over motherhood is a topic that is rarely, if ever, to be found in mainstream discourse, even by feminist writers (Donath 2015, 344). Eliane Glaser also expressed surprise at the reception of Cusk's memoir several decades after Lessing wrote about abandoning her own children. She blames this new sanctimony on a contemporary intolerance for the "selfish" mother who aims to have it all and is not ready to suffer the consequences (Glaser 2021, 138). Because mothers are now freer to achieve self-fulfilment and pursue their own careers, any complaint from them is deemed provocative and self-centred. Why should they be complaining? Cusk suspects that those women (often mothers) who have lambasted her work act as gatekeepers who seek to impose one specific narrative about motherhood, for which they will not tolerate any form of dissension. Cusk is not an art monster in the original sense of the word, in that she did not sacrifice her family for her art. Nor did she live a life purely dedicated to her art. If there is anything monstrous in her memoir, it is her attempt at lifting the veil upon the negative feelings some mothers experience towards their children, or rather towards their new identities as mothers. Some of Cusk's detractors have attempted to pathologise these feelings by accusing her of having suffered undiagnosed post-natal depression (which in any case, does not invalidate the truthfulness of her testimony). Yet to understand what Cusk is trying to express in her memoir, I found the concept of maternal ambivalence much more useful in order to make sense of the conflicting emotions mother writers routinely describe in their self-life writing.

Maternal ambivalence

The reactions to Cusk's memoir testify to the widespread belief that there is something monstrous in revealing the negative feelings the narrator experienced when she became a mother. Yet those feelings are, at least from the point of view of psychology, perfectly normal, and according to the experts specialising in the affects of motherhood, part of a healthy relationship with one's children. Donald Winnicott was the first psychologist to normalise the presence of aggression, and sometimes even outright hatred, in mothering (Winnicott [1949] 1994). Yet although these feelings are known and recognised as part of the range of emotions the "good enough mother" is allowed to feel, the contemporary discourse around motherhood, particularly the ideology of "intensive parenting" (see Chapter 1) has made them less acceptable, even causing them to be regarded with suspicion. As UK psychologist Barbara Almond observes in her book *The Monster Within: The Hidden Side of Motherhood*: "That mothers have mixed feelings about their children should come as no surprise to anybody, but it is amazing how much of a taboo the negative side of ambivalence carries in our culture, especially at this time" (Almond 2010, xiii). In *Matrescence*, Lucy Jones explains that she found it particularly hard to reconcile the two figures she had inherited from the discourse of motherhood, which opposed good and bad mothers as the antithesis to each other: the revelation was the fact that those two figures could coexist within herself (Jones 2023, 176). Even though the concept of maternal ambivalence has become a common currency in the psychoanalytic discourse about motherhood, mothers are still made to feel shame when they try to articulate the complexity of their feelings towards their children. I will try to show here that once again, self-life writing by mothers, and the practice of literature in general, is useful to make sense of the ambiguity and, ultimately, to break down the binary between good and bad mothering.

Sentences in two parts

For Jones, the historical and cultural paucity of texts taking maternal subjectivity as its main vantage point is to blame for the lack of visibility around the concept of maternal ambivalence (Jones 2023, 181). Doris Lessing and Sylvia Plath did in fact explore the coexistence of love and aggression in the relationship to motherhood, but it was Adrienne Rich, ever the pioneer in all things maternal, who would try to articulate those feelings in the oft-quoted entry of her journal which opens the chapter "Anger and Tenderness" in *Of Woman Born*:

> My children cause me the most exquisite suffering of which I have any experience. It is the suffering of ambivalence: the murderous alternation between bitter resentment and raw-edged nerves, and blissful gratification and tenderness. Sometimes I seem to myself, in my feelings toward these tiny guiltless beings, a monster of selfishness and intolerance. Their voices wear away at my nerves, their constant needs, above all

their need for simplicity and patience fill me with despair at my own failures, despair too at my fate, which is to serve a function for which I was not fitted.
(Rich [1976] 1995, 21)

This quote has it all: the oscillation between extreme opposites, but particularly the way in which the aggressive feelings she fears she may harbour towards her children are eventually turned upon herself as punishment for having even experienced them. For Barbara Almond, resisting the possibility of ambivalence creates a vicious circle in which women fail to fulfil the expectations foisted upon them by the ideology of motherhood and end up chastising themselves by holding themselves to even more impossible standards (Almond 2010, 14). The only solution, she claims, is for mothers to accept that ambivalent feelings are part and parcel of the experience of motherhood. This is the wise conclusion to which the narrator in Jane Lazarre's memoir eventually arrives, as she becomes part of a supportive network of mothers:

"I can't wait until tomorrow, when it is your day to keep the children," she would say, "but I dread leaving them in the morning." We learned always to expect sentences to have two parts, the second seeming to contradict the first, the unity lying only in our ability to tolerate ambivalence – for that is what motherly love is like.
(Lazarre [1976] 1997, 70)

But what exactly is maternal ambivalence? The experience of ambivalent feelings by mothers is documented very early by psychoanalysts such as Winnicott, as well as Melanie Klein, but it was Rozsika Parker who would really delineate its contours as a concept in and of itself. She defines it as "not an anodyne condition of mixed feelings, but a complex and contradictory state of mind, shared variously by all mothers, in which loving and hating feelings for children exist side by side" (Parker 2002, 17). It is a tension, a coexistence of contradictory emotions often felt at the same time: it is the sentence in two parts uttered by Lazarre's mothers who can't wait to leave their children in the care of someone else in order to enjoy some time to themselves while resenting the separation, it is the sigh of relief a mother may experience as she hands over her child at the day-care centre, quickly followed by a feeling of loss at the separation. It is also the alternation between fantasies of aggression against one's children and a desire to be overly protective of them. As the narrator in Rachel Cusk's memoir realises: "When she is with them she is not herself; when she is without them she is not herself; and so it is as difficult to leave your children as it is to stay with them" (Cusk 2001, 16). For Parker, maternal ambivalence can also be defined as a vortex of feelings in which tenderness coexists with aggressive impulses.

The psychoanalysts such as Rozsika Parker, or Joan Raphael-Leff, who have worked on the concept of maternal ambivalence have picked up where feminists in the 1970s left off. The "conflict between nurturance and autonomy" (Flax 1978), which made motherhood a stumbling block for women's emancipation has become internalised by modern mothers who are theoretically free to pursue a professional career even once they have become mothers. On top of the issue of the "double shift", which resulted from women being able to work outside of the home (see Bueskens 2018), mothers now have to deal with the guilt of seeking self-fulfilment while also giving priority to the care of their children, pulled on both sides by the concomitant idealisation and denigration of motherhood in public discourse (Raphael-Leff 2009). Mothers are being short-changed by the promises made under the liberal discourse in that they cannot be independent and entirely devoted to their children. Yet instead of railing against the injustice, most of them end up turning the aggression inward and see their inability at making both happen as a personal failure.

The main contribution made by Parker is that maternal ambivalence needs to be de-pathologised: she makes a clear difference between "unmanageable" and "manageable" ambivalence, arguing that manageable ambivalence can be a source of creativity in relationships in that it allows mothers to fashion their own style of mothering. For Parker, as well as other critics after her (LaChance Adams 2014; Lowy 2021), maternal ambivalence finds its root in the conflict between societal and cultural expectations of motherhood, and the need for individual mothers to retain some form of autonomy.

> The idealisation of oneness, the representation of mothers as good or bad rather than inevitably ambivalent, the frequent absence of previous experience of childcare, the often sole responsibility, the social isolation, and the eruption of emotion considered unacceptable in mothers, all combine to produce the feelings of helplessness so closely associated with the inability to transform aggression into creative care and attention, not only to the child's needs but also to her own.
> (Parker [1995] 2005, 115)

The "idealisation of oneness", combined with social isolation within the nuclear family, is at the heart of contemporary representations of good motherhood. Parker traces back the roots of this maternal imagination to 18th-century Rousseauist conceptions of child rearing based on natural instinct, through to psychoanalysis' distorted view of the mother-child relationship as central to the construction of selfhood, and the contemporary social injunctions around intensive parenting. Over the course of history, she claims, the mother's role in her child's life has become crucial not just to the child's survival, but also to her intellectual development as well as her happiness (see also Glaser 2021; Bueskens 2018). This enormous responsibility often comes at the cost of a mother's independence. Parker shows that this translates into the tensions around the possibility for the mother to go back to work and leave her children in day care, which is still to this day coded as a selfish desire on the part of mothers unable to let go of their wish for individuality. Yet for Parker, maternal ambivalence need not be an impossible quandary; it may actually be a source of creativity.

Creative ambivalence

As we have seen in Chapter 4, the difficulty of combining the care of a child with the desire to write does not only come down to the necessity of finding time away from the day-to-day care of the child, it is also about carving a space for the self as independent. I would argue that this particular issue is at the heart of motherhood memoirs such as Jane Lazarre's *The Mother Knot* and Rachel Cusk's *A Life's Work*. Both authors mourn their sense of self, particularly their creative self, which they feel is threatened by their duties as mothers, and by the injunctions to maternal fusion with their children (see LaChance Adams 2014). Yet for Parker, this fusion is not only impossible to achieve, it is also not the right signal a mother should send to her child: managing to strike the right balance between her needs and those of her child is the best way to equip her with the skills needed to reach her own independence as she grows up and becomes an adult. Although this may appear sound and healthy advice, it is often drowned under waves of guilt, as mothers are constantly bombarded with messages requiring them to become literally selfless. While Parker is aware of the guilt and the shame she believes however that acknowledging the reality of maternal ambivalence is the only way for mothers to deal with those contradictory emotions creatively. Instead of "measuring herself against maternal mythologies", the mother must carve her own path through "maternal individuation", and discover new ways to engage with her children (Parker 2002, 25).

What does creative ambivalence mean for mothers who are also writers? As we have seen in Chapter 4, the presence of a child in an author's life may in itself be a source of creativity and new-found inspiration. But I also believe that self-life writing is an apt way of working through contradictory emotions (see Juhasz 2003), as is the case for Cusk and Lazarre. These memoirs have been useful for their authors in that they have helped them make sense of their own ambivalence, but I would argue that they have also had a tremendous impact on their readers, who could see their own emotional conflicts being laid out in writing. Lara Feigel, for instance, shows that her dialogue with Doris Lessing's work, and particularly her writing on motherhood, helped her get through her own difficulties in being a wife and a mother. One of the main contributions made by Lessing, she contends, both through her work and her life story, was to place the existence of ambivalence at the heart of the maternal experience. Engaging with Lessing's legacy today, she argues, is all the more urgent as avowal to feelings of ambivalence has become less acceptable than it used to be, despite the progress allowed by feminism and the women's liberation (Feigel 2018b; see also Glaser 2021). Self-life writing has been an invaluable source of empowerment for women in that it allowed them to lay out in writing the experience of being a woman as different from that of being a man; in the case of motherhood, it has made it possible to break the taboo imposed by cultural injunctions to perfection. For Sarah LaChance Adams, we need a new care ethic with regard to motherhood, one which allows women to take into consideration the mother's wish for independence instead of conceiving of motherhood in terms of the selfless nurturing of a dependent child (LaChance Adams 2014, 16).

Bad (ambivalent) mothers

Yet as Rachel Cusk's experience has demonstrated, revelations about the darker side of motherhood do not always sit well with the public, and with some who are regarded as culturally legitimated authorities on mothering alike. Even if the concept of maternal ambivalence has become a common currency in maternal studies since the 1990s, it has also been met with unease, in keeping with the tensions within the feminist movement with regard to the issue of motherhood, as we saw in Chapter 1. In her book *What Mothers Do* (2004), psychologist Naomi Stadlen takes a very dim view of the success of this concept, which she perceives as a form of self-indulgence and as an inadequate response to the demands made by children on their mothers. She specifically blames the authors of motherhood memoirs such as Adrienne Rich, Jane Lazarre, Rachel Cusk, or Kate Figes (2013) for having instilled in the public discourse the idea that women could feel anything other than unadulterated love for their children. Stadlen completely rejects the concept of maternal ambivalence as a feminist academic fabrication which has been "over-publicised" (see Jeremiah 2018). She lumps together authors of motherhood memoirs with works by psychologists like Rozsika Parker and cultural critics like Susan Maushart, author of *The Mask of Motherhood* (1999) to show that they all fell under the dubious spell of an intellectual fallacy. "For the first time", Stadlen argues, "mothers are being encouraged to regard their ambivalent feelings as inevitable. Many mothers, say the authors of this literature, are afraid of their negative feelings, and feel guilty when they acknowledge them.

They need permission to experience their hate" (Stadlen 2004, 171–72). Stadlen believes that the women who experience these feelings suffer from their inability to see their children as separate individuals; if only they were able to understand that, they would be able to deal with their children's demands and cease to perceive them as encroachments on their independence: "Mothers in this position seem quite immature and rigid. It requires a certain maturity and elasticity for a mother to open herself and to welcome her baby" (Stadlen 2004, 178). For a book that promises to help women deal with their feelings of guilt and inadequacy, there is certainly a lot of judgement being cast around.

For Stadlen, the concept of maternal ambivalence has been created to normalise the internal conflicts experienced specifically by writers who are guilty of valuing their creative independence over the love they should be feeling for their children. If only Lazarre, Cusk *et alii* would open their hearts to motherly love, she argues, they would learn that the exhaustion, frustration, and feelings of entrapment disappear over time, and they would not contaminate their children with their ambivalent emotions. Under the guise of providing conflicted mothers with advice on how to get rid of those feelings altogether, Stadlen deploys a searing criticism of the concept and of the authors who try to represent it in their writing. Motherly love, according to her, exists as a given in all healthy relationships between a mother and her child, and failure to recognise its supremacy is tantamount to neglect. Yet it is the idealisation of motherly love which is responsible for so much of the conflict women internalise, as those who feel anything other than this pure emotion will struggle with feelings of inadequacy and guilt (LaChance Adams 2014, 4). Love is a complex emotion, and it does not exist on a purely ideal level; rather it is often mediated by the cultural and social context, as well as the mother's specific emotional history. To borrow from Lynn O'Brien Hallstein's analysis of contemporary discourses on motherhood, I would argue that there is something matrophobic in Stadlen's condemnation of specific writers in that it pits supposedly good mothers against bad, ambivalent mothers, without sufficiently looking at the context in which those mother writers experience motherhood (Hallstein 2007). It also attributes to writers such as Rich, Lazarre, or Cusk the power to shape the emotions they have felt as mothers, while they are in fact only transcribing the complexity of their lived experience as a way to make sense of it and to help other women deal with their guilt by providing them with a cathartic outlet.

Conclusion

The way the lives and works of mother writers are still probed today for signs that they could be bad mothers is, I would contend, a remanence of that prohibition on writing by mothers, which held sway in our culture, and which we believe, often naïvely, has been completely lifted. Female authors can indeed become mothers if they wish to, without facing widespread reprobation, but their parenting will be scrutinised under the assumption that a woman cannot be completely dedicated to two all-encompassing endeavours at once. To me this can be explained by the persistence of two different myths which reinforce each other: one is that a true artist can be permitted to flout our commonly held views of morality in the name of his art, and the second is that mother love requires abandoning one's self and personal desires for the benefit of the child. Although we may tolerate the excesses of the male art monster who locks himself in a cabin to write his masterpiece while his wife takes care of his children and brings him sandwiches, we cannot imagine a mother writer doing the same, or she would be immediately indicted as neglectful. The solution to this burden of contradictory injunctions is precisely more writing by mother writers: as more and more mothers take up the pen to write about their own experiences and articulate their ambivalent feelings, without fear of the type of retaliation Rachel Cusk was submitted to when she published *A Life's Work*, the field of human experience represented in literature expands beyond the expected figures and tropes which have been imposed by the male literary canon. If women are allowed to write in detail about the reality of the lived experience of mothers, it will also have an effect on our definition of motherly love and the mother-child relationship.

Mother writers also have to contend with another accusation: does motherly love make for good literature? There is always a suspicion that writing on such a topic is going to be indulgent and mawkish. But it is in fact our culture's representation of motherly love which is indulgent and mawkish: if we allow more maternal voices to emerge and to articulate a more complex and realistic representation of the range of feelings we associate with the love a mother has for her children, then we can hope that it will achieve something of a more universal status than it has at the moment. As Alicia Ostriker argues, the culturally hegemonic representation we have of motherhood is inauthentic precisely to the degree that it also requires women to renounce their selves and their independence (Ostriker 1987, 180). As Ostriker also suggests, the existence of "matrifocal" texts permits us to stretch our definition and representation of love beyond the limits of what it has predominantly been represented as in the literary canon, that is romantic, sexual love (Ostriker 1983, 131). Irish poet Eavan Boland has written on the necessity to write a poetry that would celebrate the quotidian and the domestic, to force the canon open as it were, and let mother writers walk in:

I wanted the Irish poem to live in my time. The dial of a washing machine, the expression in a child's face – these things were at eye level as I bent down to them during the day. I wanted them to enter my poems. I wanted the poems they entered to be Irish poems.

(Boland 1995, 193)

Boland defends a poetry that is written by suburban mothers, but not destined to be read only by suburban mothers, a poetry that can be written while doing laundry or while playing with a child, which does not make her a bad mother or a bad poet.

Note

1 See Chapter 2 for a discussion of that piece.

Works cited

Almond, Barbara. 2010. *The Monster Within: The Hidden Side of Motherhood*. Berkeley, CA: University of California press.

Boland, Eavan. 1995. *Object Lessons: The Life of the Woman and the Poet in Our Time*. New York: Norton.

———. 2012. *A Journey with Two Maps: Becoming a Woman Poet*. Manchester: Carcanet.

Bueskens, Petra. 2018. *Modern Motherhood and Women's Dual Identities: Rewriting the Sexual Contract*. Abingdon; New York: Routledge.

Clark, Polly. 2017. 'The Everyday Trauma of Childbirth Made Me Stop at One Child'. *The Guardian*, 25 March 2017, sec. Life and style. www.theguardian.com/lifeandstyle/2017/mar/25/the-everyday-trauma-of-childbirth-made-me-stop-at-one-child

Cusk, Rachel. 2001. *A Life's Work: On Becoming a Mother*. New York: Picador.

———. 2008. 'I Was Only Being Honest'. *The Guardian*, 21 March 2008, sec. Books. www.theguardian.com/books/2008/mar/21/biography.women.

———. 2011. 'Blue Nights by Joan Didion – Review'. *The Guardian*, 11 November 2011, sec. Books. www.theguardian.com/books/2011/nov/11/blue-nights-joan-didion-review

Dederer, Claire. 2017. 'What Do We Do with the Art of Monstrous Men?' *The Paris Review*, 20 November 2017. www.theparisreview.org/blog/2017/11/20/art-monstrous-men/

———. 2023. *Monsters: A Fan's Dilemma*. New York: Alfred A. Knopf.

Didion, Joan. 2011. *Blue Nights*. London: Fourth Estate.

Donath, Orna. 2015. 'Regretting Motherhood: A Sociopolitical Analysis'. *Signs: Journal of Women in Culture and Society* 40 (2): 343–67. https://doi.org/10.1086/678145

Elkin, Lauren. 2023. *Art Monsters: Unruly Bodies in Feminist Art*. New York City: Vintage Digital.
Feigel, Lara. 2018a. *Free Woman: Life, Liberation and Doris Lessing*. London: Bloomsbury Publishing.
———. 2018b. 'The Parent Trap: Can You Be a Good Writer and a Good Parent?' *The Guardian*, 24 February 2018, sec. Books. www.theguardian.com/books/2018/feb/24/writers-parenting-doris-lessing-lara-feigel
Figes, Kate. 2013. *Life after Birth*. London: Virago.
Flanagan, Caitlin. 2012. 'The Autumn of Joan Didion'. *The Atlantic*, 2012. www.theatlantic.com/magazine/archive/2012/01/the-autumn-of-joan-didion/308851/
Flax, Jane. 1978. 'The Conflict between Nurturance and Autonomy in Mother-Daughter Relationships and within Feminism'. *Feminist Studies* 4 (2): 171. https://doi.org/10.2307/3177468
Gilbert, Sandra M., and Susan Gubar. (1979) 2000. *The Madwoman in the Attic: The Woman Writer and the Nineteenth-Century Literary Imagination*. 2nd ed. New Haven, CT: Yale University Press.
Gilman, Charlotte Perkins. (1892) 2015. *The Yellow Wall-Paper*. London: Penguin UK.
Glaser, Eliane. 2021. *Motherhood: Feminism's Unfinished Business*. London: Fourth Estate Ltd.
Hallstein, D. Lynn O'Brien. 2007. 'Matrophobic Sisters and Daughters: The Rhetorical Consequences of Matrophobia in Contemporary White Feminist Analyses of Maternity'. *Women's Studies* 36 (4): 269–96. https://doi.org/10.1080/00497870701296895
Hanson, Clare. 2013. 'The Book of Repetition: Rachel Cusk and Maternal Subjectivity'. *E-Rea. Revue Électronique d'études Sur Le Monde Anglophone* 2 (10): 1–12. https://doi.org/10.4000/erea.3259
Huston, Nancy. 1990. *Journal de la création*. Arles: Actes Sud.
———. 2004. *Professeurs de désespoir*. Arles: Actes Sud.
Jeremiah, Emily. 2018. 'Broken Nights, Shattered Selves: Maternal Ambivalence and the Ethics of Interruption in Sarah Moss's Novel Night Waking'. In *Motherhood in Literature and Culture: Interdisciplinary Perspectives from Europe*, edited by Gill Rye, Victoria Browne, Adalgisa Giorgio, Emily Jeremiah, and Abigail Lee Six, 197–208. New York; London: Routledge.
Johnson, Greg. 1989. 'Gilman's Gothic Allegory: Rage and Redemption in The Yellow Wallpaper'. *Studies in Short Fiction* 26 (4): 521–30.
Jones, Lucy. 2023. *Matrescence: On the Metamorphosis of Pregnancy, Childbirth and Motherhood*. London: Allen Lane.
Juhasz, Suzanne. 2003. 'Mother-Writing and the Narrative of Maternal Subjectivity'. *Studies in Gender and Sexuality* 4 (4): 395–425. https://doi.org/10.1080/15240650409349236
Kachka, Boris. 2011. 'I Was No Longer Afraid to Die. I Was Now Afraid Not to Die.' *New York Magazine*, 14 October 2011. https://nymag.com/arts/books/features/joan-didion-2011-10/
Kraus, Chris. 2016. *I Love Dick*. London: Serpent's Tail.

LaChance Adams, Sarah. 2014. *Mad Mothers, Bad Mothers, and What a Good Mother Would Do: The Ethics of Ambivalence*. New York: Columbia University Press.
Lazarre, Jane. (1976) 1997. *The Mother Knot*. Durham, NC: Duke University Press.
Lessing, Doris. 1954. *A Proper Marriage*. London: Flamingo.
———. 1994. *Under My Skin: Volume One of My Autobiography to 1949*. New York: Harper Perennial.
Lowy, Margo. 2021. *The Maternal Experience: Encounters with Ambivalence and Love*. 1 vols. Women and Psychology. Abingdon; New York: Routledge.
Maushart, Susan. 1999. *The Mask of Motherhood: How Becoming a Mother Changes Everything and Why We Pretend It Doesn't*. New York: New Press New York.
Morris, Ceridwen. 2010. 'Jenny Offill: Is There Anything Literary about Motherhood?' *Literary Review* 54 (1): 175–85.
Offill, Jenny. 2014. *Dept. of Speculation*. London: Granta.
Ostriker, Alicia. 1983. *Writing Like a Woman*. Ann Arbor, MI: University of Michigan Press.
———. 1987. *Stealing the Language: The Emergence of Women's Poetry in America*. London: The Women's Press.
Parker, Rozsika. (1995) 2005. *Torn in Two: The Experience of Maternal Ambivalence*. London: Virago.
———. 2002. 'The Production and Purposes of Maternal Ambivalence'. In *Mothering and Ambivalence*, edited by Brid Featherstone and Wendy Hollway, 27–46. London: Routledge.
Phillips, Julie. 2022. *The Baby on the Fire Escape: Creativity, Motherhood, and the Mind-Baby Problem*. 1st ed. New York: W. W. Norton & Company.
Raphael-Leff, Joan. 2009. 'Maternal Subjectivity'. *Studies in the Maternal* 1 (1). https://doi.org/10.16995/sim.159
Rich, Adrienne C. (1976) 1995. *Of Woman Born: Motherhood as Experience and Institution*. 2nd ed. Women's Studies. New York: Norton.
Sandler, Lauren. 2013. 'The Secret to Being Both a Successful Writer and a Mother: Have Just One Kid'. *The Atlantic*, 7 June 2013. www.theatlantic.com/sexes/archive/2013/06/the-secret-to-being-both-a-successful-writer-and-a-mother-have-just-one-kid/276642/
Shafak, Elif. 2013. *Black Milk: On Motherhood and Writing*. Translated by Hande Zapsu. London: Penguin.
Solnit, Rebecca. 2017. 'Rebecca Solnit on Women's Work and the Myth of the Art Monster'. *Literary Hub*, 12 December 2017. https://lithub.com/rebecca-solnit-on-womens-work-and-the-myth-of-the-art-monster/
Stadlen, Naomi. 2004. *What Mothers Do*. London: Hachette digital.
Waldman, Ayelet. 2005. 'Truly, Madly, Guiltily'. *The New York Times*, 27 March 2005, sec. Style. www.nytimes.com/2005/03/27/fashion/truly-madly-guiltily.html
———. 2009. *Bad Mother: A Chronicle of Maternal Crimes, Minor Calamities, and Occasional Moments of Grace*. New York: Anchor.

Winnicott, Donald W. (1949) 1994. 'Hate in the Counter-Transference'. *The Journal of Psychotherapy Practice and Research* 3 (4): 348–56.
Woolf, Virginia. (1929) 2004. *A Room of One's Own*. Great Ideas. Harmondsworth: Penguin.
Yalom, Marilyn. 1985. *Maternity, Mortality, and the Literature of Madness*. University Park, PA: Pennsylvania State University Press.
Zambreno, Kate. 2014. *Heroines*. New York: Harper Perennial.

Conclusion
Throwing the baby out with the bathwater

As I draw near the conclusion of this analysis, I realise that some aspects of my argument need to be nuanced. As I have tried to demonstrate, women who are mothers as well as writers have had to contend with several cultural assumptions about the attributes of each of those categories. Among these, the classical liberal conception of the self as self-contained vs. the relational nature of maternal subjectivity, the superb isolation of the Romantic writer vs. the interruptions of women's work by their children's demands, and the supremacy of the medical discourse over pregnancy and childbirth vs. the lived experiences of pregnant and birthing women. Yet the necessary task of critique does not always mean criticism. None of these aspects of our culture are wrong in themselves: the affirmation and exercise of autonomy of the individual as sovereign over his/her experience, which has been the main by-product of liberalism taken in the broad sense, the freedom for artists to explore their imagination without fear of censorship, these have unquestionably represented major advances in the evolution of Western societies. Likewise, no one wishes to go back to a time when women routinely died while they delivered their children, and the introduction of medical procedures to make pregnancy and childbirth safer has been a tremendous improvement. Yet progress in itself is not synonymous with equality when it is defined by one category of the population only.

Just when I was finishing writing this book, a certain number of scandals came out in the French media, following the recent revelations of sexual abuse against actresses and women alike gathered under the #metoo hashtag. There was a period, in the 1970s and the 1980s, when it was considered acceptable for very young women to be groomed by much older men in the name of their artistic visions: at the time, these women were not considered to be abused, and they were considered lucky enough to have been chosen by great artists as their muses. There ensued endless discussions about the legacy of the sexual revolution and the necessity to

DOI: 10.4324/9781003461388-7

interrogate these times when men had been given a licence to act out on their sexual impulses in the name of freedom. Some women are finding out that the sexual revolution was in fact a male sexual revolution and that it mostly played out scenarios based on the desires of men (Perry 2022). It might seem surprising to link recent debates about sexual violence and rape culture with the question of motherhood, but as a recent memoir on motherhood argues, motherhood is also a sexual issue. In her book called *Touched Out: Motherhood, Misogyny, Consent, and Control* (2023), US author Amanda Montei explains that becoming a mother reactivated some of the trauma from her past as a young woman experimenting with sex and alcohol and allowed her to realise that she had been under the illusion that she could be in control of her sex life when she mostly found herself at the mercy of the predatory desires of other men. When the "cool girl" from her past became a mother, she realised that she had not consented to most of the sexual encounters she had had in her past, and when she decided to dedicate herself to her two young children, she became aware that she now felt the need to set boundaries to her physical intimacy with them in order to remain herself.

Yet for women, the progress we have come to designate under the denomination "sexual revolution" has also brought tremendous advances in their individual reproductive rights: the right to contraception, followed by the right to safe abortion have granted women more freedom and more control over how they experienced motherhood – or not. Those rights would probably not have been achieved had it not been for the general uprising against old moral conventions which took place in the 1970s. Women have gained a lot, but they have also lost. In spite of recent social progresses, it is now obvious that patriarchy has evolved to take new shapes: the old social constraints which imposed that women's sole fate should be motherhood have been replaced by injunctions for women to place their children's needs before their own. While the majority of women have now joined the labour market, many mothers of young children among them still feel guilty every morning when they leave them with their babysitter or at day care. Others would like to work and be mothers to their children but cannot assume the obligations specific to both tasks for lack of financial resources, while still feeling guilty and wishing they could escape the boredom of taking care of small children all day long.

My point here is that when progress is not inclusive, that is, when it does not take into account the needs of the different categories of people whom it is supposed to benefit, it can be deceptive, a trap even. Thanks to the social progress achieved in the course of the 20th century, women now have control over their reproductive and professional lives. In theory, they can choose whichever career they like, including that of a writer, and they can choose whether or not they have children and when. This freedom is curtailed by many remaining constraints: as we can see in the texts under study in this book, women still shoulder most of the work related to childcare, and they are often the ones who need to pause or altogether renounce their writing careers. The sense of guilt that permeates so many of the accounts of motherhood by women writers is testimony to the cultural assumptions they still need to battle with, and which could be summed up thus, mothers must put their children first and their personal achievements second; any departure from this rule is tantamount to neglect and warrants an accusation of selfishness. I believe that real progress will be achieved when women do not feel that they need to choose between being a mother and being a writer but when the two can seamlessly come together.

It would be wrong to say that men are not concerned by these evolutions, nevertheless. Some male authors are now exploring the joys and the travails of fatherhood in their own writing, and they are finding that they feel just as conflicted as mothers. In an article for *The Paris Review* entitled "The Pram in the Hall", an obvious reference to Cyril Connolly's aphorism, which we studied in Chapter 4, author Shane Jones also looks back to the male authors who came before him to see how they managed to combine their vocations as artists with their work as fathers. Like mother writers, Jones encounters the same sense of guilt at leaving his family in order to explore his own mental space (Jones 2014). Perhaps the most famous, or infamous example, comes from Norwegian author Karl Ove Knausgaard, who in the second volume of his autobiographical series *My Struggle* writes about his resentment at having to barter with his wife for some time to himself to write. Committed to his project of exploring in detail the most shameful aspects of his life, the narrator admits to feeling castrated by his choice to have become a stay-at-home dad, "bound to it like Odysseus to the mast" and confesses: "As a result I walked around Stockholm's streets, modern and feminised, with a furious nineteenth-century man inside me" (Knausgård 2013). That 19th-century man inside him is the splendidly isolated Romantic artist he would have been before women claimed equal access to work and self-fulfilment outside of the home. I don't think that the recent social changes will mean that parenthood is going to become a gender-neutral issue but the fact that some men are coming out to express sentiments close to those that women have been voicing for decades means that certain aspects of the parenting landscape are changing.

As a closing remark, I would like to come back to two of the women who have guided my reflection throughout this book: Virginia Woolf and Rachel Cusk. Cusk penned an article in response to Woolf's *A Room of One's Own*, trying to bring a modern viewpoint to the 1929 essay (Cusk 2009). For Cusk, the question is not so much to know where and how women will write – in the family sitting-room or in a soundproof room of her own – but what she will be writing. Should women be expected to write on the same topics as men, such as war, or adventure, in order to achieve equality? Or should they struggle to impose their own themes, the unvarying of motherhood, marriage, and domesticity, and give them equal value? Should they attempt to write the "book of change", that groundbreaking work of literary genius, or should they rather write the "book of repetition", even if it does not guarantee them literary fame? We have for too long assumed that no one wants to read about motherhood, or domesticity, but why should that be? The real issue is to interrogate the value that we grant to some topics over others and to wonder why we think a book about war is more interesting than a book about domesticity, for example. In the future, I hope to read more books and poems about suburban mothers taking the washing out while singing to their children, and I hope these works will be judged for their literary value and not just their choice of theme.

Works cited

Cusk, Rachel. 2009. 'Shakespeare's Daughters'. *The Guardian*, 12 December 2009, sec. Books. www.theguardian.com/books/2009/dec/12/rachel-cusk-women-writing-review

Jones, Shane. 2014. 'The Pram in the Hall'. *The Paris Review*, 29 January 2014. www.theparisreview.org/blog/2014/01/29/the-pram-in-the-hall/

Knausgård, Karl Ove. 2013. *A Man in Love*. Translated by Don Bartlett. London: Harvill Secker.

Montei, Amanda. 2023. *Touched Out: Motherhood, Misogyny, Consent, and Control*. Boston: Beacon Press.

Perry, Louise. 2022. *The Case Against the Sexual Revolution*. Cambridge Medford (Mass.): Polity.

Index

abject 31–2, 108, 111, 157
aggression 162–4
alienation 25: childbirth as 107; motherhood as 113, 117, 121–3, 138, 143; pregnancy as 90, 92, 99–100
allomother 22–5
anaesthetics 91, 110; *see also* childbirth
art monster 5, 63; 153–61
attachment theory 21, 31, 76, 132, 158; *see also* Bowlby, J.
Austen, J. 1, 6, 54–5, 58–9, 81
autobiographical: accounts 39–41, 72, 85, 90, 111; novel 71; subject 38–40, 42; writing 38–40, 42
autobiography 3–4, 37–42, 89; *see also* memoir; self-life writing
autonomy 1, 8, 35, 37–8, 43 173; authorial 59, 128; and motherhood 67–8, 106, 108, 164; in pregnancy 95, 97, 99, 112; in work 29
autotheory 4, 41, 144

bad mother: and good mother 151–2, 162, 167; and mad mother 156–7
body: in childbirth 107–11; maternal 30, 32, 34–5, 125, 127, 141; pregnant 89–90, 93–5; transformation of 99
Bowlby, J. 21–2
Brontës, the 1, 6, 40, 54–5, 58, 81

childbirth: fear of 94–5; first-person account of 86, 88–9, 95, 102, 105, 109, 111–12; in literature 85–90, 100–3; medicalisation of 90–2; metaphor 59–60, 62, 64; natural 96–7
childlessness 37, 46, 54, 57–9, 77–9
Chodorow, N. 31–2, 34, 38, 67, 71, 141
chora 32–3; *see also* Kristeva, J; pre-symbolic
Cixous, H. 31–3, 127, 129
Coleridge, S. T. 40, 117–18, 134
community: of experience 5, 43, 124, 133, 142; of mothers 25, 46, 94, 124; of texts 8, 145
contraception 24, 27, 54, 174
cool 33, 46, 70, 98
Cusk, R. 3, 5, 12; on childbirth 109–10; on gender inequality 29, 44; on interruption 117, 119; on Joan Didion 150–1; on maternal ambivalence 165–8; on motherhood memoirs 42, 45, 141–2; on motherhood as prison 123–6; on motherhood as work 18–21, 131–2; on pregnancy 93–7; reactions to work by 160–1; on Virginia Woolf 175; on writing about motherhood 136–9

Darrieussecq, M. 1–2, 135–8, 140
daughter-centric 41, 139; *see also* matrifocal
day care 22, 25, 35, 135, 163, 165
Didion, J. 150–5
disaffiliation 5, 39, 60, 71
disidentification 40, 55–6, 68, 71–2; *see also* matrophobia
domesticity 1–2, 61–5, 69–72, 176

écriture féminine 22–4, 127, 131
Eliot, G. 54–5, 58–60, 81
Enright, A. 12, 45, 111, 136, 141
essentialism 13, 27, 32–5, 38–40, 127–9

family: life 60–4, 81, 119–20; queer 11, 97–8; structure 15–24, 53
father: becoming a 59–60, 80, 175; involvement of 19, 22, 29, 152; relationship with 34–6, 68; role in childbirth 86, 101, 111
feminism: Black 57; first-wave 108; French 33; and matrophobia 67–9; and motherhood 13, 26–8; second-wave 22–3, 109, 127; unfinished work of 6, 24, 35, 67; *see also* sisterhood

gender: differences 31, 59; identity 27, 36, 38, 77; inequality 19, 29, 44, 52, 130, 138, 156; and motherhood 75, 140
guilt 13–15, 25–6, 44, 53, 56, 145; and maternal ambivalence 162–7; over work 18–21

heteronormativity 98–100, 110–11; *see also* queer
Heti, S. 73–9
housewife 65–6, 108, 124–5
Huston, N. 61–2, 78–80, 102, 155–6

imagination 64, 67, 75, 118–23
individual 28, 34–5, 39, 88–90, 127–8: and liberalism 6, 16–17, 37–8, 60, 173; as separate from children 132, 142, 164–7; *see also* self; subjectivity
individualism 28, 70
individuation 27, 30–2, 71
Industrial Revolution 6, 15, 21, 122
intensive mothering 16–18, 23–5, 29, 41, 44
interruption 118–21, 133–8
Irigaray, L. 31–3, 36, 72, 88, 127, 129

Kristeva, J. 31–6, 70–1, 77, 126–7, 129

Lacan, J. 31–4
Lazarre, J.: on childbirth 109–11; on childcare 24–6, 135; on maternal ambivalence 161–17; on maternal subjectivity 141–3; on motherhood memoirs 42–3, 122–4, 139; on motherhood as prison 122–4
Lessing D.: on abandoning her children 155–62, 166; on childbirth 103–6, 109–10; as literary figure 78–81, 152–3; matrophobia in 26–7, 67, 71; on pregnancy 94–5

madness 156–8
marginality 34–8, 127–9
marriage 63–5, 80–1, 98–9
material conditions: of female writers 1–4; of mother writers 34–7, 58–60, 118, 126–7, 133, 142–5
maternal: aesthetic 126–7, 132; ambivalence 161–7; instinct 14–15, 21, 76, 96–7; studies 3, 6; 13–16, 31; thinking 27, 130–1
matricide 32–3, 39, 72, 88
matrifocal 41, 138–40
matrophobia 7, 26–7, 41, 46, 66–8, 71–2, 104; *see also* matricide
medical institution 7, 68, 86–7, 90–4, 97–8, 101, 106–11; *see also* obstetrics
mother-daughter bond 66–8
motherhood: as cultural construct 14–15; as genre 132–3; as institution 13–16, 23–4, 66–8, 123–4, 130, 157–8; mask of 18, 41–4, 139

Nelson, M. 11–12, 68–70, 97–100, 110–11, 138
Ní Ghríofa, D. 124, 129–30, 132

obstetrics 87, 90–2, 94, 101, 108, 139
othermother 23–5; *see also* allomother

Plath, S: as art monster 152–8; on childbirth 103, 105–8; on the childbirth metaphor 62–7; as literary figure 78–84
pram in the hall 61–2, 155, 159, 175
pregnancy: and ideology 91–7; in literature 85–7, 112–13, 143; as queer 98–100; and subjectivity 87–90
pre-symbolic 30, 32, 34, 37

psychoanalysis 30–6, 67, 69, 71–2, 163–4

queer 97–100

relational 35–8, 88–9, 128–9, 141, 173; *see also* self; subjectivity
Rich, A.: on maternal ambivalence 161–3, 166–7; on maternal violence 156–7; on maternal writing 123–4, 143; on matrophobia 24, 26–7, 35, 41, 66–8; on motherhood as institution 124, 130, 139; on obstetrics 90–1, 96; role in maternal studies of 11–16
romantic: artist 5, 39–40, 70, 80, 117, 143, 173–5; love 113, 143–4, 168; period 1, 60

selfish 8, 45, 155–6, 161–2, 165, 175
self: -fulfilment 6, 13, 15–16, 38, 59, 68, 161, 164; lack of 31, 37; shattering of the 100, 103–5, 107, 113; splitting of the 26, 87, 89, 102–5, 109, 126, 141–2; *see also* subjectivity

selfless 30, 35–6, 41, 141, 165–6
sexuality 86, 88, 102
Shafak, E. 18, 73–9, 136, 141, 146
sisterhood 26, 68
sleep 117–20, 134, 137
subjectivity: autobiographical 40–2; maternal 6–7, 28–36, 126–31, 135, 141, 145; in pregnancy 87–90, 92, 99; *see also* individual; self
symbolic 30–7, 127; *see also* pre-symbolic

time: control over 118–22, 125–6, 132–8; cyclical 70, 126

Walker, A. 41, 56–8
Winnicott, D. 21, 162–3
Woolf, V.: as inspiration 78–81; on interruption 133–4; on mothers being writers 53–9; on women writers 1–5, 78–81, 129, 155, 158, 175
work: access to 13, 15–24, 28–9, 164–5; motherhood as 125–6, 130–2

Milton Keynes UK
Ingram Content Group UK Ltd.
UKHW031330071224
451979UK00005B/52